GREAT HOUSES
OF IRELAND

GREAT HOUSES OF IRELAND

HUGH MONTGOMERY-MASSINGBERD

CHRISTOPHER SIMON SYKES

LAURENCE KING

In memory of
our Irish Uncles Ran Antrim and Peter Montgomery
friends and colleagues at the National Trust
who opened our eyes to Ireland

Published in 1999 by Laurence King Publishing
an imprint of Calmann & King Ltd
71 Great Russell Street
London
WC1B 3BN

Tel: + 44 171 831 6351
Fax: + 44 171 831 8356
e-mail: enquiries@calmann-king.co.uk
www.laurence-king.com

Text © 1999 Hugh Montgomery-Massingberd
Photographs © 1999 Christopher Simon Sykes
This book was designed and produced by Calmann & King Ltd, London

ISBN 1 85669 172 1

Designed and typeset by Karen Stafford
Printed in China

ENDPAPERS: Gothic plasterwork at Castle Ward, Co. Down.
HALF-TITLE: Detail of mirror at Lyons, Co. Kildare.
FRONTISPIECE: Crom Castle, Co. Fermanagh.

CONTENTS

Introduction 6

INTRODUCTION

*T*WO men looked out from prison bars – as the present writer's grandmother used to say – one saw mud, the other stars. In writing about Irish country houses during most of the 20th century it has been all too easy, even in a landscape of unsurpassed beauty, to see only the mud, or rather bog enveloped in a romantic, more than faintly surreal mist.

Although cheerfulness may have broken through occasionally in the stories of Somerville and Ross and Molly Keane, the overriding mood in fictional portrayals of 'the Big House' by such writers as Elizabeth Bowen, William Trevor and Jennifer Johnston has tended to be one of intense, brooding melancholy. A Chekhovian air of nostalgia for lost dreams and general gloom pervades.

One of the most beguiling evocations of the damp, turf-scented, grand yet intimate atmosphere of the Irish country house is to be found in Siegfried Sassoon's novel *Sherston's Progress* (1936). In a deliberately dream-like description of a 'spacious and remote' house in Co. Limerick owned by a convivial and friendly foxhunter 'full of rich-flavoured Irish talk', the narrator asks:

> What could have been more delightful than to sit in a dignified dining-room and listen to such a man, while the rain pelted against the windows and a wood fire glowed and blazed in the immense fireplace, and the fine old burnished silver shone reflectively on the mahogany table?

He goes on to imagine a series of

> seldom-used rooms smelling of the past; and a creaking uneven passage with a window-seat at the end of it and a view of the wild green park beyond straggling spiral yews, and the evening clouds lit with the purplish bloom of rainy weather.

As the tour of the great house (complete with the obligatory antlers of an ancient Irish elk) continues, the narrator envisages himself in 'an unravished eighteenth and early nineteenth-century library, where obsolete Sermons and Travels in mellow leather bindings might be neighboured by uncut copies of the first issues of Swift and Goldsmith...'.

Such heady images helped give definition to inchoate impressions of Irish country houses formed by the present writer as an infant in the 1940s – a period vividly recalled in the youthful reminiscences of the writer Thomas Pakenham and the scholar-connoisseur Knight of Glin featured in the chapters on Tullynally and Glin respectively. And in the 1950s, another novel, irresistibly entitled *All a Nonsense* and telling of a young man's attempts to maintain his beloved, if crumbling, Irish family seat, struck a romantically resonant chord. Its author, Mark Bence-Jones from Co. Cork, turned out – through perusal of *Burke's Landed Gentry of Ireland* – to be a kinsman of the present writer by way of a connection with a family noted for the fact that the coffin of one of its number had been lost by some thirsty retainers *en route* to the committal in Co. Armagh.

In the 1960s – having thrilled to the Irish Georgian Society's heroic crusade for the preservation of Ireland's architectural heritage under the stylish and inspiring leadership of Desmond Guinness – the present writer joined the editorial staff of Burke's publications, where he determined to revive the series' Irish roots. In the 1970s he was fortunate enough to work with Mark Bence-Jones on several projects, including *Burke's Irish Family Records*, *Burke's Introduction to Irish Ancestry* and the original Bence-Jones *magnum opus*, *Burke's Guide to Country Houses, Volume I: Ireland* (subsequently revised and republished as *A Guide to Irish Country Houses* by Mark Bence-Jones).

PREVIOUS PAGE: Curraghmore, Co. Waterford: garden front.

BELOW Russborough, Co. Wicklow: the front hall.

Ballinlough Castle, Co. Westmeath: view across the lake.

The Knight of Glin: champion of conservation.

Bence-Jones's pioneering survey of some 2,000 Irish family seats, major and minor, standing and demolished, was memorably described by one reviewer, Lady Violet Powell (Thomas Pakenham's aunt, incidentally), as 'infinitely melancholy'. Appearing as it did in a bleak decade when confiscatory taxation had led to a haemorrhage of sales and dispersals (Malahide and Adare heading a depressing list), all too many of the entries ended with variants of the dread phrase: 'Its future is uncertain'.

The gloom-doom was so severe that some were predicting that there would soon be no more Irish country houses left in private ownership. One of the anecdotes with which Bence-Jones enlivened his architectural descriptions seemed to sum up the hopelessness of the situation: an owner of a country house reduced to two wings with only a makeshift corridor in between announced, when the corridor itself collapsed, that he was changing the name of his family seat to Ballyshambles.

The basic problem was that too many of the powers-that-be in the modern Republic persisted in seeing Ireland's remarkable stock of country houses as 'monuments of landlordism and oppression', 'hated symbols of the Ascendancy and the alien culture of the British invader', and so forth. The articulate Irish heritage lobby did its eloquent best to dispel these notions. 'The naive assumption that these houses are to be seen as merely memorials to outdated colonialism should be resisted', argued the Knight of Glin, 'because they are in fact treasure houses of Irish skills'.

In 1988 a shocking exhibition of photographs of the 'Vanishing Country Houses of Ireland', accompanied by a book of the same name by the Knight of Glin, David J. Griffin and Nicholas Robinson, catalogued the loss of some 500 Irish country houses over the past century. It brought home the acute absence of legislative machinery in the Republic to protect architecturally significant buildings from dereliction or neglect.

At last, in the 1990s, the message seemed to be getting through. It was certainly encouraging to hear the then Taoiseach, Albert Reynolds, admit that the 'blatant hostility' to country houses in the new Republic had been 'misguided' and that 'we need have no complexes about their origins'. In his opening address to the conference on 'The Future of the Country House' organised by the Irish Georgian Society in 1993, he also said: 'I fully accept that the most efficient way of protecting and preserving these houses is to help the owners as far as possible to keep and maintain them'.

Had the stars really come out at last? As the Knight of Glin, who succeeded Desmond Guinness in the presidency of the Irish Georgian Society, remarked, 'the attitude of the State has been transformed from the hatred of the colonial past to today's positively warm embrace'. Ireland's booming economy and the contribution of the European Community have also had dramatic effects.

During the 1990s the Heritage Council has become a statutory body with a very wide environmental brief and some grant-giving powers. Progress has been made towards 'listing' buildings, interiors and gardens; and the State has taken some important buildings under the wings of the Office of Public Works and Dúchas, the Heritage Service, part of the Department of Art, Heritage, Gaeltacht and the Islands. The Planning Bill, going through the Irish Parliament at the time of writing, has been hailed as a significant step forward for the protection of the built heritage, though its inadequate grant provisions strike the heritage lobbyists as little more than a gesture.

For despite the positive political goodwill that inspired the general improvements in the Irish tax structure for maintaining historic houses in private hands, the lack of implementation of specific reliefs to alleviate the practical problems is the despair of owners and their advisers. The economic difficulties of many owners without the capital assets or, indeed, the actual income to finance maintenance costs are acute; the future for their houses continues to look bleak. The Irish Georgian Society and the owners' 'trade union', Great Irish Castles, Houses and Gardens, are constantly campaigning for the cause: much more still needs to be done before the stars can truly be said to have emerged from the clouds.

What the Republic still badly lacks is – as is now perhaps permissible to mention in these days of cross-border co-operation – an equivalent 'safety net' to the National Trust in Northern Ireland, which would catch the dispersing fragments of houses, gardens and collections. Above all, there is a pressing need for a State-financed body concentrating on the architectural heritage with the muscle to rescue nationally important properties, administer proper grants and generally streamline Irish preservation.

None the less, at least as far as the few surviving great houses are concerned (and they, as the shining stars of this book, are what we are concerned with here), there is good news to impart. Castletown, Co. Kildare, surely the greatest house of all (heroically rescued by Desmond Guinness in the 1960s), is now owned by the State, which was undertaking such a comprehensive restoration when we were preparing the book that we were, alas, unable to enter. Russborough, most people's choice as the fairest house in Ireland, is lovingly maintained by the Alfred Beit Foundation. Ballinlough and Bantry have both benefited from the European Community's 'Great Gardens of Ireland' grant-aid scheme. Newbridge, now administered jointly by Fingal County Council and the Trustees of the Cobbe Family Collections, is an innovative example of a 'partnership' enterprise between a local authority and a resident family.

Essentially this book is a celebration of such families and their patronage of the arts. Most of the places included are fortunate enough to remain in the hands of their original families, whose present-day representatives are generally taking a more optimistic attitude to keeping them going than some of their predecessors did. Thus, we find the de la Poer Beresfords still at Curraghmore; the FitzGeralds at Glin; the Nugents (really O'Reillys) at Ballinlough; the Cavendishes (descended from the Boyles) at Lismore; the Crichtons at Crom; the Parsonses at Birr; the Waddingtons (descended from the Tichbornes) at Beaulieu; the Brabazons at Killruddery; the Ieverses at Mount Ievers; the Pakenhams at Tullynally; the Blackwoods at Clandeboye; the Whites at Bantry; the Gore-Booths at Lissadell; the Alexanders at Caledon; the Hamiltons at Baronscourt; and the Mulhollands still at Ballywalter. And though the great Northern quartet of Florence Court, Castle Ward, Castle Coole and Mount Stewart are now all admirably administered by the National Trust, the Coles, Wards, Lowry-Corrys and Stewarts respectively all maintain strong associations with their old family homes.

At many of these places a glorious Renaissance of restoration currently seems to be in full swing. Significantly, some of the most notable work is actually being done in great houses which have changed hands in recent years. This is the most arresting phenomenon we encountered during our travels: for the first time since the birth of the Irish Republic new money is being spent, and spent extremely well, on beautifying old houses and filling them with Irish works of art. Step forward, Mr

Castle Coole, Co. Fermanagh: stove in Saloon.

Service bell at Castle Ward, Co. Down.

and Mrs Ken Rohan of Charleville (it was Mr Rohan's company that co-sponsored the landmark 'Vanishing Country Houses of Ireland' exhibition), Dr Tony Ryan of Lyons, Mr and Mrs Martin Naughton of Stackallen and Mr and Mrs George Magan of Castletown, Co. Kilkenny – which some would say might rival Russborough as Ireland's most beautiful country house. We would like to have included further examples of this exhilarating trend, but the restoration of, for instance, Abbey Leix and Ballynatray, was not quite far enough advanced for photography at the time we were preparing the book.

Inevitably, there were several other great houses we would love to have featured but our space was severely restricted in order to keep the book to reasonably manageable proportions. On the whole, we have concentrated on places that are either lived in or at least retain the feel of domestic occupation. Hence the omission of the celebrated country-house hotels. The final choice, though, depended as much upon the practical possibility of photography, or indeed the owners' willingness to cooperate, as on any other factor. Among the absentees we especially regret, apart from Castletown, Co. Kildare, are Bellamont Forest, Carton, Castle Forbes, Charleville Forest, Dunsany, Emo, Humewood, Malahide, Portumna, Seaforde, Slane, Strokestown and Westport.

While making not the remotest claim to be comprehensive (after all, we have barely covered even one per cent of the places recorded in the Bence-Jones *Guide*), and emphatically *not* essaying any sort of guidebook, it is hoped that our informal, impressionistic approach will give something of the flavour of the 26 great houses featured in the pages that follow. Loosely arranged in a rough chronological sequence based rather more on the social history than the assortment of architectural styles, they none the less represent a broad sweep of Irish architecture – from the medieval tower at Curraghmore to Sir Charles Lanyon's mid-19th-century *palazzo* of Ballywalter.

As this is a glimpse of great houses rather than castles (in the fortress, as opposed to the romantic, sense of that word), we have blithely ignored what one might call the archaeological aspects of antiquity (though we do note a Celtic-Romanesque arch in the gatehouse at Lismore) and devoted our attentions to the post-fortified era. Beaulieu and Stackallen are the gracious and comfortable representatives of that gentlemanly style of architecture which blended Dutch and Classical influence and flourished from the late 17th to the early 18th century. Mount Ievers is a haunting example of the Irish 'tall house'; and the glories of Irish Palladianism, complete with luscious Rococo plasterwork, are illustrated by Russborough, Florence Court and Castletown, Co. Kilkenny.

Subsequently, as the Knight of Glin observed in his study of the architecture of Davis Duckart (who designed Castletown, Co. Kilkenny, and, in all probability, the wings at Florence Court), 'those well-manicured neo-classical fingers clutched the whole island in their icy grip'. As well as being busy at Curraghmore (which appears here for the first time in a book of colour photography), James Wyatt produced Ireland's most palatial neo-Classical house, Castle Coole.

After the Act of Union of 1801, the versatile and prolific Morrisons, father and son (Sir Richard and William Vitruvius), found no shortage of clients – among them the Abercorns at Baronscourt (neo-Classical), the Meaths at Killruddery (Tudor Revival), and the Longfords at Pakenham (now Tullynally), 'the Camelot of the Gothic Revival'. The Gothic style, which had first reared its head on the garden front of Castle Ward back in the 1760s, is also represented, in various guises, at Glin, Birr, Lismore and Edward Blore's Crom, Co. Fermanagh (another house appearing for the first time in a book of this sort). Elsewhere in the North, earlier in the 19th century, John Nash gave a Regency flourish to the neo-Classical Caledon – yet another comparatively 'unknown' great house making its first appearance in a book of colour photography.

The text is as much about the personalities who created these temples of the arts as their architecture and decoration, and puts particular emphasis on the present day. As well as seeking to evoke the individual magic and romance of these places, we have tried to show how the current owners are coping with the challenge of finding new ways for the buildings to survive into the new Millennium, while preserving the dual attributes of being both great houses and family homes. Their positive and practical response encourages one to see not mud but stars.

1

CURRAGHMORE

CURRAGHMORE could only be in Ireland. The name prosaically means 'the great bog', but that does scant justice to the wild and romantic beauty of the place, which thrills the senses. The magically mysterious and secret demesne – which has never changed hands by purchase and is today lovingly maintained by its present owner, the 8th Marquess of Waterford (who took over the reins from his mother on coming of age in 1955, having succeeded to the Marquessate as an infant) – is so vast as to seem like a world apart. It is certainly the largest and most splendid demesne in Ireland: the River Clodagh winds for four miles through a deep and secret valley, the boundary wall runs for no less than ten miles. The great house, with its noble recessed plate-glass windows, has a powerful presence set in a giant amphitheatre of woods, hills and mountains.

The special excitement of a visit to Curraghmore is that you feel you are being transported back in time. There is something primeval about the place. Indeed, as the peerless architectural historian Mark Girouard – whose maternal family home this was – has pointed out, the miles of silent woods are 'a fragment, basically, of the huge forests which once covered so much of Ireland'.

With beguiling ease, you can imagine that you are back in the 12th century when Robert Le Poer, a Norman soldier sent by King Henry II to Ireland and appointed Governor of Waterford, carved out a mini-kingdom of his own to the west of the town – between the River Suir, the Comeragh Mountains (which form a majestic horizon to the Curraghmore vistas) and the sea. Like many of the Anglo-Norman dynasties who established themselves in Ireland at this time, the Le Poers (alternatively de la Poers or Powers) became, as the saying went, 'more Irish than the Irish'. During the later Middle Ages they were in the habit of making predatory raids on Waterford town in company with the O'Driscoll clan from Co. Cork, so that the exasperated burgesses would offer special prayers in the Waterford churches for deliverance from them.

However, by the time of Henry VIII, the first English King to style himself 'King of Ireland', the head of the Curraghmore branch of the Powers, Richard, was considered sufficiently law-abiding to be created a peer in 1535. Forty years on, Sir Henry Sidney, then Lord Deputy of Ireland, recorded how he 'lodged the night at Curraghmore, the house that the Lord Power is Baron of' and was 'with such plenty and good order entertained'.

In the middle of the 17th century, Curraghmore featured in the *Civil Survey*, as follows:

> There stands a fayre Castle and a goodly stone house upon the land, there is also an Orcharde and Meadow upon the same and stands by the side of a fine wood, the River Clodeth running within a muskett shott thereof on the South upon wch there is a bridge not very farr from the said castle.

It is instructive to compare this first surviving description of the house with today's topography. The castle tower survives in the centre of the present house, surmounted by the crest of the Le Poers, the Stag of St Hubert with a crucifix between his antlers. The River 'Clodeth', or Clodagh, still runs romantically under the same many-arched medieval bridge (traditionally known as 'King John's Bridge'); and the 5th Marquess of Waterford – who gave the present house its mid-Victorian Classical character through a remodelling of the exterior by the little-known architect S.U. Roberts in the 1870s – had his youngest daughter christened Clodagh in tribute.

A few years after the *Civil Survey*, the Powers advanced to an Earldom of Tyrone, but the title became extinct on the death of the 3rd Earl of Tyrone, without surviving male heirs, in 1704. Shortly before he died, it would appear that the 3rd Earl carried out a rebuilding of the 'goodly stone house' mentioned in the *Survey* for, as Charles Smith notes in his description of Curraghmore in his *Ancient and Present State of the County and City of Waterford* (1746), the date of '1700' is 'on a pedestal of the doorcase'. Smith's fulsome praise for the gardens, and much else, was rightly reserved for the 3rd Earl's remarkable daughter Catherine ('Cathie'), a key figure in the Curraghmore story.

Detail of the family crest of the Le Poers, the Stag of St Hubert with a crucifix between his antlers, which surmounts the medieval tower. The coronet below is that of a Marquess – the title conferred upon the 2nd Earl of Tyrone of the later creation (who also inherited the ancient Barony of Le Poer from his mother) in 1789.

'The largest and most splendid demesne in Ireland': the view over Curraghmore up to the Comeragh Mountains.

Detail of the Beresford family crest on the roof: a dragon's head, the neck pierced with a broken tilting spear, the broken-off point in the beast's mouth. Below is a glimpse of the formal garden, with its lake and balustrade.

Cathie's marriage to Sir Marcus Beresford, 4th Bt (whose family had been prominent in the Plantation of Ulster in the early 17th century), was predicted in one of the most famous Irish ghost stories. According to a strongly believed tradition, the 2nd Earl of Tyrone (Cathie's uncle) had made a childhood pact with his friend Nichola Hamilton (later the wife of Sir Tristram Beresford, 3rd Bt) that whoever died first should 'appear' to the other. On the night of the 2nd Earl's death, aged 29, in 1693, he duly startled Nichola and, while touching on various topics (such as 'the revealed religion is the only one by which we can be saved'), told her the number of children she was going to have, how one of them would marry his niece and that she would die on her 47th birthday. Seeking confirmation of this vision, Nichola asked her old friend to touch her wrist, though Lord Tyrone warned her that it would be irreparably scarred. As he did so, the flesh and sinews shrank.

The story goes that 'forever more that lady wore a riband on her wrist'. And, sure enough, all the ghostly Earl's predictions came true – she *did* die on her 47th birthday (though she was under the mistaken impression it was her 48th) and her son Marcus married, in 1717, Lady Catherine, heiress of Curraghmore.

As well as bearing 13 children, Cathie found time to transform the place between then and her death in 1769. The interiors of the house were adorned with frescoes (now disappeared) by the Dutch painter Johann van der Hagen, the gardens elaborately laid out with canals, cascades, terraces and statues, all soon to be swept away during the late 18th-century reaction against formality. Happily, when tastes changed again in the 19th century, a formal layout was reinstated – and this still survives, together with two notable features from Cathie's time, the Wilderness and the Shell House.

Charles Smith, in the 1740s, described 'a natural wilderness of tall venerable oak' and also observed 'a shell-house erecting, which when finished promises to be very curious...' The promise was fulfilled. Today the Curraghmore Shell House stands as the principal surviving example in Ireland of the fashion started there by Mrs Delany (Mary Delany, the friend of Jonathan Swift) in the 1740s for grottoes. As the inscription on the marble statue by John van Nost of its creator recalls, 'In two hundred and sixty one days these shells were put up by the proper hands of the Rt. Honble Cathne Countess of Tyrone...'

Cathie's 'proper hands' encrusted the entire interior with shells of marine fantasy. Her proper title derived from the new creation of the Earldom of Tyrone in 1746 for her husband, Sir Marcus Beresford.

Inside the house, Cathie's chief legacy to posterity is the decoration of the great room (now the Billiard Room) on the first floor of the old castle tower, which has an exquisite coved ceiling probably by the great Italian geniuses of plasterwork the brothers Paul and Philip Francini. Foliage, flowers, busts and ribbons abound in rectangular and curvilinear compartments.

Curraghmore's most sensational feature, the magnificent forecourt, which is worthy of comparison with Sir John Vanbrugh's dramatic spectaculars at Blenheim Palace and Seaton Delaval in England – or, as Mark Bence-Jones has observed, 'seems to belong more to France or elsewhere on the Continent than to the British Isles' – is, frustratingly, impossible to pin down as to the date and the architect. Mark Girouard thinks that 1750/60 and John Roberts of Waterford are the most likely answers, though it has been suggested that at least parts of it could be rather later.

Whatever the annotation, the architecture is awe-inspiring. The approach, coming so suddenly and unexpectedly after the long, winding drive through the wooded valley, seems never-ending. On either side as you progress respectfully forward are long stable ranges (the de la Poer Beresfords, Marquesses of Waterford are legendary for their horsemanship), dominated by towering pedimented archways. The eye is caught by the crisp detailing of the stonework – rusticated arches and window surrounds, pedimented niches with statues, doorways with entablatures. This, you feel, must be the palace of a great territorial magnate.

RIGHT Catherine ('Cathie'), Countess of Tyrone, commemorated in her most remarkable creation at Curraghmore: the Shell House, a marine grotto entirely encrusted with shells. In one hand she holds a shell; in the other, a scroll with the inscription: 'In two hundred and sixty one days these shells were put up by the proper hands of the Rt. Honble Cathne Countess of Tyrone 1754'.

LEFT Cathie, Countess of Tyrone (whose portrait hangs above the chimneypiece), surveys her other principal legacy at Curraghmore: the Great Room on the first floor of the old tower (which became a Billiard Room in the 19th century), with its exquisite mid-18th-century plasterwork attributed to the brothers Francini, Paul and Philip.

Certainly by 1789, when Marcus and Cathie's eldest son, George (unkindly known as 'Squinting Tyrone'), was created Marquess of Waterford, the Beresfords had become the most powerful family in Ireland. The 1st Marquess's brothers included the ambitious politician John Beresford, one of a political triumvirate who ruled Ireland in the decade before the Act of Union with Great Britain in 1801, and two Archbishops.

The 1st Marquess was responsible for the enlargement and remodelling of the house in the 1780s, when the present Staircase Hall (with its balustrade rising in a sweeping curve) was built in the inner court. The English architect James Wyatt (who also designed Castle Coole, Co. Fermanagh – *qv*) was employed to redecorate the interiors, and created some of the finest late 18th-century rooms in Ireland – notably the Dining Room and the Blue Drawing Room. The Dining Room has delicate plasterwork on the ceiling and walls, with roundels attributed to Antonio Zucchi or Angelica Kauffmann and *grisaille* panels by Peter de Gree. The Blue Drawing Room has a ceiling incorporating roundels by de Gree and semicircular panels attributed to Zucchi. Recently the present Lord Waterford and his wife, the former Lady Caroline Wyndham-Quin, have carried out a sympathetic restoration of the principal rooms, which also include the Library and the Yellow Drawing Room.

The 1st Marquess also undertook some more melancholy building work at Curraghmore: the Irish round tower on a hill at the north-east of the demesne erected in memory of his eldest son, who was killed at the age of 12, while

ABOVE Reflected detail of the elaborate ceiling in Wyatt's Blue Drawing Room, with its panels attributed to Antonio Zucchi and *grisailles* by Peter de Gree.

RIGHT A cool neo-Classical corridor at Curraghmore, which Wyatt transformed in the 1780s.

ABOVE and RIGHT The Dining Room, one of the finest Wyatt interiors in Ireland. The ceiling roundels are attributed to Antonio Zucchi or his wife, Angelica Kauffmann, and the *grisaille* panels are by Peter de Gree. As Mark Girouard (whose maternal home this was) wrote, 'It is a room in which it is always a pleasure to be'. Prince William (later King William IV) was entertained here in 1787, when Dorothea Herbert noted 'The Ceiling and Pannels exhibiting various emblematic and Mythological Pieces painted with the utmost skill of the Artist'.

attempting, as Hansard put it in his *History of Waterford*, 'to jump with a spirited horse, a low wooden paling, which at this time ran across the entrance to the courtyard'. Consequently, Curraghmore and the Marquessate of Waterford eventually passed to the second son, whose marriage to Lady Sarah Carpenter, daughter of the 2nd Earl of Tyrconnel, brought the colourful genes of her mother's family, the Delavals of Seaton Delaval, into the family.

The wildness of the Delavals evidently came out in the adventures of the young 3rd Marquess of Waterford. Much has been written about the 3rd Marquess's erratic behaviour as a young man. (Ralph Nevill in his *Sporting Days and Sporting Ways* relished in chronicling how he 'painted the Melton tollbar a bright red, put aniseed on the hoofs of a parson's horse, and hunted the terrified divine with bloodhounds. On another occasion he put a donkey into the bed of a stranger at an inn...'.) More deserves to be known about the way he later settled down at Curraghmore with his artist wife, Louisa Stuart, to become, as his obituary in *The Annual Register of 1859* put it, 'one of the best landlords and most improving cultivators... universally popular and respected'. The Waterfords were great philanthropists and did sterling work to alleviate the terrible suffering of the Irish Famine of the 1840s.

In the 1830s the 3rd Marquess had considered some radical designs by Daniel Robertson to turn Curraghmore into a Gothic Revival pile but the plans were never carried out. Louisa Waterford built the long south-west terrace in 1843 and was probably the author of the present formal layout, with its Irish yews and round pond.

It seems almost needless to add that the 3rd Marquess, a celebrated MFH, met his end in the hunting field, for the equestrian spirit is paramount at Curraghmore. The sporting exploits of the brothers of the 5th Marquess (whose first wife is commemorated by a poignant monument by Sir Joseph Boehm in

ABOVE Sport to the fore: equine headgear in the Entrance Hall. The group portrait of *circa* 1760 (artist unknown) is of the 1st Earl of Tyrone and his family. The second son, John Beresford. who became one of the most powerful men in Ireland, is the thin-faced figure fifth from the left.

LEFT A corner of the Entrance Hall, which is hung with heads and trophies, mostly shot by the 6th Marquess of Waterford.

the family chapel up at Clonegam, overlooking the demesne) are the stuff of late 19th- and early 20th-century legend. There was Admiral Lord Charles Beresford ('Charlie B'), who had a hunt in full cry tattooed down his back, and once rode down Piccadilly on a pig; the Cavalryman Lord William Beresford, who won the VC in the Zulu War; and Lord Marcus Beresford, who managed the racing stables of King Edward VII and King George V.

The present generation has spawned a dynasty of outstanding polo players, including the present Marquess and his brother Lord Patrick Beresford; the Marquess's sons, the Earl of Tyrone and Lords Charles and James Beresford; and the budding young champion Lord Le Poer (Lord Tyrone's elder son), the first to bear that historic title for 200 years. Lord Tyrone and his brother Lord James have both recently taken out licences as racehorse trainers.

At Curraghmore, the best traditions of Irish country-house life as epitomised by the de la Poer Beresfords continue to flourish. The time-honoured pursuits of sport, architecture, horticulture, forestry and public-spirited land management are being not merely preserved but embellished and enhanced.

2

GLIN CASTLE

COUNTY LIMERICK

WHAT could be more romantic than the title of The Knight of Glin? It seems straight out of *Alice in Wonderland*. Glin Castle, too, particularly seen from a boat on the Shannon where this great river broadens into an estuary on its way to the Atlantic, has an unreal air: a cardboard battlemented fantasy surrounded by pepper-pot lodges and swooping woodlands.

Yet Desmond FitzGerald, the 29th Knight of Glin, is real enough. Indeed, as a connoisseur of the decorative arts and a campaigning President of the Irish Georgian Society, he is a substantial figure. In the words of John Cornforth of *Country Life*, the Knight 'has helped create the enthusiasm for things Irish that is one of the great changes of the past 40 years'. This has grown out of Glin, where the Knight has developed a fascinating collection of Irish furniture and paintings to complement the unexpectedly fine craftsmanship to be found behind the castle's comparatively plain and many-windowed exterior. Here, among the elaborate neo-Classical plasterwork, the fluted Corinthian columns, pedimented mahogany bookcases and the sensational 'flying' staircase, the Knight has imaginatively fashioned an integrated view of the 18th and 19th century that no other Irish country house, let alone museum, can rival.

While no one could be more passionate than the Knight as to the need to preserve Ireland's heritage of this period ('The creations of these Irish artists and craftsmen', as he says, 'should take equal place with the better-known symbols of Irish archaeology and art such as a Bronze Age gold brooch or a page from a great illustrated manuscript'), his scholarship militates against too romantic a view of the past. The Glin history is a saga of beheadings, confiscations, exile, penal cases, duelling, drunkenness, womanising, general profligacy and virtual bankruptcy.

The Knights of Glin, who have been in West Limerick from the beginning of the 13th century, are a branch of the great Norman dynasty of FitzGerald, generically known as the Geraldines of Desmond. Like the Le Poers in the

PREVIOUS PAGES The garden front of Glin Castle. A rainbow adds to the romance of the 'pasteboard Gothic' architecture.

LEFT The Hall Herman van der Mijn's portrait shows 'The Duellist' Knight of Glin being brought a challenge to a duel by his servant. The equine paintings are by Lady Rachel FitzGerald, wife of the 27th Knight and daughter of the 4th Earl of Dunraven. The table is Irish mid-18th-century Baroque mahogany and has always been in the house; the coat of arms is of FitzMaurice.

BELOW and RIGHT Three details of the carved Irish 18th-century mahogany furniture which is such a feature of the collections enhanced by the present connoisseur Knight, author of *Irish Furniture*.

previous chapter, the Knights were among those of the so-called 'Old English' who became 'more Irish than the Irish', marrying frequently into the Gaelic chieftainry families. Thomas FitzGerald built his first Norman castle on a motte at Shanid, a few miles from Glin, in about 1200, on top of an ancient ring-fort of the 1st Millennium AD.

'*Shanid Abu*' ('Shanid forever!') was the Desmond Geraldines' war cry; it was a familiar sound in the Middle Ages and is a constant motif in the decoration and objects (from bayonet holders to silver) at Glin to this day. The Knights regularly joined their kinsmen, the Earls of Desmond in rebelling against English rule. In the bloody Elizabethan death struggles the then Knight, Thomas FitzJohn, escaped execution only through a legal technicality, and his son and heir was hanged, drawn and quartered. His mother seized his severed head, drank his blood and, surrounded by a keening concourse, carried his dismembered body to be buried at Lislaughtin Abbey.

When the subsequent Knight, Edmund FitzThomas, was in rebellion the English besieged and captured the old castle of Glin (now a shattered ruin in the village). At one stage the Knight's six-year-old son was tied to the mouth of a cannon by the Lord President of Munster, Sir George Carew, who threatened to blow him to bits if the Knight did not surrender. The blunt response was that the virile Knight

The Hall: more Irish mahogany, more equine studies by Lady Rachel FitzGerald and a portrait by John Michael Wright of the armoured 1st Lord Kingston, Joint Governor of Connaught, whose wife Catherine was a descendant of the FitzGibbons, holders of the now extinct title of 'The White Knight'.

would have no trouble in producing another son, a point borne out by the tradition that the castle was defended by two dozen of the Knight's bastards.

Glin was captured again by the English in 1642 and also under the Cromwellian Settlement a decade later. Eventually, though, the ancestral estate was recovered after the Restoration of King Charles II, and during the 18th century the Knights conformed to Protestantism. Although it might be said that they were assimilated into the 'Ascendancy' through marriage, the Knights of Glin appear to have kept many of the colourful attributes of old-time Irish potentates until comparatively recently.

The wife of an 18th-century Knight carried out cattle raids in order to obtain meat for the starving people during a famine; she was known locally as the '*Bean-Tighearna*' (the 'Female Chieftain') and spoke Irish as her natural tongue. Her son Richard, Knight of Glin, known as 'The Duellist', would shout, whenever he entered a public assembly, 'Is there a *Moriarty* present?' (an allusion to the longstanding feud between the FitzGeralds and the Moriartys, who had taken part in the murder of Gerald, the Rebel Earl of Desmond in the mountains near Tralee in 1585).

The swords of The Duellist's nephew Colonel John FitzGerald, Knight of Glin, were principally for ceremonial use – notably a splendid one made by Reid

LEFT Detail of the map by William Jones depicting the Siege of Glin, 7/9 July, 1600. The castle was traditionally defended by two dozen of the then Knight's bastards.

RIGHT A general view of the Hall, with its ceiling of the 1780s attributed to Dublin stuccodores Michael Stapleton or Charles Thorpe. The trophies and shields commemorate the Volunteer movement of the same period.

of Dublin in 1800 and recently rescued for Glin by the present Knight – though he was an ardent Volunteer and formed his own regiments, the Glin Cavalry (later the Royal Glin Hussars) and the Royal Glin Artillery (which boasted its own musical band of 10) in the stirring times of the last quarter of the 18th century. The regimental colours now hang on the stairs of the house Colonel John built.

The new house, begun in the early 1780s, was a plain three-storey, double bow-fronted affair with a long service wing. This wing possibly incorporated the earlier house on the site, which, in turn, had replaced a thatched house (burnt in 1740) after the Knights of Glin had had to abandon their ancestral castle in the 17th century.

Colonel John may well have been his own architect – frustratingly for such a scholar as the present Knight, there are no documents to throw any light on the matter – working with the excellent craftsmen that Limerick could produce at a time of much confident building work in the newly prosperous country. The present Knight suggests that Colonel John's Limerick builder may have been influenced by the Italian architect Davis Duckart, celebrated for his 'Imperial', or double, staircases (and the designer of the Limerick Custom House and Castletown, Co. Kilkenny – *qv*) and by Duckart's colleague Christopher Colles, whose family had a water-powered marble works at Kilkenny. The Doric front-door case at Glin and at least one chimneypiece are made of this fossilized shell-encrusted marble.

When it comes to the decoration, the present Knight feels he is on firmer ground in attributing the neo-Classical plasterwork in the Corinthian-columned Hall to one of two Dublin stuccodores, Charles Thorpe or Michael Stapleton. Terracotta Classical plaques on an apple-green background combine with a curious mixture of flowers, foliage, Irish harps and military trophies to form a delightful piece of decoration. The ceiling also incorporates the impaled escutcheon of Colonel John and his English West Country wife, Margaretta Maria Fraunceis Gwyn from Forde Abbey and Combe Florey (later the seat of Evelyn Waugh).

Although she was something of an heiress, the money soon ran out for the expensive building operation – though happily not before the completion of the staircase, very unusual in Ireland in having two lower ramps with a single ('flying') run of steps from the half-landing to the first-floor landing. (There

ABOVE The Dining Room, with its baronial Jacobean-style furniture ordered from London in 1830 by 'the Knight of the Women' to emphasise the new 'castle' status of Glin. The group of portraits on the wall above the sideboard is dominated by General Eyre Massy, Marshal of the Army in Ireland, created Lord Clarina in 1800.

LEFT View from the Morning Room through to the Dining Room. The Morning Room is an interior much improved by the present Knight, with such additions as a chimneypiece from Tervoe (bought by his mother on the 12-year-old Knight's insistence) and, above it, William Turner de Lond's painting of *Market Day in Ennis, Co. Clare* (1820).

RIGHT The 'flying' staircase, very unusual in Ireland (and possibly inspired by Robert Adam's design at Mellerstain in Scotland). The beautifully made mahogany handrail is inlaid with harewood.

LEFT The Library, with its exceptionally fine mahogany bookcase, which has a concealed secret door. The mirror over the chimneypiece, by Francis and John Booker of Dublin, *circa* 1750/30, was a breakthrough discovery by the present Knight; bearing the Bookers' label, it was the first documented example from which many more pieces were to be attributed.

is an echo here of Robert Adam's bifurcating example at Mellerstain in Scotland.) Poor Colonel John and his wife died young and broke, with the new house incomplete and 5,000 acres of the estate having to be sold in accordance with a private Act of Parliament passed in the year of the Act of Union, 1801. This grim document noted how Colonel John had expended

> Six thousand pounds and upward in building a mansion house and
> offices, and making plantations and other valuable and lasting
> improvements.

This was certainly a hefty sum in those days, but one can only agree with the legislators that Colonel John's improvements were lasting and valuable.

In 1803, when Colonel John died and much of Glin's contents were dispersed at a Sheriff's Sale, his son the new, 12-year-old Knight, John Fraunceis FitzGerald, seemed to face a bleak inheritance. But he was a colourful and resourceful character, and managed to restore the family fortunes by successful gambling, as well as by selling large chunks of the estate. Although wild and eccentric – he was known as 'The Knight of the Women' for obvious reasons and continued the family feud with the Moriartys by fighting a Protestant clergyman of that name – John Fraunceis had many fine qualities. He was a poet, a Gaelic speaker, a just magistrate, a benevolent and improving landlord. His antiquarian tastes were given full rein in the 1820s in transforming Glin House into Glin Castle, complete with sugar-icing battlements, false arrow loops like a child's toy fort, castellated Gothic lodges, a hermitage and a folly, all in the spirit of the Romantic Movement.

In the early reign of John Fraunceis at Glin the new castle enjoyed a high noon. The hospitality and entertainment (for which the plan of the interior is ideal as all the reception rooms open off the main hall and the staircase hall

Detail of the Irish chimneypiece in the Library which was found locally.

beyond, enabling easy circulation) were lavish. But then came the Famine of the 1840s, the death of John Fraunceis from cholera, and general gloom – though at least the subsequent poverty ensured that the Victorian era left the Georgian castle untouched.

There was, however, no shortage of colour. The 'Cracked Knight' (slightly touched with concussion after an early fall from a horse) publicly horsewhipped the father of Field Marshal Lord Kitchener for evicting his tenants and is said to have ridden his horse up the back stairs at Glin. One day when the beef was not cooked to his liking 'Jack the Devil' (as the Cracked Knight was also known) threw it with its silver-plated dish and cover the full length of the dining room and out of the window. His son, the 'Big Knight', took solace in the whiskey bottle, but fortunately his sensible wife, Isabella, steered Glin safely through the late 19th-century agrarian troubles.

ABOVE View of the entrance front from the Shannon, with the service range to the right.

LEFT The prospect from the front door: castellated lodge, the Shannon and Co. Clare.

Next came FitzJohn, the 27th Knight of Glin, who had to live through even more troubled times. When the Sinn Feiners arrived in 1923 to burn the castle he roared at them from his wheelchair (he had been paralysed by a stroke, having never got over the early death of his wife, Lady Rachel Wyndham-Quin, daughter of the 4th Earl of Dunraven): 'Well, you'll have to burn me in it, boys!' The 'boys' retired to the village pub.

By the end of the 1920s Glin had fallen into a long sleep. Fortunately a princess arrived in the shape of Veronica Villiers, the wife of the 28th Knight and mother of the present Knight (duly nicknamed 'the Knight-*mère*'). She fell in love with this place of enchantment and set about restoring its beauty. After the 28th Knight's early death from tuberculosis she battled on with the generous help of her second husband, Ray Milner, a Canadian businessman, and effectively saved Glin for the next generation.

The new young Knight was inspired with a love of architecture by Stan Stewart, a Limerick pharmacist. Together the two men would explore the country houses of the area, many of them in advanced stages of decay. Outside the gaunt ruin of Ballynagarde, they discovered a headless Andromeda chained to a rock, bought her for £1 and triumphantly brought her back to Glin – where her curvaceous marble form now adorns the new rustic temple (in the idiosyncratic manner of Thomas Wright) in the walled garden.

A brilliant collector was on his way. Later the Knight persuaded his mother to buy two marble chimneypieces from the gutted Tervoe. One was duly installed in the Dining Room at Glin, the other in the Morning Room. The former turned out to be by the illustrious sculptor Sir Henry Cheere, so the Knight's 'eye' was well in.

Soon it would be sharpened through schooling in the ducal glories of Stowe, studying fine arts at Harvard, curating at the Victoria & Albert Museum and representing Christie's in Ireland. Together with Anne Crookshank, he has also produced a pioneering series of exhibitions and writings on Irish houses, landscapes, furniture, ceramics, portraits, painters and watercolours. All these interests are reflected in the Knight's stimulating collection at Glin.

The genius of the place is that, as John Cornforth has observed, it does not feel like a 'collector's house' for 'everything looks as though it has always been there, and the recent arrivals are completely at ease with the ancestors'. Both inside and out – where the Knight and his wife, Olda, Madam FitzGerald, whose first book on Irish gardens has recently appeared, have recreated and reorganised the formal and kitchen gardens – Glin is surely the *beau idéal* of an Irish country house, grand yet intimate.

To keep the roof on ('We always live with the spectre of the auctioneer's tent going up on the lawn and seeing everything scattered in a couple of days') the Knight and his family welcome paying guests, who are treated to stylish country house cuisine and hospitality at their best. The good news is that this commercial enterprise is enabling the long-naked and unfinished top floor to be handsomely clothed in order to provide more guest accommodation. Just as this book was going to press, the Knight was amused to come across the copy for an advertisement in the *Limerick Chronicle* dated April 8, 1809, during the minority of the 'Knight of the Women', which stated that: 'A proper person that would open an Hotel there [Glin House] for the Summer Season will meet with every encouragement.' The present Mine Host of Glin deserves all the encouragement going.

3

BALLINLOUGH CASTLE

COUNTY WESTMEATH

 T FIRST glance it might be thought that the Nugents of Ballinlough belong to the 'Old English' group of Irish country house owners, of whom only a handful survive. Yet closer investigation of the family history reveals something much more remarkable, indeed the very rare distinction of being a Catholic Celtic-Irish family still seated at their ancestral castle. For these Nugents are really O'Reillys: 'We changed our name for money', explains Ballinlough's present owner, the genial Sir John Nugent 7th Bt, a Count of the Holy Roman Empire.

He is alluding to how his ancestor Lieutenant-Colonel Sir Hugh O'Reilly, 1st Bt, assumed the surname of Nugent in 1812 in order to inherit a legacy from his maternal family. His mother, Barbara, was a daughter of Andrew Nugent of Dysart, Co. Westmeath, whose wife, Lady Katherine, was also a Nugent, being a co-heiress of the 4th Earl of Westmeath. Lord Westmeath was outlawed for his staunch support of the Catholic King James II in 1691, but after he had been exchanged as one of the hostages for the observance of the Articles of Limerick the outlawry was reversed and he was restored to his estates.

The name of Nugent may go back to the Normans but the O'Reillys, the princely Milesian *O'Rathallaigh*, traditionally claim descent, via Matthew 'of the Apples', to Eochaidh Moighamheadhoin, King of Ireland, AD 366. Such a wonderful span of history adds to Ballinlough's considerable romantic appeal. For, as Christine Casey and Alistair Rowan wrote in their *North Leinster* volume in *The Buildings of Ireland* series, 'All that anyone might hope for in an Irish country house is present at Ballinlough... A wooded lakeside setting, a charming and eccentric house of several building periods and a family history of distinction.'

In cold fact, the first stage of building on the present site would appear to have been in the 17th century, though family tradition maintains that the castle was built as an extension to an old tower house, the remains of which are under the ground on the north-east side of the courtyard. The year '1614' is inscribed beneath the O'Reilly coat of arms on the central attic storey, but in the view of John Cornforth of *Country Life*, 'the clue to the development of the house seems to be provided by the end chimney and fragment of steeply pitched roof beside it, which suggests to me the second half of the 17th century'. The builder would probably have been Hugh O'Reilly, who married a Plunkett and created a family mausoleum here in 1686.

His grandson, another Hugh (whose first father-in-law, the Jacobite 6th Viscount Mountgarret, is described in the correspondence of Colonel Hooke as '*fort honnête homme et zélé Catholique*'), seems to have been responsible for the second stage of construction. This gave Ballinlough a pleasant seven-bay facade with narrow windows, a breakfront centre and a segmented pedimented doorcase. The problem with dating this is that the exterior looks late 17th- or early 18th-century, while inside the joinery and plasterwork strike Casey and Rowan as being of '*circa* 1740' and suggest to Cornforth 'a date in the 1740s or early '50s'. Perhaps, as Cornforth suggests, it was just a matter of Hugh O'Reilly (who had a long reign at Ballinlough) working slowly or of completing the interior rather later than the exterior.

Leaving the experts' deliberations aside, though, it is a joy to celebrate the sheer exuberance of the Hall at Ballinlough, a truly exhilarating interior. It rises through two storeys and is spanned by an unusual bridge-gallery. There are panels of fruit and flowers in plasterwork on the walls, a cornice in the same style and a richly carved frieze of acanthus below the gallery balustrade – which, like that of the staircase, has slender wooden balusters.

The slightly clumsy, provincial handling of the scale only serves to make the Hall more endearing and the crude grimacing masks leering out of the foliate scrolls at the base of the gallery have an infectiously funny quality

PREVIOUS PAGES A corner of the panelled Hall at Ballinlough, looking through to the Drawing Room. The portrait on the right is of Lieutenant-Colonel Sir Hugh O'Reilly, 1st Bt, who changed his surname to Nugent in 1812 and earlier extended and castellated the house.

RIGHT The galleried Hall, exuberantly decorated with carved Rococo ornament and plasterwork in the first half of the 18th century.

The O'Reilly coat of arms, dated 1614, on the central attic storey of the house, high above the front door. The architecture of this facade suggests a rather later date in the 17th century.

which raises the spirits. Altogether the Hall at Ballinlough is one of the most lovable rooms in Ireland.

Casey and Rowan draw our attention to the similarities with Drewstown House across the Meath border. This has been attributed to the amateur architect Francis Bindon and 'there is certainly some reason to suppose that both interiors were designed by the same hand'. The attribution of the third stage of building at Ballinlough has also exercised the architectural authorities. At one time it was thought that James Wyatt might have been the author of the north castellated wing; admittedly the Drawing Room's fine white marble chimneypiece, with a frieze of swags and urns and supported at each end by a Roman female term, is identical to the one in the Wyatt Dining Room at Curraghmore (*qv*).

RIGHT Detail of the Drawing Room chimneypiece, a white marble transom with a frieze of swags and urns supported at each end by a Roman female term. Curiously, this chimneypiece is identical to the one in the Dining Room at Curraghmore (*qv*), designed by James Wyatt.

BELOW General view of the Drawing Room, showing its graceful rounded angles and unusual cornice decorated with Gothic pendant motifs. The arched doorway leads to the Dining Room.

LEFT The double doors dividing the Dining Room from the Drawing Room, with an arched frame incorporating both Gothic and neo-Classical touches.

RIGHT The Dining Room, hung with family portraits of the O'Reillys and Nugents. The fine chimneypiece is of polychrome marble with engaged Tuscan shafts; it appears earlier than the one in the Drawing Room next door and may have been moved from the older part of the house.

However, in *The Bulletin of The Irish Georgian Society* in 1964, Alistair Rowan put up a more convincing candidate in the person of the amateur architect Thomas Wogan Browne of Castle Browne, Co. Kildare (now Clongowes School), who is also thought to have designed the 18th-century range at Malahide Castle, Co. Dublin. Significantly, Wogan Browne was connected to both the O'Reillys of Ballinlough and the Talbots of Malahide; to complete the circle of connections, Margaret O'Reilly (sister of Sir Hugh Reilly, 1st Bt) married Richard Talbot and became *châtelaine* of that historic castle and eventually Baroness Talbot of Malahide in her own right.

Sir Hugh's Baronetcy dated from 1795 and it would appear that the new wing was added to Ballinlough within the preceding five years. A castellated range was added at right angles to the original front and given two slender round corner towers (similar to the ones at Malahide). At the same time the previous seven-bay facade was re-roofed: the breakfront was raised a storey to form a tower-like attic, which was battlemented, like the rest of the roofline.

Within the new wing are to be found highly elegant Georgian Gothic rooms with vast (18-paned) sash windows overlooking the woods and the lakes. The singular serenity of the spacious *suite* of Dining Room and Drawing Room is enhanced by the unusual feature of there being no sharp corners. Instead, the eye is treated to gently curving rounded angles, with gib doors leading into each of the corner turrets. Equally unusual are the Gothic pendant motifs in the cornices, while the double doors dividing the two rooms have a curious arched frame incorporating both Gothic and neo-Classical touches.

Having changed his name to Nugent and inherited the cash (his wife, a Miss Mathew, cousin of the 1st Earl of Llandaff, was also an heiress of sorts), Sir Hugh lived in some style at Ballinlough, as the following extract from Atkinson's *The Irish Tourist* (1815) bears out:

> The castle and demesne of Ballinlough had an appearance of antiquity highly gratifying to my feelings... I reined in my horse within a few perches of the grand gate of Ballinlough to take a view of the castle: it stands on a little eminence above a lake which beautifies the demesne; and not only the structure of the castle, but the appearance of the

trees, and even the dusky colour of the gate and walls, as you enter, contribute to give the whole scenery an appearance of antiquity, while the prospect is calculated to infuse into the heart of the beholder, a mixed sentiment of veneration and delight.

Having visited the castle of Ballinlough, the interior of which appears a good deal modernized, Sir Hugh had the politeness to shew me two or three of the principal apartments; these, together with the gallery in the hall, had as splendid an appearance as anything which I had, until that time, witnessed in private buildings. The rooms are furnished in a stile – I cannot pretend to estimate the value, either of the furniture or ornamental works, but some idea thereof may be formed from the expence of a fine marble chimney-piece purchased in Italy, and which, if any solid substance can in smoothness and transparency rival such work, it is this. I took the liberty of enquiring what might have been the expence of this article and Sir Hugh informed me only five hundred pounds sterling, a sum that would establish a country tradesman in business!

Atkinson also greatly admired the family portraits at Ballinlough, among them doubtless the dashing study of Sir Hugh's brother General Count Andrew O'Reilly of the Austrian Army, who, like the scions of many Irish Catholic families, joined 'the Wild Geese' serving on the Continent of Europe. He fought, and won, a duel, married a Bohemian heiress and distinguished himself at Austerlitz; he was Governor of Vienna in 1809 when Napoleon attacked. His nephew Count John Nugent (Sir Hugh's second son) entered the Austrian Service and became Chamberlain to the Emperor.

ABOVE Waiting for a walk: the family dogs outside the simple round-arched front door of the 17th-century facade.

LEFT A snooze by the stairs. The elaborate carved staircase has three round fluted balusters per tread.

RIGHT A corner of the gallery above the Hall, with its delightful decorative swags of foliage and flowers. The doors have oak-lugged surrounds, the walls have fielded plaster panels.

LEFT Looking out on to one of the lakes at Ballinlough. The gardens were the first recipients of a grant given by the European Union under the Great Gardens of Ireland scheme.

BELOW General view of the entrance front of Ballinlough. The seven-bay 17th-century house (to the right of the picture) was altered in the early 18th century, and extended and castellated (to the left) at the end of the 18th century.

In 1843, however, Count John succeeded his childless brother in the Baronetcy and Ballinlough. To provide work at the time of the Famine the new Baronet had a second, smaller, lake dug. It is known to this day as the Famine Lake, but had to be comprehensively dredged in the 1930s by the present Baronet's father, Sir Hugh Nugent, 6th Bt. 'It took 16 men, two horses with scoops and four with carts over three months to clear it out', recalls Sir John, the 7th Bt. During the recent restoration of Ballinlough, by contrast, two big diggers did the job in a mere 10 days. (A handsome new wooden bridge now enhances the scene.)

Sir Hugh Nugent fought a heroic battle to keep Ballinlough afloat in the 20th century. At the time he succeeded his grandfather in 1927 the prospects looked extremely bleak. In the wake of the anti-landlord legislation and the Troubles, Ballinlough – despite its long Catholic Celtic connection – had been acquired by the Land Commission, who had disposed of the supporting land and, shamefully, were proposing to demolish the castle.

With admirable tenacity, patience and perseverance, though, Sir Hugh managed to buy back the land, piece by piece, and to replant the woods and belts around the house. Eventually, towards the end of the 1930s, he and his wife, the former Margaret Puxley from a Berkshire squirearchical family, were able to tackle a thoroughgoing restoration of the house itself: 'The place had been kept alive for 10 years by Owen Quinn, a marvellous old steward', recalls Sir John Nugent. 'He lived in the house on his own with no heating, no water and rats everywhere.'

The faithful Quinn helped locate the paths buried under layers of neglect. 'He used to say to my father: "If you dig there, there *may* be a path"', recalls Sir John.

It is cheering to report that the Ballinlough saga has a happy ending, or rather a new beginning. For in 1998 Sir John Nugent and his livewire wife, 'Pepe' (Penelope Hanbury), opened the castle gardens to the public as they are currently being restored with the help of a grant given by the European Union under the Great Gardens of Ireland restoration scheme. Appropriately enough, Ballinlough is the first recipient. Visitors to this enchanting place are echoing Mr Atkinson's sentiments of 'veneration and delight'.

4

LISMORE
CASTLE

COUNTY WATERFORD

T HE VISION that suddenly dominates the horizon as you progress alongside the Blackwater on the road from Cappoquin takes your breath away. For here, perched on the top of a tree-covered cliff high above the river, is a skyline from a medieval fantasy – towers, turrets, battlements evoking the Age of Chivalry. As James Lees-Milne wrote in his biography of *The Bachelor Duke*, the 6th Duke of Devonshire, who was largely responsible for the (in his own words) 'quasi-feudal ultra-regal fortress' that we see today: 'There can be few castle sites in the British Isles more picturesque, certainly none that has changed less during our century'.

Yet while the Bachelor Duke, together with his devoted collaborator (and former gardener) Sir Joseph Paxton, fulfilled his typically 19th-century dream of recreating at Lismore everything a medieval castle should be, underneath the fantastic adornment are traces of the genuine article from the Middle Ages. Within the Bachelor Duke's massive structure of the 1850s are some of the cone-like towers of the medieval castle which housed the Bishops of Lismore. This, in turn, took the place of a castle built by King John on the site of a monastery founded by St Carthagh where in the Dark Ages the university epitomised the tradition of Ireland being 'The Land of Saints and Scholars'.

Unfortunately these spiritual ideals were less in evidence in the 16th century, when the first Protestant Bishop of Lismore, the notorious reprobate Myler McGrath, granted the castle and its lands to Sir Walter Raleigh, the Elizabethan adventurer (who in England may be remembered in chivalrous terms but in Ireland is less fondly recalled for his military activities). Sir Walter, it seems, seldom lived at the by now ruinous Lismore, preferring his house at Youghal in Co. Cork, Myrtle Grove. Luckily for Lismore, the next owner, Richard Boyle, 1st Earl of Cork, turned out to have a passionate commitment to Ireland and its improvement.

The 'Great Earl of Cork', as he came to be known, had a remarkable life. Born in 1566, he was a struggling legal clerk when, in the year of the Spanish Armada (1588), he decided to try his luck in Ireland. At that time his possessions amounted to £27 3s, a diamond ring and a bracelet. After an unpromising start, which saw accusations of embezzlement and a spell in prison (though he was acquitted, to the discredit of his accusers), he rose to become Clerk of the Council of Munster in 1600 – and subsequently one of the richest and most powerful nobles in Ireland.

Inevitably such a meteoric rise left much bitterness in its wake. In 1616, when he entered the peerage, one disgruntled chronicler noted: 'The Lord Boyle made a Baron who they say not above 16 years afore, being a poore fellowe and in prison at Monster in Ireland, borrowed 6d, and now hath a great estate and £12,000 yeerly of Irish land'. A more generous assessment is given in Sir Richard Cox's *History of Ireland*. The Great Earl of Cork, in his view,

> was one of the most extraordinary persons, either *that* or any other age has produced, with respect to the great and just acquisition of estate that he made, and the public works that he began and finished, for the advancement of the English interest and the protestant religion in Ireland, as charities, almshouses, free schools, bridges, castles and towns...

Chief among these castles and towns was Lismore, which the Great Earl rebuilt as his home from about 1610 onwards. The great coup of his career had occurred eight years earlier, when for a mere £1,500 he had bought all Raleigh's Irish landholdings (admittedly then in a poor state) in Counties Cork,

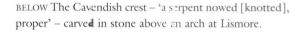

BELOW The Cavendish crest – 'a serpent nowed [knotted], proper' – carved in stone above an arch at Lismore.

LEFT The view from the castle looking east along the Blackwater. The bridge, of *circa* 1775, is by the Dublin architect Thomas Ivory.

BELOW Looking through the Riding House arch to the Gatehouse. These were both built by the 'Great Earl' of Cork in the early 17th century. The Gatehouse incorporates an old Celtic-Romanesque arch which must have survived from Lismore's monastic days.

The Dining Room, with furniture mostly designed by Augustus Welby Pugin, who is recorded as sending off drawings to Lismore in the spring of 1850.

Waterford and Tipperary. With shrewd speculation the dedicated tycoon added land in a further 13 Irish counties. The key to his success, according to his own account in *True Remembrances* (printed in the works of his son Robert Boyle, the philosopher and father of modern chemistry), was 'the introduction of manufactures and mechanical arts by settlers from England'. From his ironworks alone, apparently, he made a clear profit of £100,000.

At Lismore the Great Earl surrounded the castle courtyard with three-storeyed gabled ranges joining the old corner towers of the castle, which were given contemporary (Jacobean) ogival roofs. Then, as now, the principal living rooms of the castle were on the side above the River Blackwater, with the parlour and dining-chamber in a wing projecting outwards to the very edge of the precipice. The dining-chamber was lit by an oriel, or 'compass', window, from which there was a sheer drop to the river far below.

When King James II dined here in 1689, as Smith relates in his *History of Waterford*, he strolled over to look out of this window and 'started back in surprise'. The shock is no less potent today, even if now the dizzy-making view is to be had from the Drawing Room bay, successor to the Great Earl's compass-windowed dining-chamber.

There are, though, some notable survivals from the Great Earl's copiously documented building works at Lismore, especially the Gatehouse (incorporating an old Celtic-Romanesque arch which must have survived from Lismore's monastic days), the fortified garden walls and the Riding House, which originally sheltered a mounted guard. Progress, however, does not seem to have been particularly brisk. In 1637, over a quarter of a century after he had embarked on the castle's enlargement, the Great Earl was complaining that 'our masons here are bunglers, and slow in dispatch'.

Eventually, it was not so much the Great Earl's death in 1643 (there is an elaborate tomb at Youghal) which brought the building works at Lismore to an end as the violent upheavals of that period. Although the stoutness of the garden walls helped repel the Confederate Army siege of 1642, three years later the castle was sacked. *The Civil Survey* of 1654/6 describes Lismore as 'ruinated'.

The 2nd Earl of Cork, who married the north English heiress Elizabeth Clifford and also became Earl of Burlington in the English peerage, is described as a more cautious figure than his father. But he made Lismore habitable again and may have been responsible for the Doric portico (long since disappeared) opposite the Gatehouse and also, as Mark Girouard suggests, 'the impressively gloomy avenue of yews in the lower garden', which survives.

Thereafter Lismore fell into neglect. The 4th Earl of Cork, who preferred to be known as the 3rd Earl of Burlington and spent all his time in England or the Continent pursuing his passion for Palladian architecture, took no interest in Ireland. Lismore Castle did not appeal to his refined tastes and it would appear that this brilliant amateur architect went so far as to dismantle the north range there so as to save running costs. Yet his only surviving child and heiress, Charlotte, was to marry into a family that came to form a great love for Lismore, the Cavendishes, Dukes of Devonshire.

Charlotte's husband, the 4th Duke of Devonshire, Lord Lieutenant of Ireland and Prime Minister of Great Britain, was preoccupied with matters of state. But her son, the 5th Duke (better known as the husband of the flamboyant Georgiana Spencer, the 'Face Without A Frown' immortalised by Gainsborough and Reynolds), was responsible for the elegant bridge designed by the Dublin architect Thomas Ivory, *circa* 1775, which still spans the Blackwater. It forms a graceful prelude to the dramatic creation of his son and successor, 'Hart', the 6th 'Bachelor' Duke.

A singularly attractive and sympathetic character, the Bachelor Duke – who, as the present Duchess of Devonshire has written, was a 'mixture of grandeur and humility' – had an obsessive love of building and gardening. Lismore was to be his pet project. After seeing it for the first time as a boy he was, 'haunted by the magical setting' of what he called his 'enchanted castle' for the rest of his life.

His first visit as Duke came in 1812, when he escorted his tempestuous cousin Lady Caroline Lamb to Ireland after her torrid affair with Lord Byron. Lady Caroline's romantic notions of an Irish castle (ghosts, knights in armour, echoing dungeons and, as she put it, 'vast apartments full of tattered furniture and gloom...') were dashed by the reality of the patched-up structure. As her mother, the Countess of Bessborough, wrote:

> Hart handed her into, not a Gothic hall but two small dapper parlours
> neatly furnished in the newest Inn fashion, much like a Cit's villa at
> Highgate... She also persists in its being very damp...

Detail of door-lock at Lismore.

One of William Atkinson's gentle Gothic interiors of 1811, with vaulted ceilings: the Drawing Room was refashioned from the previous dining chamber. Its tapestries, depicting scenes from *Don Quixote*, previously hung at another Cavendish family seat, Compton Place, Eastbourne.

Lady Caroline annoyed the Bachelor Duke by treating a toad on the premises as if it was the rightful proprietor. Possibly stung by her impertinence, he made all haste with a remodelling by the English architect William Atkinson. a Gothic specialist probably best known for his work at Scone Palace in Scotland. The rooms above the river were done over with delicate groined ceilings supported on brackets in stucco, slender panelled doors and quasi-medieval chimneypieces in black marble. The Drawing Room superseded the dining chamber and its celebrated window; and outside battlements replaced the Great Earl of Cork's gables.

Subsequently the Bachelor Duke was busy in England with improvements at Chatsworth, the family's principal seat in Derbyshire, but towards the end of his life in 1858 Lismore loomed ever larger in his affections. 'Chatsworth is stupendous', he once wrote, 'but after Lismore seems to me a splendid desert'. A week at Lismore, he found, 'goes like an hour anywhere else'. He revelled in the lack of snobbery among his neighbours : 'They have got a natural *bonhomie* and want of pretension', he wrote, 'that makes them very captivating, never wanting to appear what they are not'.

The Bachelor Duke's own lack of snobbery is exemplified in his great working friendship with Paxton. Together, in the early 1850s, they rebuilt the three remaining sides of the courtyard at Lismore with impressive battlemented towers and turrets in cut-stone shipped over from Derbyshire. The ruined chapel of the old Bishops of Lismore was triumphantly recreated as a sort of ecclesiastical Banqueting Hall, complete with choirstalls, a huge Perpendicular stained-glass window at either end, and richly coloured Gothic stencilling on the walls and roof timbers.

This amazing interior has been aptly called (by Mark Girouard) 'a kind of miniature House of Lords', and the rebuilt Palace of Westminster's interior designer Augustus Welby Pugin, the high priest of Gothic Revival, certainly had a hand in its decoration, and in that of the other refashioned interiors at Lis-

ABOVE The first breathtaking glimpse of Lismore along the road from Cappoquin. The gardens, noted for their shrubs, are a popular attraction for visitors.

LEFT 'A miniature House of Lords': the stupendous Banqueting Hall by Pugin and Crace. The chimneypiece was exhibited in the Medieval Court at the Great Exhibition of 1851. The ping-pong table is a reminder that for all its grandeur, Lismore is essentially a much-loved holiday home.

more. Pugin's magnificent Banqueting Hall chimneypiece, originally designed for the Barchard family of Horsted Place in Sussex, had been exhibited in the 'Medieval Court' at the Great Exhibition of 1851. Pugin's principal craftsman at Lismore was John Gregory Crace, who had previously worked on the Bachelor Duke's private library at Chatsworth.

Without wishing to echo Lady Caroline Lamb, one is struck at Lismore by how much more modest the interior is, the grandiloquent Banqueting Hall aside, than one might expect from the building's rambling extent. The particular charm of the place is that it has the atmosphere of a much-loved holiday home – which, of course, is exactly what it has been for the last 150 years.

Today it is not just the holiday home of the Cavendish family, as the owner, the Marquess of Hartington, son and heir of the present Duke of Devonshire, lets it out on an occasional basis to other families too. There could be no more delightful or invigorating place for a relaxed house-party. One of the castle's amusing features is a bathroom celebrating the dancing skills of the legendary Hollywood star Fred Astaire and his sister Adele, who married Lord Charles Cavendish, younger son of the 9th Duke of Devonshire. Indeed, Adele was the *châtelaine* of Lismore for a dozen years and lived here in considerable style.

Although available for rented parties, the castle is not open to the public, but the gardens are a popular attraction from April to September every year. The present Duke and Duchess of Devonshire have carried out many improvements to the gardens during their regular visits for the fishing. The lower garden provides woodland shelter for a fine collection of shrubs, including magnolias and camellias. It is linked to the upper garden by the staircase to the Riding House (built by the Great Earl of Cork), a characteristically charming and unexpected feature of lovable Lismore.

5

CROM CASTLE

*I*RELAND'S 'LAKELAND' of Co. Fermanagh (where tradition has it that there is more lake than land) may not have received the same amount of publicity as the Romantic poets bestowed on England's Lake District, but it is surely no less beautiful in its way and all the more bewitching for being so comparatively little known. Although some of the great waterway of Lough Erne, which runs majestically for some 40 miles, has been colonised by the cabin-cruiser fraternity, the glories of the Upper Lough – where the sheet-glass surface of the water reflects a magical landscape of fields, hills, trees and mountains in a kaleidoscope of ever-changing colours – remain delectably undiscovered.

One's romantic expectations are raised by various 'eye-catchers' dotted around on the little islands in the Upper Lough, such as the round battlemented Crichton Tower on Gad Island. These are preparing you for the thrill of catching sight of Crom Castle, the seat of the Crichtons, Earls of Erne, who acquired this picturesque property in the 17th century. The present impressive Victorian pile by Edward Blore remains in the ownership of the present Earl of Erne, Lord Lieutenant of Co. Fermanagh. The 1,350-acre estate, a notable haven for wildlife, from whooper swans and red Irish hares to purple-hairstreak butterflies and silver-washed fritillaries, is now in the care of the National Trust.

Not far from the 19th-century Tudor Revival castle, which sits magnificently above the lacustrine landscape, the eye is caught by what appears to be a Picturesque folly on the lake shore. But on closer investigation this romantic ruin turns out to be real enough : the fragments of a Plantation castle that has evidently taken some buffeting.

Old Crom Castle was built in 1610 by a Scottish planter, Michael Balfour. In the official inspection of 1619 it is described as having 'a bawn of lime and stone' 60 feet square and 12 feet high, with two flankers and with 'a house

PREVIOUS PAGES The present Crom Castle, with its boathouse in the foreground, seen from the island of Inisherk on Upper Lough Erne. The battlemented boathouse was designed by George Sudden, *circa* 1850.

LEFT A canine perspective on the scale of Edward Blore's giant *porte-cochère* at the entrance to Crom. The colour of the local limestone changes according to the vagaries of the weather.

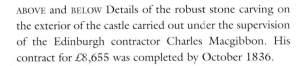

ABOVE and BELOW Details of the robust stone carving on the exterior of the castle carried out under the supervision of the Edinburgh contractor Charles Macgibbon. His contract for £8,655 was completed by October 1836.

of lime and stone' inside. Soon after this inspection, the castle became the home of James Spottiswoode, Bishop of Clogher, whose daughter Mary married Abraham Crichton.

The Crichtons had previously been a prominent family in Scotland, originally seated at Crichton (the ruined castle immortalised in Sir Walter Scott's *Marmion*) and latterly at Brunston Castle near Edinburgh (in the 16th century Alexander Crichton was described as 'a zealous promoter of the reformed religion'), and were already well established in the Plantation of Ulster, having acquired the neighbouring estates of Aghalane and Dromboory. Abraham obtained the freehold of Crom and became High Sheriff of the county and the local MP. A redoubtable character, Colonel Crichton became celebrated for defending Crom Castle in 1689 against the army of the Catholic King James II not once but twice, the first time in March, the second in July. Two years later he commanded his own regiment at the Battle of Aughrim, Co. Galway. His sons also distinguished themselves in the military, the youngest (and eventual successor to Crom), David, by rising to the rank of Major-General and the governorship of the Royal Hospital.

The Crichtons stayed on in the old castle, having withstood the sieges, right up to 1764 when, as tradition has it, another Abraham Crichton (the General's son) attending the house-warming party at Florence Court (*qv*) noticed an ominous glow in the sky to the south. He galloped back to Crom to find his own house had been rather more than warmed; it had been burnt down.

After the fire the Crichtons seem to have spent most of their time at another of their properties, Knockballymore, on the Co. Monaghan border. Abraham, who had been an MP for 41 years, was raised to the peerage as Baron Erne in 1868. His son John, who was advanced to a Viscountcy in 1781 and then created Earl of Erne eight years later, married as his second wife, Mary, the eldest daughter of that most worldly of ecclesiastics, the 'Mitred Earl' of Bristol, notorious for dispensing his benefices as Bishop of Derry to the winners of curates' races held on the sands below his eccentric cliffside palace after sumptuous repasts.

The Mitred Earl (of whom Lord Charlemont sagely observed 'his ambition and his lust alone can get the better of his avarice...') took a jaundiced view of the Erne marriage. 'Your poor sister', he wrote to another of his daughters in 1778, 'is worn out, exhausted and can do no more. He tires her to atoms by his silly difficulties and his endless irresolutions. Great God, how ill she is matched!'

Whatever the justice in these complaints, the Ernes seem to have led largely separate lives, mainly away from Ireland, though the new Earl did build a small lodge or summer residence on the island of Inisherk on Upper Lough Erne, where the present walled garden is situated. Possibly one of his 'irresolutions' concerned a desire to build a new family seat: his will of 1828 specifically bequeathed £20,000 in consols to his eldest grandson, John Crichton, 'to build Crom Castle'.

Young John (who eventually succeeded to the Earldom of Erne in 1842 upon the death of his eccentric bachelor uncle) did not lack for resolution. Within a year of his grandfather's death he was discussing plans for the new castle with the English architect Edward Blore, a specialist in the Gothic Revival style and *protégé* of Sir Walter Scott (for whom he had worked at Abbotsford on the River Tweed). Gervase Jackson-Stops suggested in *Country Life* that John Crichton had probably admired Blore's designs for Weston House in Warwickshire, exhibited at the Royal Academy in 1828. Certainly there are striking similarities between Weston (demolished, alas, in the 1930s) and Crom.

Poor Blore – his surname's proximity to 'Bore' does not help matters – has received an unkind press over the years. Yet Mark Girouard, the great authority on Victorian country houses, has argued that Blore was the perfect architect for the Tory gentry, designing houses for them in the good Old English style, as opposed to the Italianate *palazzi* which Sir Charles Barry built for Whig grandees such as the Duke of Sutherland. (It was the Duchess of Sutherland who notoriously branded Blore as 'the *economical* architect' after he underbid to complete John Nash's Buckingham Palace.) 'Gently picturesque and gently Elizabethan' is Girouard's summing-up of Blore's traditional style – and it nicely captures the flavour of Crom.

Built of local limestone (in a colour that changes according to the vagaries of the weather) with sandstone dressings, it is certainly a house to be reckoned with. The key feature is its unrivalled position on the high ground north of the old castle which benefits both the house and the surrounding landscape in providing an infinite variety of marvellous views. Much credit is due to Crichton and Blore's landscape architect William Sawrey Gilpin, a nephew of the Picturesque pioneer the Reverend William Gilpin and also a fine painter, for his role in helping to choose the site, as well as in planning the vistas and the mixed planting of trees that give Crom much of its charm.

The house, erected from 1834 onwards, has a tall battlemented entrance tower, which incorporates a *porte-cochère*, but the garden front (where Blore placed the three principal rooms) enjoys the panorama through its vast mullion windows and deeply projecting bays. Inside, the most spectacular feature is the great Staircase Hall, with its double-return 'Imperial' staircase (similar, as Alistair Rowan has pointed out in his *North-West Ulster* volume in *The Buildings of Ireland* series, to the one at Lowther Castle, Cumberland, by Sir Robert Smirke, for whom Blore worked as a draughtsman). This remarkable interior has the feel of a cathedral, a feeling enhanced by the late Perpendicular arcade, crisply detailed in timber and plaster, which frames the staircase, and also by the armorial stained-glass windows by Thomas Willement.

The contract of the builder Charles Macgibbon of Edinburgh for £8,655 was completed by October 1836, though two years later a conservatory pavilion and arcade were added to the west wing. But then, in January 1841, disaster struck. Another fire fell upon Crom.

RIGHT The Staircase Hall, with its late Perpendicular-style arcade detailed in timber and plaster, is one of Edward Blore's most magnificent interiors. It was designed in 1835 and rebuilt in the same form after the fire of 1841. The double-return staircase has been compared with Sir Robert Smirke's at Lowther Castle in Cumberland.

BELOW Blore's dramatic entrance staircase rises in a straight flight from the base of the *porte-cochère* up to the central Staircase Hall, which is guarded by the impressive Gothic portal seen at the top of the picture. To increase the sense of theatre in this ascent, Blore placed the *porte-cochère* in a sunken courtyard.

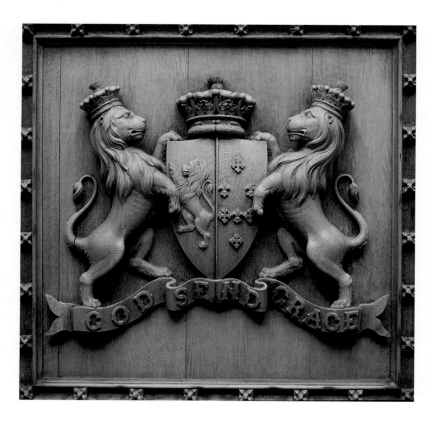

ABOVE Heraldry is a particular feature at Crom, as at so many Victorian castles. This is a detail of an armorial panel in the Library, showing the coat of arms of the 3rd Earl of Erne impaling those of his wife, Selina Beresford.

RIGHT 'One of the most comfortable country house libraries in Ireland': the Library, formerly the drawing room, was rearranged in the 1880s when its bookcases and panelled fireplace were moved here from their original position in what is now the Drawing Room. The 'Jacobethan' overmantel and the bookcases were designed by Edward Blore and are similar to ones at Merevale in Warwickshire, which came after Crom.

LEFT The Drawing Room, formerly the Library, which was rearranged in the 1880s, and redecorated in the 1950s by Felix Harbord. The fine late 18th-century white marble chimneypiece installed here is by Peter Bossi.

BELOW Every window at Crom tempts the visitor to look out over the lacustrine landscape. The castle commands a picturesque prospect above Upper Lough Erne.

The story goes that John Crichton's idiosyncratic uncle the 2nd Earl of Erne was at the barber's in England when someone rushed in and announced: 'Milord, your house has burnt down'. He replied, 'Well, build it up again,' before resuming his perusal of the newspaper. And this is what his nephew, soon to be the 3rd Earl, duly did, albeit at considerable expense (nearly £15,000 was spent on the painstaking rebuilding and refurnishing).

Macgibbon and the others involved, including the Edinburgh furniture-makers Trotters, reassembled, though this time under the supervision of the Dublin architect George Sudden rather than of Blore who by now (*pace* the Duchess of Sutherland) was too expensive for the Ernes. Soon, if not suddenly, the house was as good as new once more, with its enfilade of rooms on the garden front (Dining Room, Saloon and Library) adorned with 'Jacobethan' ceilings, and quatrefoil-studded cornices.

In the late 19th century the 4th Earl of Erne converted the Library into a Classicised Blue Drawing Room, complete with scagliola columns. Blore's splendidly 'Jacobethan' overmantel and panelled bookcases were removed to form a comfortable new Library in the original drawing room beyond. As Gervase Jackson-Stops remarked in *Country Life*, this room, 'with its cigar-coloured walls matching the fumed oak of the woodwork, its leather bindings and blazing log fire, must be one of the most comfortable country house libraries in Ireland'. Latterly, the barrel-vaulted Billiard Room in the north wing, which also dated from the 4th Earl's time, has been ingeniously remodelled by the architect Nicholas Johnston into a family dining room.

This is one of a number of sympathetic improvements made by the present Lord and Lady Erne, whose passion for Crom is engagingly infectious. When Lord Erne came of age in 1958 and took on the running of the place, the castle had not been lived in for the best part of a century as his grandfather had been killed in the First World War and his father in the Second, during which Crom was occupied by the military. One of the first things the young Lord Erne had to do was to install electricity.

LEFT Jolly boating weather: the present Earl of Erne on Upper Lough Erne. Everything at Crom revolves around the great lake. The Lough Erne Yacht Club was founded here by the three local landowning families.

ABOVE A view of the lake showing the round battle-mented Crichton Tower on Gad Island. It was built in 1847 as an observatory. The demesne was landscaped by the artist William Sawrey Gilpin, who planned the vistas and mixed planting of trees.

Forty years on, it is gratifying to see that the Victorian architecture of the great house is now much more widely appreciated than it was by previous generations. The castle is the focal point of an estate dotted around with an enchanting group of picturesque small buildings. Perhaps the most delightful is the Victorian Boathouse, an intriguing mixture of bargeboards and battlements which was once the headquarters of the Lough Erne Yacht Club, founded by the three local landowning families, the Crichtons, the Sandersons and the Massy-Beresfords. It is richly evocative of jolly regattas and recalls Crom's essentially aquatic way of life in which everything – from going to church to transporting livestock – revolved around boats negotiating the watery jigsaw of the labyrinthine lough.

6

BIRR CASTLE

BIRR IS not only bang in the centre of Ireland, it is also very much at the centre of Irish life. Unlike the other great houses in this book, it is by origin (and setting aside for a moment its beautiful and botanically important gardens) essentially a town castle, situated as it is in the middle of the model Georgian heritage town of Birr. Indeed, until the castle was turned round to look out over the demesne as part of the Gothicisation carried out in the 19th century by the 2nd Earl of Rosse, the castle faced the town, in what is still called Castle Street, which led straight up to its entrance.

Socially as well as architecturally the history of the town, the castle and the Parsons family, Earls of Rosse, happily still very much here today, are entwined. Not for nothing was Birr long known as Parsonstown.

Back in the 1620s Sir Laurence Parsons, a shrewd lawyer who was Joint Receiver-General of Crown Lands with his brother Lord Justice Sir William Parsons, came up from Myrtle Grove at Youghal, Co. Cork (celebrated as the house where Sir Walter Raleigh is said to have smoked the first pipe of tobacco and planted the first potato in Ireland), and proceeded to lay the first town ordnances. Subsequent generations of the Parsons family were responsible for laying out the attractive Georgian malls and commissioning the splendid range of buildings – from churches to the ravishing Classical temple, John's Hall, now the town's Heritage Centre – which undoubtedly make Birr what Mark Girouard in *Country Life* described as 'pleasant, well kept and pretty a town as any in Ireland'.

The present castle stands some 60 yards north-west of the now vanished Black Castle of the O'Carrolls. Between 1620 and 1627 Sir Laurence rebuilt the gatehouse of the old fortress and added two flanking towers. These are still extant and inside one of them is a fascinating frieze of early 17th-century plasterwork.

The room which the frieze adorns is now the castle's Muniments Room. This is a major repository of archives that have provided material for exhibitions not only at Birr but also on the continent of Europe, in America and in

Britain – where the Royal Institute of British Architects' Drawings Collection has recognised the hitherto under-appreciated importance of Birr's Irish Georgian architectural archive.

It would certainly take many years of research in the archives to disentangle the complicated history of the castle's vicissitudes in the 17th century, an unruly period of siege and counter-siege. There is, though, as the present Lord Rosse points out, one survival of the 17th-century sieges that visitors can at least still see: the siege lines and pits in the park which were excavated for the artillery from which to bombard the castle. Another survival from the 17th century is what the topographer Thomas Dinely described in 1681 as 'the fairest staircase in Ireland'. Built of yew not long before Dinely's visit to Birr, it has bold turned balusters, an exquisitely curved handrail and must be one of the earliest wooden staircases in Ireland.

PREVIOUS PAGES The Saloon, Birr's most celebrated interior with its tent-like Gothic vaulting and gold flock Victorian wallpaper. The photograph on the extreme right of the picture is of Anne Countess of Rosse, who did much to restore Birr's interior.

ABOVE View of the castle from the banks of the River Camcor which runs through the gardens. The castle was 'turned round' to face the demesne rather than the town during the early 19th-century Gothicisation by the 2nd Earl of Rosse. To the right is the wrought-iron suspension bridge of *circa* 1810 – probably the oldest of its kind in Ireland.

Fortunately the 18th century passed comparatively uneventfully. The great lawn was laid out in front of the castle; the old O'Carroll keep and the 17th-century office ranges were swept away; and the interiors were treated to contemporary decoration, including a series of chimneypieces and some plasterwork in the Yellow Drawing Room and Study and an elaborately coffered ceiling in the Library.

The Birr Castle we see today from the gardens, which blend so harmoniously with the Gothic architecture, is largely thanks to the patriot statesman the 2nd Earl of Rosse, an uncompromising opponent of the Act of Union with Great Britain and described by Wolfe Tone in his days as an MP as 'one of the *very few* honest men in the Irish House of Commons'. Besides enlarging and remodelling the castle in the Gothic style from about 1801 onwards, he also built the impressive Gothic entrance to the demesne.

The 2nd Earl's architectural achievement – he seems to have been his own architect, with help from a little-known professional called John Johnston – was to give a unity to the facade of the old castle which it must have been lacking before, by effectively turning the building round, away from the town and facing the demesne. He faced the exterior in ashlar and added a new two-storey porch in the centre, with a giant pointed arch over the entrance door. On the

The Great Telescope, the jewel in the crown of Ireland's Historic Science Centre at Birr, completed in 1845 by the 'Astronomer (3rd) Earl' of Rosse. Once the biggest reflecting telescope in the world, it was recently fully restored.

RIGHT A first-floor corridor at Birr showing the Gothic vaulting and plasterwork which is such a feature of the decoration. It dates from after the fire of 1832 which destroyed the original 17th-century hipped roof.

LEFT A flourish of heraldry in the gateway to the castle featuring the Parsons's leopard. The cast-iron Gothic gates are said to have been designed by the multi-talented Mary, Countess of Rosse, wife of the 3rd Earl. Indeed, she is even supposed to have taken a hand in their making in the estate forge.

The remnants of the darkroom of the pioneer photographer Mary, Countess of Rosse (wife of the 3rd Earl), which is being recreated to form part of Ireland's Historic Science Centre, now burgeoning at Birr.

end of the castle overlooking the River Camcor he built a single-storey extension above an undercroft to house the Saloon, a deliciously Gothic interior with an elegant plaster vault on slender columns. In 1832, after a fire had destroyed the original hipped roof of the 17th century and also damaged the staircase, the 2nd Earl added a third storey to the castle. At the same time the staircase was repositioned under a new ceiling of plaster Gothic vaulting.

Another of the 2nd Earl's architectural legacies at Birr is the graceful wrought-iron suspension bridge of *circa* 1810 – probably the oldest of its kind in Ireland. This is now in a fragile state but it is gratifying to learn that the bridge will shortly be restored as part of the programme of restoration being carried out in connection with Ireland's Historic Science Centre, which is now burgeoning at Birr.

This exciting new stage in Birr's history has come about through the enterprise of the forward-looking 7th and present Earl of Rosse, a former member of the Irish Government's Advisory Council on Development Co-operation, and his artist wife, Alison. An earlier Countess of Rosse, Mary – wife of the 3rd Earl, the celebrated astronomer who built the world-famous Great Telescope at Birr in the 1840s – was a pioneer Irish photographer. And her darkroom is one of the features of Ireland's Historic Science Centre opened in 1999 in the stable block she herself designed.

ABOVE Looking up to the Gothic ceiling of the Staircase Hall which was installed after the fire of 1832. The fire damaged the 17th-century staircase which was then re-erected.

LEFT 'The fairest staircase in Ireland', as Thomas Dinely described it on a visit to Birr in 1681. Built of yew, it must be one of the earliest wooden staircases in Ireland. Note the bold turned balusters and the exquisitely curved handrail. The knobbly Gothic decoration of the landing – delightfully suspended in mid-air – dates from after the fire of 1832.

This major new museum celebrates inventions and scientific achievements both from Birr and from elsewhere in Ireland. A particularly notable example is the turbine-propelled vessel, the *Turbinia*, designed by the Astronomer Earl's youngest son, Sir Charles Parsons, whose development of the steam turbine made him one of the great pioneer figures of modern science. After the *Turbinia* made rings round the British Navy at the Naval Review of 1897 the steam-turbine was promptly adopted for the propulsion of ships around the globe.

The jewel in the crown of Ireland's Historic Science Centre at Birr is, of course, the Astronomer Earl's Great Telescope, 'the Leviathan of Parsonstown'. As completed in 1845 it became the biggest reflecting telescope in the world, and remained so for 70 years. Recently it has been ingeniously restored to full working order with the help of smooth, computer-controlled hydraulic motors – and in 1999 a new speculum mirror, 72 inches in diameter, was added to the Telescope ensuring that its eye is as powerful now as it was when built 150-odd years ago. To see this extraordinary contraption being skilfully operated by Birr's resident expert John Joyce (himself a cousin of the Irish Chieftain Joyce of Connemara) is one of Ireland's most memorable experiences.

The Dining Room in full fig, complete with Connors, the Birr butler. The Victorian flock wallpaper is of the same date as that in the Saloon; the chandelier hanging from the opulently Gothic ceiling is of ormolu.

RIGHT Looking through the Library, with (to the right) its ingenious 'jib' door. The books displayed on it have dummy spines.

What strikes one at Birr is the way the so-called 'Two Cultures', the Arts and Sciences, supposedly poles apart, knit naturally together. Thus the Great Telescope is not just a technical curiosity but a thing of beauty in itself. Its vast walls are embellished with Gothic arches and battlements typical of their time so that the observatory is an ornament in the demesne's parkland.

In short, the 3rd Earl of Rosse was something of a Renaissance Man. As *The Proceedings of the Royal Society* put it in an appreciation of his achievements:

More heraldic leopards (the armorial beasts of the Parsons family Earls of Rosse), this time supporting the massive Gothic sideboard in the Dining Room. The piece probably dates from shortly after the marriage in 1836 of the 3rd Earl of Rosse to Mary Wilmer Field.

> He was not exclusively devoted to astronomy or mechanics. In fact few minds of our day have grasped so wide a range of knowledge. He was a master of political economy... He also devoted much attention to the great question of national education... He was a good chemist, would have attained a high position as a civil engineer, and possessed a large amount of military and nautical knowledge.

His son, the 4th Earl of Rosse, also a Fellow of the Royal Society, was hardly less distinguished. But when the 5th Earl died of wounds received in action in the First World War, an event shortly followed by a fire which destroyed the Library ceiling, the future at Birr must have seemed uncertain. The new Earl, Michael, was only a boy of 12.

Yet under his imaginative stewardship and that of his bride, Anne Armstrong-Jones, sister of the stage designer Oliver Messel, Birr was to enjoy a new Golden Age. To mark their marriage in 1935 the Rosses created a stylish formal garden in the form of a monastic cloister, with windows looking inward. The white seats at either end were designed by Anne Rosse with the crossed initials of herself and her husband. Such formality was perfectly in keeping with Birr's famous

box hedges, reputed to be the tallest in the world, which must have formed part of the formal garden laid out here in the mid-17th century by William Parsons (the Receiver-General's son).

As well as being inspirational gardeners, Michael and Anne Rosse were pioneer conservationists of 18th- and 19th-century architecture. The intensely romantic Birr was particularly well suited to Anne's flair for combining period authenticity with contemporary fun. As Mark Girouard wrote in a perceptive appreciation of her life for *The Daily Telegraph*, the castle 'was, and is, like a house in a novel' (indeed it is said to have inspired Kinalty in Henry Green's *Loving*, which was filmed here for television):

> its plaster-vaulted Gothick drawing-room and the wild cream-and-gold Gothick furnishings in her bedroom both looked like sets designed by her brother Oliver Messel, but were in fact genuine products of the early 19th century. Anne had the sensibility to see their point, and arrange, light and set them off with contemporary good taste, as few others would have done.

Her spell as *châtelaine* of Birr has passed into Irish folklore. 'It's just a shabby old Irish house', she would say of the castle, though during her reign it became a byword for luxury. There were stories of her pruning roses resplendently adorned with diamonds or of sweeping into a humble cabin, brushing aside the occupant's apologies for its rude simplicity with 'My dear, don't change a *thing*!' Yet she had a genuine love of Ireland and understanding of the Irish. She would recall 'sneaking off in the deep countryside of the Midlands of Ireland to take part in "Dancing at the Cross Road"' or relishing 'being allowed to take part in an Irish wake in our beloved Birr'.

Although Anne Rosse had an English dimension to her life (she restored her family's gardens at Nymans in Sussex and was instrumental in founding the Victorian Society at the London treasure-house of her grandfather Linley Sambourne, the *Punch* cartoonist), her son Brendan, the present Earl, is as committed to Ireland as his name suggests. He took over the running of Birr in 1980 after working for the United Nations.

As a director of the Irish Houses and Gardens Association for 11 years, Lord Rosse was a leading advocate of finding a new role for country houses in a heritage and educational context. His ideas have been successfully put into practice through the Birr Scientific and Heritage Foundation on the castle demesne, where the award-winning gardens, with their trees, imaginative planting, lake, rivers and waterfalls, and now Ireland's first Historic Science Centre are a vital part of the attractions of the heritage town of Birr.

Representing the 14th generation at the castle, Brendan Rosse is determined, as he says, that it 'should continue to thrive and flourish for another 14 generations'. So vibrant is the atmosphere at Birr and so versatile the Parsons family that one can have no doubt that it will.

Lady Rosse's bedroom. The extraordinary mirror was made for the marriage of the 3rd Earl of Rosse to Mary Wilmer Field in 1836.

7

BEAULIEU
HOUSE

BEAULIEU is very special. The singularly satisfying house, which forms a compact group with its church, yard, trees and sloping gardens beside the Boyne estuary, is the supreme example in Ireland of that delectable style of architecture which blended Dutch and Classical influence and flourished from around the middle of the 17th century right up to the age of Queen Anne. That it has passed through descent to the redoubtable present owner, Mrs Nesbit Waddington, makes Beaulieu even more exceptional.

The place's extraordinary, almost tangible, quality of unselfconscious intimacy, might be thought to militate against the appellation 'Great'. Yet there is a sublime grandeur about Beaulieu's architecture – one thrills, for instance, to the depth of the overhanging eaves of the hipped roof and to the height of the two-storey Hall, adorned with wonderfully robust carvings – which is all the more effective for being somehow unpretentious. As Mark Girouard has put it, there is something generous about Beaulieu, combining vigour and magnanimity. Paradoxically, it is its essential modesty that makes it truly great. Above all, Beaulieu is a reminder of why this lovable pre-Georgian style of building – nicely summed up by Professor Alistair Rowan as 'one of comfortable relaxation and ease' – is such an architectural favourite. Country houses, one feels, had a gentlemanly, well-mannered air then: nothing too flashy or clever.

Beaulieu (pronounced, and sometimes spelt, 'Bewley') came into the family through the exploits of Sir Henry Tichborne, soldiering scion of the Tichbornes of Tichborne in Hampshire, who had made his name in the Siege of Drogheda in 1641/2. As governor in charge of the defence of this key port, Tichborne was hemmed in by some 17,000 Ulster rebels under the command of Sir Phelim O'Neill, who had made his headquarters at the Plunkett stronghold of Beaulieu, along the Boyne. Although outnumbered ten to one, Sir Henry showed remarkable resilience. Eventually through a mixture of luck (on one occasion his loose horse 'galloping madly', as he put it, gave the rebels a false impression of the garrison's strength) and careful management of supplies, he was able to retaliate. There was a skirmish on the slopes below Beaulieu and the odd daring raid for extra provisions, such as sheep and cows. And then in February 1642 fate intervened when a storm carried away the boom that the rebels had put across the Boyne.

The next month Sir Phelim O'Neill left Beaulieu, which was promptly occupied by Sir Henry. He went on to capture Dundalk and, as the Protestant hero of the hour, was appointed one of the Lord Justices of Ireland. It would appear from a deed of sale that Sir Henry eventually acquired Beaulieu through formal purchase from the Plunketts rather than by confiscation. Irish state papers show that in 1654 Sir Henry petitioned the Lord Protector, Oliver Cromwell, stating that he was owed £868 for 'money spent in public service in Ireland' and that, by order granted him by the Protector at Clonmel, Co. Tipperary, in May 1650, he possessed and enjoyed 'the house and lands of Bewly', which he prayed to be granted to him outright in settlement of his debt.

Sir Henry's prayers were not finally to be answered until, after an anxious tenancy under the Cromwellian Commonwealth, the newly restored monarch, King Charles II confirmed him in possession of the Beaulieu estate and, for good measure, appointed him Marshal of the Irish Army. The old soldier died at his beloved Beaulieu in 1667. In his will he asked to be buried at Drogheda 'at or about 10 of the clock in the night-time without either sound of the trumpet, beat of drum, or volley shot'.

The trumpets and the muskets flourish to his memory, though, in the riot of carved trophies in the Hall at Beaulieu and his defence of Drogheda is commemorated by the important topographical picture of the town set into the overmantel of the fireplace. This fascinating picture, which shows the medieval fortifications of the old port still virtually intact, as well as a beguiling glimpse of the newly built Beaulieu itself, is attributed to William van der Hagen and dates from the early 18th century. Recent research by the architectural historian Dr Edward McParland shows that the house we see today also probably dates from this time.

PREVIOUS PAGES The entrance front of Beaulieu. This exceptionally early non-fortified country house is the supreme example in Ireland of the style of architecture which blended Dutch and Classical influence and flourished from around the middle of the 17th century right up to the age of Queen Anne.

RIGHT The great two-storey Hall, adorned with robust carvings. The overmantel of the fireplace contains an important early 18th-century topographical picture of Drogheda by William van der Hagen, which includes a vignette of the newly built Beaulieu. The antlers above the doorway to the right of the picture belonged to an ancient Irish elk.

LEFT Detail of the overdoor in the Hall's east doorway showing the imposing coat of arms of the 1st (and last) Lord Ferrard of Beaulieu, who commissioned not only the wood carvings in the Hall but also remodelled (even largely rebuilt) the house in the early 18th century.

LEFT Detail of the elaborate wood carvings in the overdoor of the Hall's south-east doorway showing a bandful of musical instruments.

McParland discovered some correspondence in the Molesworth papers in the National Library of Ireland between the then Lord Molesworth and the 1st (and last) Lord Ferrard of Beaulieu, grandson of Sir Henry Tichborne, that suggested the building work carried out at Beaulieu between 1710 and 1720 was much more extensive than had previously been imagined. The tradition had always been that Beaulieu was built on the site of the old Plunkett Castle by Sir Henry and his son Sir William, MP for Louth, who died in 1693, but the historian Harold O'Sullivan believed that an existing house on the same site may have served as the family residence in the late 17th century.

A significant clue in McParland's researches emerged from one letter written on September 4, 1722, by Lord Ferrard to Lord Molesworth from Beaulieu:

> ... yesterday I turned the joyners and carpenters out of the south end of my house I am now painting and hope in three weeks time to begin to furnish I have taken up the loft for my great staires which I dayly expect from Dublin and then will have done till next year...on Monday the carpenter tels me he will be with you his wages are twelve [?] and his victuals I will send by him Hackluit and your plan of which I have taken a Coppy and Curle and I have done something at itt which may be some help by takeing out what you like and rejecting or altering the rest, as soon as he is able to travell we will wait on you...

ABOVE Another corner of the Hall, featuring a fine example of Irish 18th-century furniture. The portrait is of Miss Sidney Montgomery, whose half-brother the Reverend Robert Montgomery (died 1825), married Sophia Tipping, great-granddaughter of Lord Ferrard and heiress to Beaulieu.

RIGHT View from the Hall (taking in yet another delectable overdoor) through to Lord Ferrard's grand staircase of the 1720s to the north. Like the staircase at Stackallen (*qv*), it has thin Italianate balusters and Corinthian newel posts.

ABOVE First-floor corridor above and behind the Hall, which can be glimpsed through the window to the right. It provides a useful vantage point for observing what is happening below.

LEFT The panelled Drawing Room facing south, with its compartmental plasterwork ceiling. The central panel contains a Classical *trompe-l'oeil* scene painted in the manner of Antonio Verrio. The Classical chimneypiece was inserted in the early 19th century.

ABOVE Backstairs Beaulieu: an evocative view of the service area.

LEFT A Beaulieu bathroom: no-nonsense country house comfort. The racehorses on the plain walls are a reminder of the place's strong Turf associations. The present *châtelaine*, Sidney Waddington (*née* Montgomery) used to run a stud farm here together with her late husband, Nesbit Waddington, who was manager of the Aga Khan's stud farms.

The clue is 'Curle' – John Curle, the architect, who worked closely with Lord Ferrard, and who had also designed, in 1702, the original Castle Coole (*qv*), a house of similar type to Beaulieu, complete with steep roof and overhanging eaves.

The idea that Lord Ferrard – rather than merely embellishing the Hall and inserting the grand staircase, as had previously been thought – actually remodelled, even largely rebuilt, an existing house may take some digesting for those familiar with Beaulieu's proud status as 'the finest example of Irish domestic architecture to survive from the Restoration period'. But in reality it makes not a scrap of difference to its inherent quality or indeed architectural importance, let alone its invincible charm. Ultimately the precise dates and minutiae of expert scholarship matter little in the face of such beauty and magnificence.

The two 'show' fronts, the entrance on the west, the garden towards the Boyne on the south, are of very pleasing design. As Alistair Rowan and Christine Casey observed in their *North Leinster* volume in *The Buildings of Ireland* series: 'There can be little doubt that an architect of experience was employed here'. The windows (thin Georgian sash bars replace the original cross-framed timber mullions) are framed by flat brick surrounds; the entrance doorcase has two Corinthian pilasters supporting a segmental-headed pediment; and the dormer windows in the roof are artfully balanced, in the classic 17th-century manner.

Inside, the central Hall knocks you for six. After taking in the mighty chimneypiece and the arched doorways, the eye falls upon the series of stupendous wood-carvings. They repay almost endless study, for the detail is so exuberant and unexpected – all manner of military impedimenta, musical instruments and luxuriant foliage are intertwined. The riot of heraldry includes the coat of arms of Sir Henry's son and successor at Beaulieu, Sir William Tichborne (who also acquired the estate of Blessingbourne, Co. Tyrone – later, incidentally, the seat of the present writer's family, the Montgomerys), impaling those of his wife, Judith Bysse, a considerable heiress as the daughter of the Lord Chief Baron of the Exchequer.

There can be no doubt that these elaborate carvings date from the reign at Beaulieu of their son Henry Tichborne, who was created a Baronet in 1697 and, as *The Complete Peerage* notes, 'for his services in promoting the cause of William III in Ireland', Baron Ferrard of Beaulieu in 1715. Rowan and Casey, who support the 'revisionist' McParland thesis on Beaulieu's building history, point out that the style of the carvings bears a striking resemblance to contemporary plasterwork at Stackallen (*qv*), built *circa* 1710 for the future Lord Boyne. They also suggest that Lord Ferrard's new Staircase Hall to the north (there is a significantly earlier, 17th-century-style oak staircase to the south) is almost certainly by the same craftsmen who worked at Stackallen. Although not so grandiose as the stair at Stackallen, it has the same thin Italianate balusters and Corinthian newel posts.

By contrast with the Baroque splendours of the Hall, the rest of the interiors are small and cosy. The Drawing Room is wainscotted with the bolection-moulded panelling that is such an attractive feature of Beaulieu's late 17th-century character, and has a plasterwork ceiling in which garlands of foliage and flowers frame an oval central panel containing a Classical *trompe-l'oeil* scene in the manner of Antonio Verrio, celebrated for his painted rooms at the great English treasure-house of Burghley (see *Great Houses of England & Wales*).

Lord Ferrard died of apoplexy in 1731 and the peerage died with him; both his sons had predeceased him, the elder being drowned when making the perilous crossing to England in 1709. So Beaulieu passed to his daughter Salisbury Aston. The portrait of her husband, William Aston, in the Hall shows him pointing towards the lakes in the demesne which he created 'to give labour to the poor in time of scarcity'.

During the time of their grandson, another William Aston, Beaulieu was let to Lord Chief Justice Singleton, the patron of a local poet and playwright, Henry Jones, who began life as a bricklayer's apprentice at Beaulieu. Thanks to Singleton's introduction to the influential Earl of Chesterfield, Jones found himself catapulted to popular success with his tragedy *The Earl of Essex* (though *The Dictionary of National Biography* considered 'its literary quality is of the poorest'). Unfortunately fame undid poor Jones: 'his drunken habits, indolence, coarse manners and arrogant temper soon disgusted most of his patrons', as the *DNB* tells us. He died in the workhouse after being run over by a wagon when he was on a bender.

On the younger William Aston's death in 1769, Beaulieu was inherited by his aunt Sophia Tipping, whose daughter and heiress, Sophia, married the Reverend Robert Montgomery, Rector of Monaghan. This rather unworldly clergyman was of the family of Montgomery of Ballyleck, the Monaghan branch of the Norman dynasty which settled in Ireland in such numbers from Scotland in the early 17th century. Their son Alexander also went into the Church but proved more successful in managing the estate. A formidable, though generous, personality, he is said to have gone about with a loaded pistol in his pocket

Over the garden wall: Beaulieu forms a compact group with the neighbouring church (of the familiar Church of Ireland 'hall and tower' type). Mrs Waddington's ancestor Sir Henry Tichborne, Governor of Drogheda, acquired the property from the Plunketts in the mid-17th century.

(where it once blew up) and to have had, according to a nephew, 'a voice that used to make trespassers start when he shouted at them'. Various 19th-century 'improvements' were made, but thankfully nothing too drastic to affect Beaulieu's 'untouched' feel.

In 1939 Alexander's great-granddaughter Sidney succeeded her father, Richard Johnston Montgomery, at Beaulieu. Earlier in the year she had married Nesbit Waddington, a well-known figure on the Turf as the long-serving manager of the Aga Khan's stud farms. The Waddingtons, an immensely popular and hospitable couple with two daughters, also had their own stud farm at Beaulieu. Nesbit Waddington died a few years ago but Sidney Waddington, who takes a particular interest in the historic walled gardens by the church, battles bravely on to preserve this rare and magically atmospheric gem among Irish houses.

8

KILLRUDDERY

COUNTY WICKLOW

THERE is nowhere quite like Killruddery: it has a bewitching quality, whereby romance and formality are delicately balanced, that is all of its own. The house (part 17th-century, part 19th-century, and reduced in size in the 1950s) is magnificently laid out facing ornamental water, with a steep hill down which a cascade flows on one hand, while the vista on the other is closed by further hills. Beyond the entrance gates to the north, though, is the ever-encroaching urban sprawl of Bray, and the survival of Killruddery, a sylvan oasis in the desert of suburbia, reflects enormous credit on the late Earl of Meath, who died in 1998 after a nigh on 50-year reign over this enchanted realm, and on his widow, Betty.

A tour of Killruddery with Betty Meath is an unforgettable experience. Nicely described by her friend Lady Violet Powell in *The Departure Platform* as 'slim with a deceptive air of fragility', Lady Meath knows every inch of the place – in the 1960s she carried out virtually single-handed the mammoth task of repainting the ceiling of the neo-Classical Great Drawing Room and is still often to be seen working in the famous gardens – but the knowledge is lightly and sympathetically conveyed in her beguiling soft voice.

Lady Meath explains how, in the early 1950s, she and her husband, Tony, were confronted with a savage infestation of dry rot in the then vast house which consequently had to be shrunk to almost two-thirds of its previous size. The architect Claud (later Lord) Phillimore was commissioned to dismantle and reconstitute a substantial portion of Killruddery, using the same materials – numbered before demolition – in order to produce a house of more manageable size. This resulted in a new and simplified entrance front, and some remodelling inside.

Outside, though, the appearance of the formal gardens has changed hardly at all (apart from the natural growth which has, of course, enhanced their beauty) since they were laid out in the late 17th and early 18th centuries.

Their significance, not to mention their magic, cannot be overstated. In an article on Killruddery for *Country Life*, the Knight of Glin and John Cornforth described their ambitious formal layout as 'not only the most poetic as well as the most extensive pre-naturalistic design in Ireland but... among the most important gardens of its type in the British Isles'.

The pattern of design reminds Lady Violet Powell of La Granja, near Segovia, and of Chatsworth (thus bringing 'Co. Wicklow, Old Castille and Derbyshire together, distant in geography, but near in feeling'). The Knight of Glin and John Cornforth can find no English or Irish precedent for 'the Long Ponds', the twin canals at Killruddery, though Lady Meath murmurs on our tour that the gardens of the Château de Courances, south of Paris, have a similar design of twin canals on approach to the house. Apart from the view they offer, these Killruddery *miroirs d'eaux* (550 feet long) were also used, as Lady Meath points out, 'to stock fish for the house'.

Killruddery's other remarkable design feature is its *patte d'oie*, or less highfalutingly 'The Angles', an ingeniously planned series of walks flanked by hornbeam, lime or beech hedges which meet at two centre points. Such is the joy of exploring these groves, one is tempted to wax lyrical about all the remaining aspects of what Lady Meath calls 'the garden of entertainment' – the Sylvan Theatre (which inspired Sir Walter Scott in *St Ronan's Well*), the Beech Hedge Pond, the Round Pond and Fountain, the ha-ha and Cascades.

The Meaths' ownership of Killruddery dates to 1618, when Sir Edward Brabazon, later the 1st Earl of Meath, was granted the property. His grandfather Sir William Brabazon, descendant of a long-established Leicestershire knightly family, had established himself as a powerful figure in Tudor Ireland, rising to the posts of Lord High Treasurer and Lord Deputy. The 1st Earl of

PREVIOUS PAGE: The Statue Gallery at Killruddery, which houses the marble sculptures collected in Italy in the early 19th century by the 10th Earl of Meath through the agency of Gaspare Gabrielli. It was built in 1852 by the Scottish architect William Burn after the fashion of Crystal Palace in London. The original glass roof, which had become unsafe, has recently been replaced.

BELOW Looking down the Long Ponds, or canals, to the south front. The demesne has the most extensive early formal layout surviving in Ireland. The pierced parapet on the conservatory to the left is said to have been based on Lady Meath's tiara. The gables to the right indicate the line of the 17th-century house.

Meath is described in *The Complete Peerage* as 'a great sufferer by the troubles of those times' (the Civil War) and in 1644 was packed off to the Tower of London. Not the least of his sufferings was the destruction of his house at Killruddery.

The *naif* picture of the Killruddery Hunt (*circa* 1740) at Killruddery shows a Caroline house with a recessed centre and hipped roof not dissimilar in style to Beaulieu (*qv*) that must have been built by his son, the 2nd Earl of Meath, who succeeded to the title in 1651 and managed to recover part of the family estates. But he was drowned off Holyhead on his way to England in 1675, though his eldest son and heir, William, was saved. The 3rd Earl had already had a lucky escape four years earlier, when he was granted a pardon for killing an ensign in a duel.

Yet we learn from the correspondence of the 3rd Earl's steward, one Cheney, that it was his younger brother Edward Brabazon (later the 4th Earl) who was responsible for 'great improvements' at Killruddery in the 1680s, including a deer park, pond and duck decoy. 'Ye decoy', reported Cheney, 'will be the finest in ye kingdom or I believe in ye 3 kingdoms'. He had also

> made ye hous very handsome. Ye wainscoted rooms ar al now
> varnished 2 ye door in ye hal next the garden which had only a little
> window at ye top thereof, is now a window.

Instead of concentrating on cultivating his garden, however, the 4th Earl of Meath, by training a military man, could not resist being caught up in the Williamite Wars. He was to the fore at the battles of Carrickfergus, the Boyne and Limerick, where he was wounded in 1690. By 1704, when he married,

as his second wife, Dorothea Stopford (immortalised by Jonathan Swift as 'Count-ess Doll... such an owl') the 4th Earl had let out Killruddery and was installed in a house in Dublin, where he was Ranger of Phoenix Park.

An advertisement for the remainder of the lease at Killruddery in 1711, four years after the 4th Earl's death, gives some idea of the extent of his improve-ments, listing:

> [a] pleasure Garden, Cherry Garden, Kitchen Garden, New Garden, Wilderness, Gravel Walks, and Bowling Green, all Wall'd about, and well planted with Fruit Trees, with several Canals or Fish-ponds well stor'd with Carp and Tench.

The Great Drawing Room, showing the enfilade through to the Conservatory in the far distance. This fine neo-Classical Morrison interior is celebrated for its plasterwork. When Lady Meath, the wife of the 14th Earl, was repainting the ceiling in 1968, she noticed the signature of Simon Gilligan, 1824, on top of the cornice to the right of the chimneypiece (ordered in Italy from Giacinto Micali in 1817).

ABOVE Detail of the elaborate carved gilt mirror hanging at the head of the Staircase. The glass reflects some of the remarkable plasterwork by a local man, Henry Popje of Bray.

RIGHT Detail of the chimneypiece in the Dining Room (originally the small drawing room). The silk walls are original.

It would appear that his nephew the 6th Earl of Meath was responsible for extending the formal layout of the gardens in the 1730s – about the same time as his neighbour, the 1st Viscount Powerscourt, was creating his garden terraces at Powerscourt. Mrs Delany keeps us informed of the 6th Earl's matrimonial career:

> We have had a wedding lately [she wrote in December 1731], Lord Meath, a man of good sense and great fortune, who was married unfortunately when he was a boy to his aunt's chambermaid. He never lived with her and she died about a month ago. Yesterday he married Miss Prendergast: he has been in love with her several years; she has little or no fortune and is far from handsome.

Almost miraculously, the formal layout of the gardens at Killruddery survived untouched through the age of 'naturalisation'. Presumably the succeeding Earls of Meath had other things on their minds; the 9th Earl, for instance, was fatally wounded in a duel in 1797. And by the time of the 10th Earl the layout was beginning to be appreciated on antiquarian grounds. In 1827 one visitor, G.N. Wright, observed that 'the grounds are laid out in an old-fashioned, formal style of Dutch pleasure-grounds, and are, in this country, quite unique'.

If the aesthetic 10th Earl of Meath – who collected marbles and chimney-pieces in Italy through the agency of the landscape painter Gaspare Gabrielli of Lyons, Co. Kildare (*qv*), fame – was happy to leave the gardens as they were, he had no such sentiments for the surviving 17th-century house. As Wright put it, old Killruddery was 'unfit for the residence of a nobleman of taste and fortune'. Various rebuilding schemes were considered, including a bizarre Gothic affair (complete with Baronial gateway) by Francis Johnston. Eventually, though, Lord Meath settled for the Tudor Revival style being pioneered in Ireland by William Vitruvius Morrison.

Together with his father and partner Sir Richard Morrison (better known for his Classical work), in June 1820 William Vitruvius produced a detailed estimate for a major remodelling of the 17th-century house. Building work went on for nine years around the resident Lord and Lady Meath; as one of the family recorded 'it was done bit by bit and they moved from one part to the other'. The Morrisons' bill in June 1829 mentions a figure of £20,000 as the cost of the house.

Expensive as that was then, the Meaths surely got their money's worth. The three 'show' fronts became a delightful vision of East Anglia meets Wicklow granite: bay windows, pepper pots, late-Tudorish chimneystacks. The entrance front was moved round to the north side, and the old east front, which had faced a forecourt and a road, now enjoyed a garden aspect.

Inside, the Morrisons' creation was adorned with very fine plasterwork by a local craftsman, Henry Popje of Bray, who made liberal use of the Brabazon crest, a goshawk or falcon rising. It is seen to particularly good effect in the dome of the Staircase Hall, where the architectural detail is an intriguing mixture of Classical and Tudor Gothic. One of Popje's men, a Simon Gilligan, inscribed his name on top of the cornice in the neo-Classical Great Drawing Room, as Betty Meath discovered in 1968, when she was repainting the ceiling.

Some 'Louis Revival' touches were added to the decoration of the interior by Matthew Cotes Wyatt (celebrated for his exotic Elizabeth Saloon at Belvoir Castle in England) in the mid-to-late 1820s. Later, in the 1840s, the 10th

ABOVE The central dome above the Staircase adorned by Popje with swirling clouds. The stained glass window to the right, by Millner (1853) depicts the arrival in England in 1066 of William the Conqueror, with his standard-bearer Jacques le Brabacon ('the Great Warrior'), traditionally the ancestor of the Brabazons.

LEFT The Library, with Chippendale-style bookcases. This room is part of the 17th-century house.

The Staircase, which was originally designed on an 'Imperial' plan but reduced to a single flight as part of the 1950s alterations. The hanging gilt lantern came from Adare Manor, the principal family home of Lady Aileen Wyndham-Quin, wife of the 13th Earl of Meath.

Earl of Meath commissioned Daniel Robertson, who had been working at Powerscourt next door, to make various improvements, including the garden balustrades.

The 11th Earl of Meath, who had done his best to provide relief on the family estates during the Famine, succeeded to Killruddery in 1851 and promptly brought in the prolific Scottish architect William Burn to add the conservatory. Its pierced parapet is said to have been based on Lady Meath's tiara. Now known as the Statue Gallery, it houses the 10th Earl's impressive collection of marbles.

Further alterations were made by William Slater and then, a century later, came Claud Phillimore's radical reduction. Effectively, the north and east (save for a projecting gable) side disappeared, the west wing being left intact. A new and simplified entrance front was built on the same axis as its Morrison predecessor, but standing further back. The entrance is now by way of a vestibule with a curving stone stair directly into the Staircase Hall, which retains its Morrison decoration – as do the two Drawing Rooms, the smaller of which became the Dining Room; the original dining room along with the entrance hall and great hall was among the rooms demolished.

The present Earl of Meath is carrying on the campaign fought so gallantly by his parents to conserve the suburb-girt Killruddery, which he opens regularly to the public. Its jaunty architecture – all pointy, curvy gables, pinnacles and oriels – and, above all, its unrivalled gardens make Killruddery's survival as a much-loved family home a vital need for Ireland's heritage.

9

STACKALLEN HOUSE

---

*I*F THE FORMAL gardens at Killruddery, featured in the previous chapter, are the oldest surviving in Ireland, the one installed in 1998 at Stackallen for its owners, Mr and Mrs Martin Naughton, must be the newest – and no less striking for that. The story is simply told: the Naughtons took the splendidly bold move of buying 'lock, stock and barrel' a gold-medal winning Chelsea Flower Show garden called *Bosquet de Chanel*.

This elaborate *cabinet de verdure* encompassed by high beech hedges designed by Tom Stuart-Smith for the *couturiers* Karl Lagerfeld and Chanel, was duly dismantled after the show and shipped to Co. Meath, where it was recast and substantially enlarged by Stuart-Smith in collaboration with Todd Longstaffe-Gowan of the Landscape Agency, a new company specialising in all aspects of landscape restoration, conservation and design. It was refashioned to fit into a former paddock north of the house. The garden took a mere six weeks to assemble, and, hey presto, there it was – an adornment that, quite understandably, gave immediate gratification to the Naughtons.

The 'instant garden' is only one of a highly impressive range of improvements made by the Naughtons at Stackallen during a thorough and sympathetic restoration of the house and its demesne. The leading Irish garden designer Jim Reynolds has also been busy here; and there is an exotic new Painted Room by the muralist Michael Dillon. The exterior of the house has been handsomely repointed and the interior immaculately renovated under the direction of David Sheehan of the Dublin practice Sheehan & Barry. It forms a fine setting for the important collection of Irish 20th-century art imaginatively assembled by the Naughtons in recent years. Carmel Naughton is a connoisseur of paintings and chairman of the National Gallery of Ireland in Dublin, where her husband, Martin, the founder in 1973 of the Glen Dimplex group in Newry, is also actively involved in the creation of the stylish new Georgian town-house hotel The Merrion, in Merrion Square.

All this enthusiastic rejuvenation is tremendously encouraging for every-one who cares about Ireland's heritage being a living, breathing entity. It is particularly exciting that it should have happened to such an important build-ing as Stackallen, an exceptionally early great house, indeed one of the very few surviving grand Classical Irish country houses of the 18th century.

Until recently it was usually assumed that Stackallen was built *circa* 1716, the year after its builder, General Gustavus Hamilton, who had distinguished himself at the Battle of Boyne nearby (where his horse was shot under him) and at the storming of Athlone, was created a peer as Baron Hamilton of Stackallen. But this, as Christine Casey and Alistair Rowan have pointed out in their author-itative *North Leinster* volume in *The Buildings of Ireland* series, is to miss several points.

PREVIOUS PAGES Like a lovable doll's house, the garden front (originally the entrance front) of Stackallen sits prettily above its recently re-landscaped formal gardens and new plantations of trees. The house and demesne were immaculately restored by Mr and Mrs Martin Naughton in the 1990s.

OPPOSITE The Staircase Hall, dominated by one of the largest and grandest staircases in Ireland, which rises in one broad, long flight under an elaborate plasterwork ceiling.

ABOVE Detail of a marble chimneypiece at Stackallen.

LEFT The ceiling of the Staircase Hall, with its swaggering armorial achievement in the central panel displaying the coat of arms of General Gustavus Hamilton impaling those of his wife, Elizabeth Brooke of Brookeborough. The Ionic columns at the foot of the stairs were installed in the early 19th century, when the new entrance was created.

First, the General would have been approaching his mid-seventies by this time (rather late in the day to be building a triumphal pile). Secondly, the style of the building also suggests an earlier date. And thirdly, it is surely significant that neither the coat of arms in the oculus of the pediment on the south facade (now the garden front but originally the entrance front) nor the amazingly elaborate one on the ceiling of the Staircase Hall incorporates a nobleman's coronet, whether that of a Baron or a Viscount (Hamilton was advanced to the Viscountcy of Boyne in 1717). Casey and Rowan conclude that these armorial adornments would seem to have been put in place and the house completed before Hamilton's elevation to the peerage – 'and since a dated gutter head of 1712 has been found, the years 1710–12 seem the most likely date'.

Certainly, on stylistic evidence, Stackallen belongs to the culmination of that delectable type of 17th-century country house which flourished from the Restoration of King Charles II right up to the Age of Queen Anne and which we have joyfully encountered at Beaulieu (*qv*), a mere 20 miles away. As Casey and Rowan observe, the arrangement of the windows in such houses differs significantly from buildings of the Georgian period and is marked by the fact that the ground-floor and first-floor windows are of equal height. At Stackallen they are all sash windows with 15 panes of glass, and only the top floor reduces in size to sashes of nine panes. There are nine bays on the present garden front, seven on the present entrance front; this and the fact that the window surrounds are more elaborate on the former confirm that the south facade was the 'show' side.

Hamilton, who had received a substantial grant of forfeited lands beside the River Boyne in the 1690s, would doubtless have wanted to make a splash with his new house. A scion of the illustrious Ulster House of Hamilton, Earls (and later Dukes) of Abercorn, he derived his exotic Christian name from his father Sir Frederick Hamilton's military service with King Gustavus Adolphus of Sweden. Before joining the Army himself, young Gustavus matriculated at Trinity College, Dublin – where, in 1712, was laid the foundation stone of the Library designed by the military engineer and architect Thomas Burgh of Oldtown, Co. Kildare, to whom Desmond Guinness, in his *Great Irish Houses and Castles*, attributes the architecture of Stackallen.

Burgh, like Hamilton, had been a Williamite soldier. Hamilton, who had estates in Co. Fermanagh and married into another prominent Ulster dynasty, the Brookes of Brookeborough, first came to prominence in 1688 as the Protes-

LEFT Details of carved faces adorning the Irish mahogany furniture at Stackallen, where the Naughtons have assembled an important collection of Irish art. Carmel Naughton is chairman of the National Gallery of Ireland.

– 104 –

ABOVE The Painted Room at Stackallen, with
murals by the artist Michael Dillon, youngest son
of the 20th Viscount Dillon.

The Drawing Room at Stackallen, stylishly decorated by Carmel Naughton, with a view through to the Painted Room.

tant Governor of Enniskillen. The next year, as Colonel of the 20th Foot, he was to the fore in the defence of Coleraine and Derry against Jacobite attack. The story goes that at the successful storming of Athlone he waded through the Shannon at the head of his troops.

Garlanded with honours, he rose to be a Privy Councillor under Queen Anne before finally retiring to enjoy his new estates in Co. Meath. The interior of his elegant new house at Stackallen was to be dominated by one of the largest staircases in the whole of Ireland, a broad, long flight under a spectacular plasterwork ceiling of oak-leaf borders, military trophies, flowers and musical instruments. And there, swaggering in the centre, is General Hamilton's coat of arms impaled with those of his wife, Elizabeth Brooke of Brookeborough.

The proud old couple were not, though, to enjoy the splendours of Stackallen for long. Elizabeth died there at Christmas 1721, the General two years later, in his 84th year. It is probable that their full plans for Stackallen were never finished for as Casey and Rowan expertly note, the house 'reads' as a great cube and, as built, lacks a full range of rooms on its east side.

The General was succeeded in the Viscountcy of Boyne by his bachelor grandson who, in turn, was followed by a cousin embroiled in marital difficulties. It was never clear whether his first marriage, to a blacksmith's daughter from Tullamore, had been valid or not; in any event, his children by his second wife, the eldest of whom assumed the title of Viscount Boyne, were regarded as illegitimate. So it may have been his brother, the 4th Viscount Boyne, who was responsible for making various improvements to Stackallen later in the 18th century, including the stables (similar, when built, to those by 'Capability' Brown nearby at Slane, seat of the Conynghams) and the reworking of the staircase.

Further, more radical, alterations occurred in the early 19th century. A painting by Henry Brocas, senior, of *circa* 1820 shows the house and the stables before the entrance was moved from the south front, so the switch-round must have happened shortly after that date. At the same time a pair of Ionic columns was introduced by way of a screen to open up the new Hall directly into the Staircase Hall.

This would have been in the time of the 6th Viscount Boyne, who married Harriet Baugh, the heiress of Burwarton House in Shropshire (which, rebuilt by Anthony Salvin in the 1870s as a sprawling Italianate pile, was eventually to become the Boynes' principal residence). The 7th Viscount married an even more prosperous heiress in the form of Emma Maria Russell of Brancepeth Castle, Co. Durham, which also passed into the Hamilton family, causing them to assume the additional surname of Russell. Miss Russell's mother was a Tennyson of Bayons Manor, Lincolnshire, and thus an aunt of the poet Alfred, and of her paternal grandfather, William Russell, we read:

> Mr Russell commenced his fortunate career at Sunderland as a general merchant... and, as his opulence increased, speculated extensively in collieries, and... acquired immense wealth. He died in 1817, one of the richest commoners in England.

So wrote John Burke in his *Commoners of Great Britain and Ireland* (1833/5). And by a nice coincidence it was Burke's descendant, Major Anthony Burke, MFH, who eventually came to live at Stackallen in the second half of the 20th century. This was after various vicissitudes, including a spell when the Boynes let the house out in the 19th century as a school, which subsequently developed into St Columba's College, near Dublin.

The Burkes are celebrated as a dynasty of heralds and genealogists: Tony Burke's grandfather Sir Henry Farnham Burke was Garter King of Arms, and his great-grandfather Sir Bernard Burke, Ulster King of Arms, was a leading populariser of pedigrees through such works as *Burke's Peerage & Baronetage* and *Burke's Landed Gentry*. (There is another interesting link with Stackallen in that Sir Bernard, like Carmel Naughton, had a strong association with the National Gallery in Dublin.) Tony and his second wife, Elizabeth, formerly Lady Milborne-Swinnerton-Pilkington, were more concerned with equine pedigrees; they ran Stackallen as a successful stud farm and the house became legendary in the world of horse-racing for its hospitality (as the television commentator Julian Wilson's racy autobiography attests).

After Tony was killed in the hunting field in 1964, as his first wife had been before him, Elizabeth Burke lived on at Stackallen into the 1990s, when the Naughtons arrived to give the old house an invigorating new life. What Martin and Carmel Naughton have achieved in a short time both inside and out (some 4,000 trees, for instance, have been planted around the house), is remarkable, admirable and extremely cheering.

The present entrance front of Stackallen, created in the early 19th century. This is of seven bays whereas the garden front is of nine bays.

10

FLORENCE COURT

*T*HE house-warming party at Florence Court mentioned in the chapter on Crom Castle, to the south of the lush lakeland county of Fermanagh, was supposedly held in 1764. This would have been during the ownership of the 1st Lord Mount Florence, formerly MP for Enniskillen, who died in 1767, and a year after the marriage of his son William, later 1st Earl of Enniskillen, to Anne Lowry-Corry, sister of the 1st Earl of Belmore, builder of Fermanagh's other great house, Castle Coole (*qv*). However, the house-warming story is only a legend and precise dates about Florence Court's building history are hard to come by.

Pedantry on such matters, though, would be quite out of place, for Florence Court's winning combination of charm and romance sweeps scholarship aside. The setting against the brooding Cuilcagh mountains, with Ben Aughlin rearing up dramatically to the south, takes the breath away, while the architecture of the long, golden-grey 'show' facade has, as Mark Bence-Jones put it so well in his *Guide to Irish Country Houses*, 'a dream-like Baroque beauty that is all the greater for being somewhat bucolic'. And inside is the wonderful treat of luscious Rococo plasterwork – a riot of overflowing acanthus, puffing cherubs and hovering birds of prey.

Some of the original 18th-century decoration was destroyed during a disastrous fire in 1955, two years after the National Trust took on the care of Florence Court from the 5th Earl of Enniskillen. But fortunately much of the Rococo plasterwork (attributed to the Dublin stuccodore Robert West) was saved thanks to the foresight of the then Countess, who had holes bored through the surviving ceilings in the main block affected by the fire in order to let the water – often the most damaging element in such conflagrations – drain away. And then the National Trust, with the help of the scholarly Georgian Revival architect Sir Albert Richardson, carried out a most thorough and sensitive restoration so that today visitors would have to have a very expert eye to detect the difference.

For some years after the fire the Trust experienced difficulties in furnishing Florence Court with enough of the original contents, but it is heartening to report that in 1998 there was a glorious restitution. This came about owing to the generosity of a subsequent Countess of Enniskillen, Nancy, widow of the 6th Earl, who bequeathed 'family pictures and historic items' owned by him 'to the National Trust as he wished'. This simple statement, as Peter Marlow, the Trust's Northern Ireland Historic Buildings Representative, said, 'masks the transformation of Florence Court by the addition of over 250 items of great beauty, historical interest and family association'.

Among the family portraits in this bounty is an attractive study of *circa* 1710 of Florence Cole (only daughter of a Cornish Baronet, Sir Bourchier Wrey), after whom the house is named. Her husband, John Cole, MP for Enniskillen, was the first of the family to settle at this rural outpost of the family estates, which he had inherited in 1710. The Coles, to the fore in King James I's Plantation of Ulster a century before, had previously been seated at the old Maguire castle of Enniskillen, where Sir William Cole was the town's first Provost in the 17th century.

Initially it seems that John Cole may have built the first Florence Court as a shooting-box and continued to base himself at Enniskillen Castle, which Sir William had renovated. None the less, as Alistair Rowan points out in his *North-West Ulster* volume in *The Buildings of Ireland* series, Cole was described as 'of Florence Court' and is said to have 'begun very costly and sumptuous buildings' on his estate before his death in 1726.

The central block of the house we see today, though, is dated variously around 1758 and 1764 (the year of the alleged house-warming). Tim Knox, the National Trust's architectural historian, has discovered a reference in the Bagshawe manuscripts which suggests that John Cole's son and namesake, the 1st Lord Mount Florence, was 'attending to the finishing of my House' in November 1761. The next generation, in the shape of William Cole, eventually 1st Earl of Enniskillen, was following hard on Lord Mount Florence's heels, though, and it is probable that William was closely involved in the building operations. A memorandum of November 5, 1767, added to Lord Mount Florence's will three weeks before his death, directed that William should inherit 'all the marble chimney pieces and cut stone for the colonnade at Florence Court'.

The 'colonnade' is obviously an allusion to the wings, those delightful flanking arcades leading to single-storey pavilions which give Florence Court such distinction. Accordingly, this addition is usually dated *circa* 1768. Stylistically, the design of the wings is considerably more sophisticated than that of the central block and the Knight of Glin has attributed them to Davis Duckart of Castletown, Co. Kilkenny (*qv*), fame. The mason is known to have been one Andrew Lambert.

Thanks to the wings, the 'show' facade at Florence Court extends to a frontage of no less than 260 feet, and very impressive it is too, though closer study tends to dismay the architectural purists. Professor Rowan, who generally considers Florence Court's architecture 'endearing rather than fine', does not, in the best blunt Belfast way, mince his words when it comes to describing the detail. The main front is 'quite crazy', and he refers to the 'vaingloriousness of a provincial hand'. Rustication, keystones, and lugged surrounds run riot. The window surrounds are not the same on any two floor levels. The centre, projecting slightly, is a 'welter of jumbled scales'. And so on and so forth. Yet who could resist such a lovable creation?

As Rowan says, it is undoubtedly the finest early Georgian house in North-West Ulster. 'Early' may seem to be pushing it a bit for a house of the mid-18th

PREVIOUS PAGE: A corner of the handsome 'architectural' Hall. The unusual seven-panel design of the doors is a feature of the decoration at Florence Court.

BELOW The plain, unornamented back of the house, with its three-sided bow. Begun in the 1720s, Florence Court was finished later in the 18th century.

ABOVE Looking east out of the seven-panelled front door towards Lough Erne. The demesne is celebrated for its trees, including 'the Florence Court Yew', *Taxus baccata* 'Fastigiata', a freak plant discovered here in 1767.

BELOW The entrance front seen in its glorious mountainous setting. The flanking wings, attributed to Davis Duckart, are dated *circa* 1768 and are of a considerably more sophisticated design than the endearingly bucolic central block, with its 'quite crazy' detail.

century, but the style of the plan is clearly old-fashioned for its date and could well have been drawn up many years before it was built.

Inside, the main feature apart from the celebrated plasterwork is the woodwork, especially the staircase with its splendid joinery. There are three fluted banisters per tread, a mahogany rail and a pine floor. It leads up to many people's favourite interior at Florence Court, the Venetian Room, preceded by a vaulted lobby and lit by the great Venetian window. The gorgeous ceiling here is one of those restored after the fire of 1955, though the elaborate affair in the Dining Room downstairs is original. The Classical chimneypiece in the Dining Room may well be one of those mentioned in Lord Mount Florence's will.

The beneficiary, his son William, was a man of taste and had done the Grand Tour on the continent of Europe in the 1750s before filling what had virtually become the Cole family's Parliamentary seat of Enniskillen. As a politician, though, he was no mere time-server and, while Horace Walpole may have sneered at 'the mob of nobility' which flooded the Irish peerage in 1776 (the year of 'reckless profusion', as *The Complete Peerage* sniffed), when William was advanced from the Barony of Mount Florence to the Viscountcy of Enniskillen, he did not deserve to be bracketed with the tuft-hunting toadies. The astute, if anonymous, chronicler of *Sketches of Irish Political Character* in 1799 – 10 years after William was advanced again to the Earldom of Enniskillen – remarked that

This nobleman has the character of great spirit and intrepidity, of which his eloquence partakes. He is one of the boldest speakers in the House [of Lords, in Dublin], without the overbearing obtrusive manner of *certain* other speakers... His Lordship *opposes* the Union.

ABOVE Detail of the luscious Rococo plasterwork at Florence Court, which has been attributed to the Dublin stuccodore Robert West.

LEFT The Staircase Hall: a treasury of superb plasterwork and woodwork. The staircase has three fluted banisters per tread with a finely carved mahogany handrail and a pine floor.

RIGHT Looking back down the stairs into the two tiers of windows in the central bay at the back of the house. The Rococo panels in plasterwork have been compared with those in the common room of Trinity College, Dublin; the cornice is in the Gothic style.

BELOW The Venetian Room, with its great window (to the right) and gorgeous plasterwork ceiling. This was one of the rooms damaged in the fire of 1955; the plasterwork was faithfully restored.

The 2nd Earl of Enniskillen, who succeeded to the title and to Florence Court two years after the fateful Act of Union, also earned a good press from a more illustrious source, Daniel O'Connell, 'The Liberator' himself. Lord Enniskillen, O'Connell declared, was 'one of the finest looking Irish gentlemen' he ever saw and he described him as 'that rare good thing in Ireland, a resident nobleman, spending his income amongst his own tenantry'.

One of the projects upon which he spent his income was the relandscaping by John Sutherland of the beautiful 90-acre demesne. It was in the 2nd Earl's time that were planted many of the now magnificently mature beeches, oaks and sycamores, as well as the rhododendrons and magnolias growing in exuberant clumps in the valley below the house. The grounds are famous for their superb examples of the Florence Court weeping beech and specimens of the original Irish, or 'Florence Court' yew, *Taxus baccata* 'Fastigiata', a freak plant discovered here in 1767 – and which can only be reproduced from cuttings.

'The Liberator', who led the campaign for Catholic emancipation in Ireland, may not have been quite so generous in praise of the 2nd Earl's son and successor, the 3rd Earl of Enniskillen, a prominent figure in the Orange Order. Among the heirlooms mentioned in his will, proved in 1887, a year after his death, are 'King William's trunk, mustard pot and spurs'.

This 'mustard pot', a notably rare and important 17th-century piece of silver gilt, is among the treasures to have recently been returned to Florence Court in accordance with the wishes of the late 6th Earl of Enniskillen.

LEFT The Dining Room, which boasts what the purists insist is the best original plasterwork ceiling at Florence Court – an elaborate affair of scrolls, shells and rocaille work round a circular panel featuring Jupiter's eagle and the four winds.

Several of the items also recall the 3rd Earl's Orange associations, including a pair of silver mounted cannon balls retrieved from the Siege of Derry and a rifle presented to him in 1848 by the Orangemen of Dublin.

Restored to their traditional place at Florence Court, too, are the pair of mighty cannon on the front steps (supposedly won in a wager by the 2nd Earl of Enniskillen from his neighbour the 2nd Earl of Belmore at Castle Coole) and the marble bust of King William III in the Front Hall. Three majestic 18th-century landscapes of Enniskillen, Devenish and the Belleek Rapids are also back where they belong, together with a mass of memorabilia – including material

ABOVE and BELOW Details of the eclectic collection of furniture at Florence Court, the contents of which have lately been enhanced by the bequest of the 6th Earl of Enniskillen, whereby over 250 items of historical interest and family association came back to the house.

The 'downstairs' rooms at Florence Court are full of atmosphere, evoking a vanished way of life. The roof of the Kitchen, shaped like a giant umbrella, is made of fire-proof material.

on the 6th Earl's role in forming the Kenya legislature in the 1960s – which brings the family history alive.

Not the least of the attractions at Florence Court is the sympathetic way in which the National Trust presents the 'downstairs' aspect of Irish country-house life. This naturally interests the visitor as much as, if not more than, the grandeur 'upstairs'. The service rooms in the basement are artlessly evocative of a vanished way of life, with the stone-flagged Kitchen being memorably atmospheric. Under its fireproof ceiling resembling a vast umbrella, this room looks out on to the cobbled courtyards containing coaches, a dairy, a laundry, drying rooms and all the other domestic nuts and bolts that underpinned the smooth running of this exceptionally pretty place.

11

MOUNT IEVERS
COURT

COUNTY CLARE

*I*F FLORENCE Court, featured in the previous chapter, has a dream-like quality, Ireland's other celebrated 'Court', Mount Ievers in the depths of Co. Clare, positively makes one want to pinch oneself to check consciousness. Its shimmering beauty haunts the imagination. There is an aura about Mount Ievers, happily still the home of the Ievers family who built it in the 1730s, which transcends architecture and has learned architectural historians reaching for the adjectives.

As Mark Girouard has written, 'Magic is an overworked word, but there is undoubtedly a magic about Mount Ievers. It is a mysterious house, shut away among woods with no outlet to the outer world... high, thin and ghostly'. Desmond Guinness, Maurice Craig and the Knight of Glin have likened its verticality to a doll's house; Mark Bence-Jones has commented on its air of melancholy. All this is true, yet Mount Ievers's extraordinary appeal remains elusive to description. Nothing can prepare you for the experience of trying to absorb its tantalising images – silvery limestone ashlar one side, achingly romantic faded pink brick the other – which flicker in front of you, as if in a film. (Hardly surprisingly, the house has recently been 'discovered' as an ideal location for film and television companies.)

A prig might argue that Mount Ievers is not, strictly speaking, a 'great' house, that it properly belongs to the 'provincial smaller Georgian' category. To which one can only respond: 'Pish!' For quite apart from its poetic qualities, paramount in themselves, a strong case can be made for the house's remarkable architectural distinction. The design, as Mark Girouard remarked in his *Country Life* article on Mount Ievers, 'perfectly combines strength, simplicity, and sophistication'. A particularly sophisticated refinement is the way each stage of the house is set back a few inches from the stage below. Mount Ievers's special significance is that it is the quintessential Irish 'tall house', indeed probably the precursor of all the rest.

PREVIOUS PAGES Framed by woodland, the silvery limestone ashlar north front of Mount Ievers, built by Colonel Henry Ievers in the 1730s to the designs of John Rothery. The stone was probably quarried on the estate.

LEFT The house's most impressive internal feature: the Staircase, a handsome example of early Georgian joinery with alternate barley-sugar and fluted balusters leading up to the lancing. The ceiling has a modillion cornice and bold geometrical panels.

BELOW The first-floor landing, hung with family portraits of the Ieverses. The late Squadron Leader Norman Ievers, who took over the place in 1945, restored the original thick glazing-bars of the windows which had been replaced by thin late Georgian astragals in the mid-19th century.

The style would appear to have been influenced by Chevening in England's 'garden county' of Kent, traditionally attributed to the great 17th-century architect Inigo Jones and the seat of the Lennard family, who were – surely significantly – kinsmen of Mount Ievers's builder, Henry Ievers. (He would also presumably have seen it illustrated in the second volume of *Vitruvius Britannicus* (1717).) This explains Mount Ievers's quaintly 'old-fashioned' appearance, complete with 17th-century-style hipped roof. The similarities between the two houses are certainly striking, and Mark Girouard's expert eye has spotted the unusual feature in common of 'the stone cornice with pulvinated frieze below the eaves'.

Yet, as Mark Bence-Jones has robustly put it, Mount Ievers is 'as Irish as Chevening is English'. The essential difference is in the detail and the proportions – thus at Mount Ievers the mass of windows are grouped closer together than at Chevening, resulting in a narrower and taller effect.

Henry Ievers's architect was John Rothery, who died in 1736, shortly before the house was finished. The job was completed by John's son Isaac Rothery, and another member of the family, Jemmy, also appears to have been involved in the operation judging from the building accounts – which are unusually extensive, especially for a house in such a remote part of Ireland. These Rotherys seem to have been something of an architectural dynasty, as Maurice Craig has discovered references to Samuel and William Rothery working as masons and builders in Dublin at the end of the 17th century.

Looking through the two front doors from north to south. Mount Ievers's distinguished architecture 'perfectly combines strength, simplicity and sophistication'.

Isaac Rothery is thought to have gone on to build Bowen's Court in Co. Cork for the Bowen family – the house immortalised by the novelist Elizabeth Bowen in *The Last September* but sadly demolished in the early 1960s. Although it is dated 40 years later than Mount Ievers, Bowen's Court had several similarities to the earlier house, notably an unfinished long gallery, or ballroom, on the top floor – a feature more familiar in Elizabethan or Jacobean England than Georgian Ireland.

The Mount Ievers building accounts reveal some diverting details. An average weekly entry shows, for instance, 11 masons employed at five shillings per week and 48 labourers at only five pence, plus food, clothes, shoes and coarse linen (woven on the premises). The oak timbers for the roof were floated down the Shannon and then hauled overland for 20 miles. The slates (at 9s 6d a hundred) came from Broadford nearby and – though not documented – the stone was probably quarried on the estate, whereas the brick is traditionally said to have come from Holland. The entire cost was listed as £1,478 7s 9d, plus various extras such as £15 for 'two horses I gave Rothery'.

If the Rotherys had a proud dynastic tradition, so too, of course, have the Ievers family, who claim descent from Sir Hugh de Eure (d. 1295) of Eureham in Buckinghamshire, a village that eventually changed its name to Iver. (The present Mr Ievers of Mount Ievers points out that a good reason for the family to change its name in the 17th century was to dissociate itself from the regicide Eure.) An alternative, and no less romantic, theory is that Ievers is an English form of the Irish *OhLómhair* (O'Hever). In any event, by the time the traveller Thomas Dinely (who praised the staircase at Birr Castle – *qv*) came to call at Mount Ievers in 1680, he found 'Henry Ivers, Esq' well established in a 'castle... well situate and capable of very considerable improvement'.

Dinely noted that:

> The gentleman owner hereof, came over (a young man, clerk to one Mr Fowles, a Barrister) since the King's Restoration, and hath in this time by his Industry, acquired one Thousand pounds a year. The first and chiefest of his rise was occasioned by being concerned in the Revenue as Clerk to the King's Commisioners for setting the Quit Rents, and afterwards became their Deputy receiver, is now in Commission one of his Majesties Justices of the Peace, not worth less than sixteen hundred pounds a year.

In fact, Ivers 'came over' much earlier than the Restoration of King Charles II. The pedigree of the family in *Burke's Irish Family Records* mentions the date of his settling in Co. Clare as 1643; he is certainly on record in 1657 as owning land in that county. This grew into a considerable estate, including Mount Ievers, or Ballyrella, as it was then called, which appears to have been acquired in the summer of 1679.

Dinely's sketch of the castle at Ballyrella the following year shows a high, square tower of the sort familiar in this part of Ireland. The impressive stone fireplace in the Hall of the present house comes from the old castle and is dated 1648.

Henry Ievers shrewdly remained a staunch Protestant, even though his patron, the 2nd Viscount Clare, for whom he acted as steward, joined the Jacobite cause. Henry's eldest son was disinherited for marrying, without his father's consent, 'a person of noe fortune' – presumably a Catholic – and so the Mount Ievers property passed on his death in 1690 to the second son, Colonel John Ievers of the Clare Dragoons, who adopted the present spelling of the family surname.

The Colonel, who went on to become MP for the county, died at the end of 1729 and soon afterwards his son and successor, Henry Ievers, wasted no time in pulling down the old castle and building Mount Ievers Court. Henry, an ambitious young barrister, became the third of his family to serve as High Sheriff of Co. Clare, and also officiated for Co. Limerick, where he had business interests in the city and was Mayor in 1745. At Mount Ievers he established a spinning school (which not only promoted local industry but also ensured that its trainees were brought up as Protestants in the predominantly Catholic west) and a barracks for a company of the Clare Militia Dragoons, of which, like his father before him, he was Colonel.

The high basement of the new house doubtless helped the security arrangements, as did the water around the house and the high walls of the courtyards. These features are emphasised in the charming study of Mount Ievers set into an overmantel in one of the downstairs rooms in the house. A contemporary oil painting in the *naif* manner of the mid-18th century, it shows the north (brick) side of the house surrounded by an elaborate formal layout which has since largely disappeared.

By comparison with the grandeur of the exterior, the inside of Mount Ievers is simple – and none the less pleasing for that. The best feature is the Staircase, a fine example of early Georgian joinery with alternate barley-sugar and fluted balusters leading up to a spacious landing adorned with a modillion cornice and a ceiling of bold geometrical panels.

One of the key points about Mount Ievers is how little it seems to have changed since it was built. Fortunately, the family have tended to leave Henry's masterpiece well alone, though in the middle of the 19th century the first-floor sash windows were changed to ones with bigger panes. Thin late Georgian astragals replaced the endearingly chunky glazing-bars of the original design.

This would presumably have been in the time of Eyre Ievers, who in 1808 had inherited Mount Ievers as a boy from his father, George, in strange circumstances. The story goes that George, a local magistrate, had most unwisely agreed to be a second in a duel held in a nearby churchyard. When a Mr MacNamara (perhaps a kinsman of Dylan Thomas's colourful in-laws from these parts) duly dispatched his opponent, a Mr Hammond, poor George Ievers collapsed with apoplexy. As he died that night at Mount Ievers, his pack of hounds are supposed to have escaped from their kennels and to have run past the house in full cry.

Today, though, the thick glazing-bars of the first-floor windows are back where they belong, thanks to the faithful restoration carried out by the late Squadron Leader Norman Ievers, who took over the place in 1945 and devoted his life to preserving its beauty. The roof was renewed and two ponds to the south of the house, on the site of those shown in the *naif* 18th-century painting of Mount Ievers, were created. The Squadron Leader's admirable efforts were supported by the Irish Georgian Society, who continue to give encouragement and practical help to his widow, Breda, and his son, also called Norman, in their devoted nurturing of this rare and ravishing gem.

Detail of a chimneypiece at Mount Ievers – a rare decorative flourish in an interior noted for its panelled simplicity and unaffected plainness.

RIGHT The shimmering beauty of the south front, with its faded brick, traditionally from Holland. Mount Ievers is the quintessential Irish 'tall house'.

12

NEWBRIDGE HOUSE

EWBRIDGE IS important not only on account of its Georgian architecture and a set of interiors that must rank among the finest in Ireland but also as a precursor of a partnership between country-house-owning families and official bodies that augurs well for the future of the Irish heritage. As discussed in the Introduction, the Republic of Ireland does not, at present, enjoy the advantage of a safety net in the form of a property-owning National Trust, though the pioneering arrangement at Newbridge shows a practical way forward in such circumstances.

In 1985 the Cobbe family, who had been at Newbridge since the 1730s, when their ancestor Bishop Charles Cobbe (later Archbishop of Dublin) started putting the estate together, found themselves obliged to sell up. That could have been the end for Newbridge as it was for so many other Irish country houses in the bleak era of the 1970s and early 1980s. Yet the enterprising pair of Michael Lynch, of Dublin County Council's Parks Department, and Matt McNulty, of *Bord Failte* (the Irish Tourist Board), who had already rescued the historic Malahide Castle nearby to be a tourist attraction, stepped in with an ingenious solution. The Cobbes could continue to reside in the house in return for leaving most of the contents – the original Irish furniture, pictures and works of art on display – *in situ* on loan.

The scheme works remarkably well. Visitors to Newbridge are struck by the intimate and emphatically non-'museumy' atmosphere which only a true family seat can retain. The haphazard mixture of objects – from China Blue porcelain to Abyssinian buffalo heads – speaks of centuries of Cobbe ownership. And the special bonus of the set-up, now in the care of Fingal County Council and the Trustees of the Cobbe Family Collections, is that it benefits from the unrivalled eye and sympathetic advice of the connoisseur and designer Alec Cobbe, one of the family, whose brilliant work at Harewood, Powis, Sledmere and other places was celebrated in an earlier volume in this series, *Great Houses of England and Wales*.

PREVIOUS PAGES The Red Drawing Room, which was added to Newbridge *circa* 1760 by Thomas Cobbe as a gallery for his notable collection of Old Masters and as a *salon* for his hostess wife, Lady Betty Beresford. The ceiling has Rococo plasterwork by Richard Williams. Through the door at the end of the room can be seen, in the little drawing room, the fine Irish mahogany bureau bookcase bought by the Cobbes in 1764 for £11 17s 6d.

LEFT Looking through the noble entrance to the 45-foot-long Red Drawing Room, with its pedimented doorway and fluted engaged Corinthian columns. The chandelier is English crystal.

RIGHT View through an arch into the Inner Hall at Newbridge.

BELOW Marble busts form a conversation piece in this corner of the Inner Hall.

One can detect Alec Cobbe's 'eye' and influence, for example, in the marvellous hanging of pictures in Newbridge's (and, one could almost add, Ireland's) most spectacular interior, the Red Drawing Room, and also in the astonishing Museum of Curiosities, a cornucopia of diverse objects displayed in a room with pretty Chinese prints recalling the original decoration of *circa* 1790. As well as arranging the interiors to show off Newbridge's exceptional collections of Irish furniture and *objets d'art*, the Council also carried out a thorough restoration of the exterior of the house (replacing the glazing-bars in the windows, missing since Victorian times), courtyard and demesne.

The first chunk of the estate, including the 'townland' of Newbridge, was acquired in 1736, when, as the unusually detailed family accounts tell us, Charles Cobbe, Bishop of Kildare, paid £5,526 5s 6d for 490 acres. Six years later the Bishop added a further 510 acres nearby for £6,425. He was eventually to form a huge estate of some 35,000 acres north and south of Dublin.

The Cobbes were originally a Hampshire family, seated at Swaraton near Fleet, where their coat of arms was recognised in the heraldic Visitation of Hampshire in 1575. (At this period one of the family, Richard Cobbe, was described as Vice-President and benefactor of Corpus Christi College, Oxford.) In the late 17th century Thomas Cobbe rose to be Governor of the Isle of Man and then in 1717 his youngest son, Charles, completed the journey across the Irish Sea by arriving in Dublin as Chaplain to his cousin and fellow Wykehamist,

LEFT Tapestry and sculpture combine to form one of many arresting images in the eclectic interior.

RIGHT The Library, formerly the drawing room, with its Baroque-style ceiling and bow window overlooking the gardens. The painting above the chimneypiece is of the School of Schweikhardt.

Detail of a characteristic carved head on a piece of Irish furniture at Newbridge.

the 2nd Duke of Bolton, the new Lord Lieutenant (or 'Viceroy') of Ireland. Charles must have had a difficult time coping with the idiosyncratic behaviour of his patron, who, as Bishop Burnet noted, 'for many weeks he would not open his mouth till such an hour of the day when he thought the air was pure' and would hunt by torchlight. When he did open his mouth it might have been better if he hadn't: Jonathan Swift considered the Duke '*a great Booby*' and Tom Hearne thought him 'a most lewd, vicious man, a great dissembler and a very hard drinker'. It cannot have been easy to act as spiritual adviser to a man who, as *The Complete Peerage* records, believed in 'seriously recommending the castration of all unregistered priests and friars, with a view to making the common Irish protestants'.

Fortunately, for Ireland, the dreadful Duke did not last very long in the job, and Charles Cobbe survived this baptism of fire to advance rapidly through the ecclesiastical ranks; he was appointed Dean of Ardagh in 1718, Bishop of Killala in 1720, Bishop of Dromore in 1727, Bishop of Kildare in 1732 and finally Archbishop of Dublin in 1746. The present house at Newbridge dates from three years after his elevation to the Archbishopric. Its architect, George Semple, was a friend of the Archbishop's and in the same year also added the 100-foot spire to St Patrick's Cathedral in Dublin.

As built, Newbridge was austerely Classical, with the Entrance Hall panelled in plaster, paved with chequered flagstones and adorned with a carved armorial stone chimneypiece. The Archbishop evidently did not share the extravagant tastes of his early patron the Duke of Bolton. Yet after the Archbishop handed over Newbridge to his son Thomas Cobbe in 1755 on his marriage to Lady Elizabeth ('Betty') Beresford from Curraghmore (*qv*), sister of the 1st Marquess of Waterford, the new proprietors decided to make a bigger splash at Newbridge. The lavish marriage settlement confirms that there was no shortage of cash available.

Above all, Thomas, who followed his maternal grandfather, Speaker Sir Richard Levinge, 1st Bt, into the Irish House of Commons, and Lady Betty, a celebrated hostess, were determined to make Newbridge a fashionable place for entertaining. They promptly extended the house by adding the Red Drawing Room, a highly impressive chamber, 45 feet long, entered through a monumental doorway with a pediment and fluted engaged Corinthian columns. The glorious ceiling of Rococo plasterwork, and also the one which enlivened the Archbishop's Dining Room, is by the Dublin stuccodore Richard Williams, a pupil of Robert West of Florence Court (*qv*) fame.

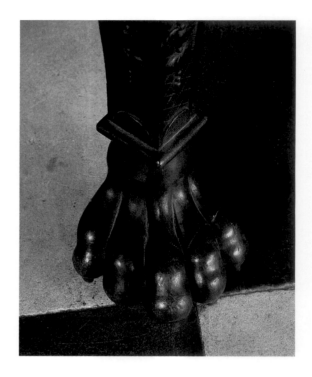

ABOVE Detail of a hoof on another Irish piece of furniture at Newbridge.

LEFT Looking across the panelled Entrance Hall, with its chequered flag-stones of Portland stone and Welsh slate. The head above the door is of an Abyssinian buffalo shot in 1908.

RIGHT Although open to the public and a deservedly popular tourist attraction, Newbridge very much retains the flavour of an intimate family house as this homely assortment of Cobbe artefacts and memorabilia illustrates.

Besides serving as Thomas and Lady Betty's *salon*, the Red Drawing Room was also in effect a picture gallery to show off the magnificent collection of Old Master paintings which they formed with the expert advice of the local clergyman the Reverend Matthew Pilkington. For as well as being Vicar of Donabate (where the Cobbe family pew was also decorated by 'Williams the Stuccoer', as he is described in the Newbridge accounts), Pilkington was, by a happy chance, the author of *The Gentleman's and Connoisseur's Dictionary of Painters* (1770), the first such work of reference to be published in English.

Superb as the surviving Old Masters in the Red Drawing Room are, it is also, as the present-day guidebook to the house says, 'nice to note as you go through Newbridge that many of its treasures were in fact made here in Ireland'. For instance, in the little drawing room next door can be found a rare example of Irish furniture that is actually documented: the fine mahogany bureau bookcase was bought by the Cobbes in 1764 for £11 17s 6d.

Although Newbridge's most fascinating room, the Museum of Curiosities, also contains objects of specific Irish origin – such as bog butter found in Co. Donegal in 1849 and an ostrich egg laid in Dundalk, Co. Louth, in 1756 – it is essentially a miscellaneous repository that reflects the Cobbes' wanderings around the world over the last 200 years. As a family museum dating from *circa* 1790 it is very rare in Ireland and Great Britain; the equally eccentric collection at Dunrobin Castle featured in *Great Houses of Scotland* dates from only the 19th century.

The entrance front of Newbridge, designed by George Semple for his friend Archbishop Cobbe in 1749. The property is now administered in an innovative partnership between Fingal County Council and the Trustees of the Cobbe Family Collections. The recent restoration work included the putting back of the Georgian glazing bars in the windows, which had been missing since the 19th century.

ABOVE and BELOW Exotic birds enlivening the rooflines at Newbridge. The peacocks (above) are among the assorted livestock housed in the Courtyard. The stone hawk (below) is a representation of one of the Cobbe family crests.

The variety of curiosities is mind-blowing. Here are specimens of black brain coral, a stuffed buzzard, an Indo-Persian spiked helmet and bricks from Babylon; there are an African Chief's umbrella, pieces of the Nanking Cargo, a hookah pipe and the mummified ear of an Egyptian bull. Among the artefacts are mementoes of Lady Betty Beresford's medical experiments.

For Lady Betty fancied herself as a physician. One of her pet cures was derived from a tub of 'tar-water', the ingredients of which kicked off with six gallons of brandy. Her most famous invention was the Chilblain Plaister, which became a commercial success in England.

It was perhaps partly for reasons of health that Lady Betty persuaded Thomas Cobbe to leave the delights of Newbridge, where they had laid out a naturalistic demesne (probably to the designs of Charles Frizell from Wexford), for the then fashionable English spa of Bath. Fortunately, though, their grandson Charles Cobbe returned to live at Newbridge early in the 19th century and set about improving the place once more.

Charles and his heiress wife, Frances Conway, from Morden Park in Surrey, were responsible for adding the Regency furniture to the Newbridge collections. Much of this was supplied by the Dublin firm of Mack, Williams & Gibton, who also made the curtains for the Red Drawing Room in 1828. A few years later two of the best pictures in this room – masterpieces by Poussin and Hobbema – were sold by Charles Cobbe for the worthiest of causes: in order, as he himself put it, to raze the 'wretched mud cabins' of his tenantry and replace them with proper cottages. (The Newbridge Hobbema, incidentally, fetched £3,000 and is now in the Metropolitan Museum, New York.)

Such warm-hearted Christian philanthropy balances the traditional view of the 'Ascendancy' portrayed by Charles's spinster daughter Frances, a traveller, journalist and pioneer feminist, who summed up Irish Society at the end of the 18th century as having

> combined a considerable amount of aesthetic taste with traits of genuine barbarism; and high religious pretension with a disregard of everyday duties and a *penchant* for gambling and drinking which would now place the most worldly persons under a cloud of opprobium.

Be that as it may, the Newbridge of today exudes a notably friendly atmosphere in which the present sits peacefully with the past. Nostalgically stocked kitchens, laundries and outbuildings help present a rounded picture of life in an Irish country house. The coaches on display in the stables include a splendid State Coach built in 1790 (about the same time as the square cobbled courtyard itself was laid out) for 'Black Jack' FitzGibbon, the Lord Chancellor of Ireland.

'Black Jack' was notorious for his remark that he would 'tame the Irish like cats'. Hardly surprisingly, his coffin had dead cats thrown at it. Newbridge's model farm houses less controversial creatures, such as chickens and pigs. They contribute a reassuringly homely touch to this exemplary Heritage showplace, a model of partnership.

13

TULLYNALLY CASTLE

COUNTY WESTMEATH

*T*HIS', wrote the young John Betjeman in September 1930 to his friend Patrick Balfour (later the 3rd Lord Kinross) in a letter from the Irish country house where he was staying, 'is an early 19th-century Gothic Palace in the remotest part of Ireland, to right and left rise round towers (hold this page up to the light and you will see one), ruined abbeys, ruined castles and prehistoric camps, I am in heaven'.

Indeed, as his daughter and editor of his *Letters* Candida Lycett Green has written, this 'Gothic Palace' of Pakenham Hall (which has reverted to its original Irish name of Tullynally Castle under the present ownership of the writers Thomas and Valerie Pakenham) was to become the budding poet's 'spiritual home in Ireland'. Betjeman's host and hostess were Thomas Pakenham's Uncle Edward and Aunt Christine, the 6th Earl and Countess of Longford, prominent figures in the Irish theatre in the days when The Gate and The Abbey in Dublin were known as 'Sodom and Begorrah'. Edward, who ran The Gate, is remembered by his nephew Thomas as 'a spherical figure of 24 stone (so stout he had to sit in the back seat of a car in order to drive it), who wore a wide-awake hat, wrote plays, translated from the Irish, Greek and Latin, and was a passionate Irish Nationalist'. The celebrated Irish actor Micheál MacLiammóir recalled in his memoirs Edward 'striding into the theatre with his sudden infectious cackle of laughter, his magnificent expanse of grey flannel trousers and dazzling pullover, and billowing breast where an orchid curled incongruously on the gingerbread homespun...'.

MacLiammóir thought of Edward Longford in Betjemanesque terms – 'oh, *jolly, jolly tuck shop*' – and, as Christine Longford wrote in her unpublished memoirs, John Betjeman and Edward had much in common. They 'shared interests in churches, protestant hymn-tunes, ballads and comic peers' and she considered that Betjeman 'gave Edward – if one could give one's friends marks – more pleasure for 30 years than anyone else in our lives'.

Sometimes Betjeman's love of Orange songs could be taken too far. Lady Violet Powell, Edward's third sister, recalls how she 'had to explain that it would be injudicious to attempt to buy them in Mullingar'. And a fellow guest at Pakenham, the *enfant terrible* novelist Evelyn Waugh, grumbled in his diary that 'John B. became a bore rather with Irish peers and revivalist hymns and his enthusiasm for every sort of architecture'. Yet the jollity engendered by John Betjeman and Edward Longford made Pakenham a byword for entertainment in Irish country houses. As Waugh himself wrote, in an obituary of Edward in 1961:

> I have seen at Pakenham what I have seen nowhere else, an entirely sober host literally rolling about the carpet with merriment... His butler and attendant footmen would gravely bestride the spherical form in its velvet smoking-suit as they carried their trays.

Christine Longford noted that in fact there was only one footman at Pakenham and that it was Waugh who wore a velvet jacket rather than her husband, but otherwise the reminiscence was 'true enough'. Moreover, there was certainly nothing affected about Betjeman's enthusiasm for Pakenham,

PREVIOUS PAGES 'Hill of Swans': looking up from the lake to the castellated facade of Tullynally. The new conservatory can be spotted to the right of what Sir John Betjeman called a 'Gothic palace'.

BELOW The Drawing Room, with its ceiling of geometrical design: scene of much entertainment presided over by the Pakenham family.

RIGHT Gothic Valhalla: the vast Hall at Tullynally, which benefited from a pioneering experiment in central heating in the early 19th century by the Pakenhams' neighbour, Richard Lovell Edgeworth.

BELOW The family crest of the Pakenhams – 'an eagle displayed *gules*' (hence the red scarf) coming 'out of a mural crown *or*'.

where his visits inspired, as his biographer Bevis Hillier put it, 'some of his best poems and his most sustained piece of architectural research, into the life and work of Francis Johnston'.

It was Johnston who had been brought in between 1801 and 1806 by the 2nd Earl of Longford to Gothicise the previously plain Georgian box which was transformed, on the builder's bills, from 'Pakenham Hall House' to 'Pakenham Hall Castle'. Johnston gave the house slim round corner turrets and a battlemented parapet appropriate to the family's military traditions – for whereas today the Pakenhams are celebrated on account of the pen, in former times it was the sword that gave lustre to the name.

Both the 2nd Earl's brothers – Sir Edward Pakenham (who subsequently came to grief at New Orleans, after which his corpse was pickled in rum for carriage back to burial in Co. Westmeath) and Sir Hercules Pakenham – were Peninsular War Generals. And their sister Kitty married the great Duke of Wellington, whose biography was written by Elizabeth Longford, wife of the present Earl, the Labour politician, penal reformer and campaigner against pornography.

The Tullynally estate was acquired in the 1650s by another military man, Henry Pakenham, Captain of a troop of Dragoons in the service of Oliver Cromwell's Parliament. The Pakenhams, a long-established East Anglian

family, already had links with Ireland through the service of Edmund Pakenham (Henry's grandfather) as secretary to his cousin Sir Henry Sidney, Lord Deputy of Ireland in Elizabethan times. Captain Henry's son Sir Thomas Pakenham rose to be Prime Serjeant-at-Law for Ireland by the end of the 17th century; and in 1756 the family entered the peerage when Sir Thomas's grandson and namesake, who was MP for Longford, was created Baron Longford. His widow, a great-grandniece of Ambrose Aungier, 2nd and last Earl of Longford of an earlier creation, was subsequently elevated to a new Earldom of Longford in her own right.

Their eldest son, Edward, who succeeded to the Barony but not to the Earldom (as he predeceased his mother), was described by Sir John Blaquiere as 'a tolerable speaker and a very respectable good-humoured man'. The Lord Lieutenant of Ireland in the 1780s, the 1st Marquess of Buckingham, was rather warmer in his praises of Lord Longford: 'He has been indefatigable, and with his brother T. [Captain, later Admiral Sir Thomas] Pakenham, has helped us more than any family in Ireland'.

It was during Edward's reign at Pakenham Hall (as Tullynally had been renamed) that the previous house, which in turn had succeeded a plain 17th-century structure, was remodelled by Graham Myers, architect to Trinity College, Dublin. A five-bay Classical facade was topped up with a third storey. A draw-

'Everything a library should be': the Library at Tullynally, John Betjeman's favourite room in the house. The recently installed jib door can be seen to the right, by the steps. The portrait of Major-General Sir Edward Pakenham (killed at New Orleans in January 1815, after which his corpse was pickled in rum for carriage back to Co. Westmeath) is a reminder that the Pakenhams were formerly as celebrated for the sword as they now are for the pen.

ing by Edward's Uncle George, from 1738, shows the earlier house of two storeys surrounded by an elaborate formal layout of basins, cascades and canals – soon to be swept away by the romantic tide of 'naturalisation'.

The romantic tastes of the 19th-century owners of Pakenham were so powerful as to result in what Mark Bence-Jones has aptly called 'a Camelot of the Gothic Revival'. With its long, picturesque skyline of towers, turrets, battlements and gateways stretching among the trees of its rolling parkland, the Tullynally we see today covers a greater area than any other castellated country house in Ireland. Indeed it looks not so much like a castle as a small fortified town.

Not content with Francis Johnston's gentle Gothicisation, in the 1820s the 2nd Earl of Longford (Edward's son, who succeeded his grandmother in the Earldom) engaged the architect James Shiel to go the whole hog. Inside, the vast Hall took on even more of the appearance of a vaulted Gothic Valhalla and a three-sided bow was added to the garden front. One of the 2nd Earl's most remarkable innovations was the installation of a pioneering central heating system devised by his eccentric neighbour Richard Lovell Edgeworth of Edgeworthstown. In a letter of 1807 Edgeworth's daughter the novelist Maria (author of *Castle Rackrent*) describes 'the immense hall so well-warmed by hot air that the children play in it from morning to night. Lord L. seemed to take great pleasure in repeating 20 times that he was to thank Mr Edgeworth for this'. To this day, as Mark Girouard wrote in a fascinating study of Tullynally's domestic appliances for *Country Life*, the Hall has remained the warmest room in this rambling house.

It was to ramble yet further in the early years of the reign of the 3rd Earl of Longford, a bachelor known as 'Fluffy'. The ubiquitous architect Sir Richard Morrison enlarged Pakenham once more, from 1839 to 1842, with a two-storey battlemented range on the entrance front (containing a private apartment for the family) and a kitchen wing with battlemented gables on the garden front. Morrison's achievement was to tie the whole composition together. The battlemented range on the entrance front was ingeniously linked to the house by a tall octagonal tower with a turret, and his two wings joined the house to the stable court beyond, which is entered by a castellated gateway. The finishing touch was added in 1860, when J. Rawson Carroll (architect of Classiebawn, Co. Sligo, built for Lord Palmerston and eventually Lord Mountbatten's Irish holiday home) designed the tower at the corner of the stable court for the new 4th Earl of Longford.

Two views of the cavernous 'downstairs' service area of Tullynally, which houses a veritable museum of Victorian domestic gadgetry.

The multitudinous Victorian improvements made at Pakenham by the 4th Earl, Under-Secretary of War in the British Government (though, as Lady St Helier wrote in her *Memories of Fifty Years*, he was 'an Irishman, and a soldier, and a man of the world, a good talker, and had a strongly characteristic Irish sense of humour'), particularly absorbed John Betjeman's attention. He delighted, for instance, in the wheezy organ (by Henry Bevington of Greek Street, London) in the Hall and the cavernous Kitchen, with its mighty iron-range and such artefacts as a butter-maker and marmalade-cutter. As Bevis Hillier has remarked, it may well have been of Pakenham especially that Betjeman was thinking when he wrote: 'in a country house I do not like to see the state rooms only, but the passages to the billiard room, where the Spy cartoons are, and the bedrooms where I note the hair brushes of the owner and the sort of hair oil he uses'. Today the atmospheric 'downstairs' area of Tullynally remains a veritable museum of Victorian domestic gadgetry.

Betjeman's, and surely every visitor's, favourite interior in the great house was, of course, the Library. As Mark Bence-Jones has put it, this is 'everything that a library should be; spacious and comfortable, with oak bookcases going up to the ceiling and windows facing south over idyllic parkland'. Recently Thomas Pakenham has devised a brilliantly deceptive jib-door, indistinguishable among the bookcases, which gives into Shiel's octagonal, vaulted Dining Room and affords that room a striking new vista.

Thomas Pakenham points out that it was in the Library that Evelyn Waugh spun the globe to decide on the destination of his travels in the 1930s. The outcome was Abyssinia and 25 years later the young Pakenham – who preceded his elder sister Antonia Fraser into print – followed Waugh's footsteps to what was now Ethiopia, where he discovered an unrecorded medieval church at Bethlehem. This led to Thomas Pakenham's first book, *The Mountains of Rasselas*, and to an absorption in African affairs which resulted in his books on *The Boer War* and *The Scramble for Africa*. He is also the author of *The Year of Liberty*, a stirring account of the abortive 'Great Irish Rebellion' of 1798. In 1992 he received the prestigious W.H. Smith Literary Award, previously won by his uncle the great novelist Anthony Powell, whose first visit to Pakenham in 1934, as described in his memoirs, was at the invitation of his future sister-in-law Elizabeth, matriarch of the Literary Family Pakenham.

Thomas Pakenham naturally spent the £10,000 cash prize on what he describes as 'this crumbling house'. Among his many improvements has been the banana-shaped conservatory, a light and airy confection beside the kitchen wing. He recalls the time in 1961 when his Uncle Edward 'suddenly went pop' and he found himself 'the owner of this 80-room pile with a 1,500-acre demesne of woods and lakes'. Fortunately, he had long nurtured a passion for Ireland. At the age of 11 he was first exposed to 'the intense romantic appeal' of the island. The impact of the Gothic atmosphere ('without petrol or electric light') of the Irish Midlands in the mid-1940s was, he recalls, 'absolutely overwhelming – it was like going back to the world of Le Fanu and *Uncle Silas*'.

'Coming from a suburban garden in north Oxford [where his father had been a don], you can imagine what it was like exploring this marvellous demesne as a boy', he recalls as he shows his plans for new arboreta and ambitious new water-works. Thomas and his wife, Valerie, have done much to restore the pleasure-grounds and gardens of Tullynally, which like the castle are open to the public.

They encompass two ornamental lakes, a fernery walk and grotto, a Chinese garden and a walled garden with extensive flower borders and a magnificent avenue of 200-year-old Irish yews. John Betjeman loved the 1780 Coade stone sphinxes framing the gate to the kitchen garden. There is also a circular woodland walk around the demesne.

Trees are something of an obsession with Thomas Pakenham: his eye-opening book *Meetings with Remarkable Trees* spawned a television series, and the Tullynally demesne contains some splendid specimens. As we walk round the lake a pair of swans glide into view – appropriately, for the Irish name of Tullynally, now happily restored, means 'Hill of Swans'.

The 'Camelot of the Gothic Revival': Tullynally covers a greater area than any other castellated country house in Ireland, stretching from the stables, to the right, to the lake front of the house, to the left, and dotted with towers, turrets and battlements.

RUSSBOROUGH

HOUSE OPENING TIMES.

		EASTER SUN. & MON.	10.30 – 5.30
APRIL, OCTOBER		SUNS. & BANK HOLS.	10.30 – 5.30
MAY, SEPTEMBER		MONS. TO SATS.	10.30 – 2.30
		SUNS. & BANK HOLS.	10.30 – 5.30
JUNE, JULY, AUGUST		DAILY	10.30 – 5.30

14

RUSSBOROUGH

COUNTY WICKLOW

*T*HERE ARE great Irish houses, there are beautiful Irish houses, and then there is Russborough, surely the fairest of them all. A sparkling vision in Golden Hill granite, facing the Poulaphouca reservoir and the majestic Wicklow mountains, this Palladian palace designed in the 1740s by Richard Castle for Joseph Leeson, later 1st Earl of Milltown, is hardly short of perfection. Both literally and metaphorically there is too much for the eye and mind to take in, for the length of the entrance front, complete with pairs of colonnades and wings, seems to stretch towards infinity. And inside the sumptuous plasterwork, carved chimneypieces, inlaid floors and lavish use of San Domingo mahogany, not to mention the fabulous art treasures, leave one bemused with joy.

That all this, the pride of Ireland's heritage, can be enjoyed by the visiting public is thanks to the generosity, foresight and unwavering faith of the late philanthropist Sir Alfred Beit, 2nd Bt, and his widow, the former Clementine Mitford. After rescuing and splendidly restoring Russborough in the 1950s, they filled it with the celebrated Beit Collection of pictures and works of art (dominated by Dutch, Flemish and Spanish masterpieces, but also including a wonderful range of English, Scottish, Italian and French paintings). This resulted in an exquisite ensemble, for the great house was enhanced by the collection and the collection was enhanced by being shown in such glorious surroundings.

Then, in 1976, the Beits fulfilled their ideal of forming a charitable educational foundation, the Alfred Beit Foundation, whereby Russborough would become a centre of fine arts and be opened to the public, which came to pass a couple of years later. The over-ruling objective of the Foundation has been to maintain for all time this outstanding example of Palladian architecture for the enjoyment of the public and to further interest in the arts.

As so often in Ireland, the history of Russborough's building and decoration is frustratingly undocumented. It is, though, known that Joseph Leeson, then aged 30, bought the place from a John Graydon in 1741, when there was already a house on the site; but of this there is no record. Leeson's father and namesake, a prosperous Dublin brewer and businessman, had died earlier the same year; according to *The Gentleman's Magazine* he was worth more than £50,000, a tidy sum in those days. The family fortunes had been founded by Hugh Leeson, a soldier-turned-tycoon who came over to Ireland from Northamptonshire in the early 17th century.

As befitted a new landed proprietor, young Joseph went into Parliament and also did the Grand Tour. The great authority on that cultural experience, Sir Brinsley Ford, discovered that Leeson had his portrait painted by Pompeo Batoni in Rome in 1744 and also that, in the following year, Horace Mann mentioned in a letter to Horace Walpole that the *Augustus Caesar* 'with £60,000 worth of goods, and many statues, pictures etc; of one Mr Leeson, a rich Irishman' had been captured by the French. (The £50,000 mentioned by *The Gentleman's Magazine* appears to have been something of an undervaluation.)

These treasures, presumably recaptured, were destined for Leeson's 'noble new house forming into perfection', as it was described by one chronicler in 1748, by which time it was evidently not finished. John Cornforth, writing in *Country Life*, considers that it was probably not finished until the mid-1750s – after Joseph Leeson, this time with his son and namesake, had paid another visit to Rome in 1751, the year in which his architect, Richard Castle, had dropped dead on the site of another of his commissions, Carton, the remodelled seat of Ireland's 'first family', the FitzGeralds, Earls of Kildare and soon to be Dukes of Leinster.

Castle (or Cassels), who hailed from Hesse-Cassel in Germany, had succeeded Sir Edward Lovett Pearce as the leading figure in Irish Palladianism. As the Knight of Glin has pointed out, he cribbed the idea of the balustraded upper landing lit by a lantern window at Russborough from Pearce's superb Palladian villa of Bellamont Forest, Co. Cavan, built *circa* 1730 for his uncle Lord Justice Coote (and recently immaculately restored by the designer John Coote from Australia).

PREVIOUS PAGES Gateway to Paradise: the Palladian archway which leads to Russborough, designed in the 1740s by Richard Castle for Joseph Leeson, later 1st Earl of Milltown, and now opened to the public by the Alfred Beit Foundation.

BELOW A view of the vast entrance front, showing one of the colonnades to the left of the central block. In total, the south frontage runs to 700 feet.

RIGHT Close-up of the entrance across the forecourt.

BELOW View from the Front Hall on to the entrance steps and the demesne, with the Wicklow mountains beyond.

The Knight of Glin has also spotted that Castle (whose other commissions included Powerscourt, the other side of the Wicklow mountains from Russborough) was influenced by the architectural engravings in William Adam's *Vitruvius Scotius*. The curved colonnades at Hopetoun (featured in an earlier volume in this series, *Great Houses of Scotland*), for instance, have echoes at Russborough.

John Cornforth suggests that Castle may, too, have been inspired by Castle Howard (see *Great Houses of England and Wales*). 'If the power and drama of the Vanbrugh design are taken away', he wrote in *Country Life*, 'there is a sense of spread and mass similar to that achieved at Russborough.' Yet marvellous as Russborough is, there is a slight flaw in the design – which could be said to add to its extraordinary charm. Cornforth put his finger on it when he remarked that the centrepiece, the central block on the 'show' facade, is 'not bold enough to hold one's attention... the result is that one's eyes tend to move constantly from side to side across the forecourt, being tossed back and forth by the more richly modelled concave colonnades'.

Inside, the lofty Hall boasts a mighty black Kilkenny marble chimneypiece and a ceiling similar to the one Castle designed for Leinster House in Dublin (now the Irish Parliament). A marble table-top, presumably bought in Rome, was until recently the only Leeson item to remain at Russborough, but then Sir Alfred Beit, with remarkable forensic skill, succeeded in tracking down the four oval marine scenes by Joseph Vernet which had formerly adorned the Drawing Room to the left of the Hall. He bought them back from an American stockbroker and they now hang happily within the plaster mouldings originally created around them at a date that seems almost certain to have been after 1751.

LEFT The Saloon, Russborough's principal interior, with its plasterwork attributed to the Francini or Lafranchini brothers. The walls are hung with 19th-century Genoese velvet; the 18th-century candelabras are by Falconnet; the floor is inlaid; and the paintings are Dutch and Flemish of the 16th and 17th centuries.

RIGHT A corner of the chimneypiece in the Saloon by Thomas Carter the Younger.

BELOW Detail of one of the candelabra on the Saloon chimneypiece by Falconnet.

Behind the Hall is Russborough's principal interior, the Saloon, with its superlative plasterwork ceiling attributed to the Italian stuccodores the Francini or Lafranchini brothers, who also worked at Carton and Castletown, both in Co. Kildare. Putti bearing emblems of the Seasons and the Elements dance round the cove between abundant scrolls and foliage and beneath crisp garlands. The Lafranchinis – if it was they, and it seems highly likely it was – were also busy in the Music Room, with its coffered saucer dome, and the old dining room (now the Library).

The style of the plasterwork in the Staircase Hall is obviously by another hand. It is spectacularly over the top, not so much Rococo as, to coin a phrase, 'Cor-I-Should-Coco!'. The sober chronicler Mr Sibthorpe judged it as 'the ravings of a maniac', adding that he was sure the maniac in question must have been Irish. Yet, of course, this riot of exuberance is terrific fun – and delightfully photogenic.

Although far from being a maniac, Joseph Leeson's bachelor eldest son and namesake, who had accompanied his father to Rome, was described by Sir Herbert Croft in *The Abbey of Kilkhampton* (1780) as 'an incorrigible Simpletor'. He succeeded to his father's peerages, the Barony and Viscountcy of Russborough and the Earldom of Milltown (created in 1763), and to Russborough itself on old Joseph's death in 1783. Old Joseph's third wife and widow, incidentally, Elizabeth French, lived on to a very great age until 1842 – a century after her husband had begun building operations at Russborough.

LEFT The barrel-vaulted Tapestry Room, which takes its name from the Soho tapestry hung here, made in London by John Vanderbank, *circa* 1720. The bed and matching furniture were also made in London by Wilsons of the Strand, 1794. Russborough's architectural beauty is enriched by the fabulous treasures of the Beit Collection.

RIGHT 'Cor-I-Should-Coco!' The riot of exuberant Rococo plasterwork which leaves visitors gasping in the Staircase Hall.

BELOW The Drawing Room, with its plaster mouldings created to contain the four marine scenes by Joseph Vernet commissioned by the 1st Lord Milltown. The paintings, which had been sold, were brought back to Russborough by Sir Alfred Beit, 2nd Bt.

The Leesons remained at Russborough throughout the 19th century and fortunately few changes were made to its then unfashionable Palladian features during the Victorian era, apart from the inevitable replacement of the original glazing-bars by the ubiquitous plate glass in the windows. (Naturally, the glazing-bars returned in the 1950s' restoration by Sir Alfred and Lady Beit.) The succeeding Earls of Milltown made little mark on the outside world either, though the 6th Earl, a minor politician, earned himself a 'Spy' caricature in *Vanity Fair* in 1883.

Eight years later the title became dormant on the death of his bachelor brother, the 7th Earl, though an heir appeared to exist among the collateral branches of the family. The 6th Earl's widow, the former Lady Geraldine Stanhope, daughter of the 5th Earl of Harrington, lived on at Russborough until 1914, but by this time the family collection of pictures in the house had been given to the National Gallery of Ireland. This 1902 benefaction turned out to be by no means Russborough's only link with the National Gallery, for in 1986 Sir Alfred Beit, who was a governor of the Gallery, presented it with part of the Beit Collection – so that today Russborough could be said to be effectively an 'outstation' of the National Gallery.

Meanwhile, in 1931, the 6th Earl of Milltown's nephew Sir Edmund Turton, 1st Bt, MP, a Yorkshire squire (whose father-in-law, Sir Spencer Ponsonby Fane, was a co-founder of the I Zingari cricket club and built the pavilion at Lord's), had decided to sever the Leeson links with Russborough, and to sell up. The future of the great house seemed uncertain. But fortunately Colonel Denis Daly, a scion of the Dalys of Dunsandle, Co. Galway, stepped in and did a valiant job in preserving the place at a difficult time.

During the Daly ownership, in 1937, Sir Alfred Beit, then decorating a house in London's Kensington Palace Gardens with the help of Lady Colefax, was

struck by the beauties of Russborough as photographed in an article for *Country Life*. He decided to copy the dining room chimneypiece in his own library.

Russborough remained in his heart and by chance 15 years later, when he was out in South Africa and thinking of settling there permanently, he saw the self-same house of his dreams advertised for sale in *Country Life*. He wasted no time, and instantly bought it by telegram.

South Africa was a key element in the Beits' story, for Sir Alfred's uncle and namesake (who, like Russborough's architect, originally hailed from Germany) was one of the 'Randlords', a friend and partner of Cecil Rhodes. He amassed a huge fortune based on diamonds and gold-mining in the business that became de Beers. The Beit Collection, started in the 1890s by Alfred senior and expanded by Sir Alfred's father, Sir Otto Beit, 1st Bt, developed into one of the most important collections of the 20th century – one indeed which is worth an illustrated volume of its own. And Russborough was to be its supremely satisfactory showplace.

Young Alfred succeeded to the Collection (which he was imaginatively to expand) and the Baronetcy in 1930, and entered the British House of Commons the next year. He and his wife, Clementine Mitford (whose father, if he had survived the First World War – as Evelyn Waugh enjoyed pointing out to his friend Nancy Mitford – would have become Lord Redesdale instead of her own father, portrayed as the fiery 'Uncle Matthew' in her novels), were celebrated as 'the handsomest couple in London'. They fell in love with Ireland, and Ireland reciprocated. Their hospitality at Russborough passed into legend. As Desmond Guinness wrote in *Great Irish Houses and Castles*, 'the guests were drawn from artistic and intellectual circles as well as the *beau monde*... Kenneth Clark, Peter Quennell, Christopher Sykes [uncle of the photographer of this book], Gaston Palewski, Charles de Noailles and Diana Cooper would be found staying'.

Even two terrible burglaries did not dim the Beits' determination to do their best for Russborough and Ireland. First in 1974, 19 paintings, including a Goya and a Vermeer, were taken by terrorist thugs, who assaulted the Beits. The pictures were recovered within a month. Then, in 1986, a further 18 paintings (four of which were destined for the National Gallery) disappeared in what was described at the time as the most lucrative art robbery ever. Gradually, most of them were tracked down around the globe and it was gratifying that some turned up before Sir Alfred's death in 1994.

The previous year the President of Ireland, Mary Robinson, had made him and his wife honorary Irish citizens. No honour could have been more richly deserved for these public-spirited patrons of the arts who have endowed Ireland's most beautiful house for posterity.

Echoes of Hopetoun: the curved east colonnade at Russborough, with statuary adorning the niches.

15

CASTLE WARD

COUNTY DOWN

C ASTLE WARD, now in the care of the National Trust, is celebrated
for its contrasting styles of architecture: one side of the mid-
Georgian house is Classical, the other Gothick. This curious
state of affairs came about because the owner, Bernard Ward,
the local MP (later 1st Viscount Bangor), and his wife, Lady Anne,
simply could not agree on matters of taste – or, it seems, much else.
Amusing and unusual as this is, though, it is surely the glorious setting of Castle Ward above Strangford Lough, the most stately of
Northern Ireland's great waterways, that makes the strongest impression. Every
prospect pleases in a swooping landscape of woods, farmland, pleasure-
grounds and lakes, including the artfully created Temple Water overlooked
by a pretty Palladian pavilion. And down by the shores of the Lough is Audley's
Castle, not just a picturesque 'eye-catcher' but one of the many fortified
tower houses built in these parts.

The original Castle Ward was another of those little tower houses by the
Lough, and still survives not far away. It was probably built in about 1610 by
Nicholas Ward, formerly Clerk, Comptroller and Surveyor-General of the Ord-
nance and later Deputy-Surveyor-General of Lands. The property had been
acquired from the Earl of Kildare by Nicholas's father, Bernard Ward, a Cheshire
man, and was previously known as *Carrick na Sheannagh* ('Rock of Foxes').

As the 17th century progressed, the Wards of Castle Ward expanded their
estate and established themselves as prominent figures in Co. Down. The Bernard
Ward of the day was High Sheriff of the county in 1690, when he became
embroiled in a furious quarrel with Jocelyn Hamilton of Tollymore in the Grand
Jury Room at Downpatrick. They promptly went outside to settle matters
near the Abbey ruins in a most unruly manner: the High Sheriff shot, and mor-
tally wounded, Hamilton, with a pistol, but the dying man managed (as one
report put it) 'so brave a thrust' with his sword that Ward was run through almost
to the hilt.

Hardly surprisingly, the High Sheriff's son Michael Ward grew up to have a healthy respect for the proprieties and became a Judge of the King's Bench. He was also an enterprising businessman with interests in the linen trade, Ulster's main industry, and agricultural improvement. Contemporary visitors to Castle Ward in the Judge's time record much landscaping activity. The *Topographical and Chronological Survey of the County of Down* (1740) mentions 'handsome Improvements in Parks, Gardens, Canals, a Decoy, and great Plantations...'. The Temple Water, a great rectangular pond, dates from this period, though the pavilion itself was added by the Judge's daughter-in-law Lady Anne.

The Judge must also have extended the old tower, or built a new house nearby on the low ground near the shore of the Lough, though no record of this survives. In any event, on his death in 1759, his son and successor, Bernard Ward, wasted little time in embarking on a new Castle Ward in a prime position up on the hill. But he had a battle on his hands when it came to settling on the style of architecture.

For Bernard had not only succeeded to the Parliamentary seat of his late friend Robert Hawkins Magill of Gill Hall (reputedly the most haunted house in Ireland), but had also taken on his widow, Lady Anne, daughter of the 1st Earl of Darnley. A visit by Mrs Delany in August 1763, by which time the new house must have been well under way, gives some hints of the trouble in store:

> Mr Ward is building a fine house, but the scene about it is so
> uncommonly fine it is a pity it should not be judiciously laid out. *He*
> wants taste, and *Lady Anne Ward* is so whimsical that I doubt her
> judgement. If they do not do *too much* they *can't* spoil the place for it
> hath every advantage from Nature that can be desired.

The portrait of Bernard Ward, by Francis Cotes (1767), which now hangs in the Saloon at Castle Ward, leaves one in no doubt as to what his own taste was, wanting or not. He is holding a plan of the new house clearly showing the conventional Classical side. The 'whimsical' Lady Anne fancied the Gothick taste. The resulting compromise produced one of the most unusual buildings in Ireland.

Outside, at least, Mr Ward appears to have got the better of the bargain for it is not only the original entrance front that is Classical but the sides as well; whereas it is, on closer inspection, really only in the endearingly dotty detail of the garden front – ogee arches to the windows, battlements and exceedingly whimsical pinnacles – that the Gothick asserts itself. Inside, though, it is another matter. For while the husband may have rejoiced in the Doric columns of the Hall, and succeeded in securing a Classical advance into the middle of the house with his Staircase, the wife's Gothick interiors on the garden side undoubtedly steal the show.

The Gothick ceilings in the Saloon and the Boudoir, for instance, are quite extraordinary. The Saloon ceiling was likened by Mark Girouard in *Country Life* to 'a gigantic decorated halma board, complete with pieces'. The one in the Boudoir, or sitting room, positively induces hilarity with its riot of voluptuous, billowing curves calling to mind a ballooning tent or even a giantess's set of bloomers.

In less fevered fact, a letter from Lord William Gordon to Bernard Ward in 1764 makes it clear that the fan-vaulting was based (as at Arbury Hall in Warwickshire, the seat of the FitzRoy Newdegates, Viscounts Daventry) on King Henry VII's Chapel at Westminster Abbey:

PREVIOUS PAGES Castle Ward sitting splendidly in its prime position above Strangford Lough. It was built in the 1760s for Bernard Ward (later 1st Viscount Bangor), with one front Classical and the other Gothick as he and his wife disagreed over architectural styles – and much else besides.

RIGHT The Classical in the ascendant: looking through the Hall to the Staircase. The Doric columns to the right are of scagliola. The parquet floor replaced the original inlaid floor of oak and mahogany in the 19th century.

BELOW Detail of the endearingly rustic plasterwork on the walls of the Hall probably carried out by a team of stucco workers from the nearby village of Dundrum 1828/9. Some of the objects depicted are actually the real thing plastered over – an ingenious labour-saving device. By contrast, the ceiling plasterwork is more sophisticated and shows the expert hand of Dublin stuccodores *ante* 1775.

ABOVE Detail of gilt decoration in the Saloon. The wallpaper is 19th century.

LEFT The Saloon: one of the three Gothick interiors at Castle Ward. In the middle right, behind the piano, is an Italian 17th-century cabinet veneered with tortoiseshell, ivory and ebony. The portrait above is of Judge Michael Ward, father of the 1st Viscount Bangor.

I left a Commission in England to send Lady Ann drawings of the Roof of Henry the eights [*sic*] Chapel, a Chineise Bed & a Temple, which I hope her La has got & I shall not forget the Painted Glass...

None the less, in execution at least, the Boudoir ceiling hardly puts one in mind of religion.

Unfortunately the plan of Castle Ward Bernard Ward is seen holding in his portrait in the Gothick Saloon – on reflection, perhaps not a place he would have chosen – does not reveal the name of the obviously adaptable architect. The tradition is that, like the stone with which the house was built, he was brought over from Bath (where Lady Anne herself eventually decamped) or Bristol. Mark Girouard conjectures that it could possibly have been one or other of the Bristolians James Bridges and Thomas Paty, both capable of switching between the Classical and Gothick styles.

The National Trust's guidebook points out that the Classical features of the exterior, and also the Staircase, bear a close resemblance to the pattern-book *Collection of Designs* (1757) by Abraham Swan, which is still to be found in the panelled Library. The inspiration for the Gothick touches, which were slow to cross the Irish Sea, could well have come from a visit the Wards made in 1754 to Inveraray Castle, which had been tricked up with Gothick ornament by the English Palladian architect Roger Morris for the 3rd Duke of Argyll (see *Great Houses of Scotland*).

RIGHT A Gothick glimpse of the extraordinary decoration in the Boudoir, inspired by King Henry VII's chapel at Westminster Abbey, but its billowing voluptuous curves call to mind more a ballooning tent or even a giantess's set of bloomers.

The building of Castle Ward appears to have taken almost 10 years, for when Sir James Caldwell came to stay in the autumn of 1772 it was 'still not quite finished' even though the family was in residence by then. Sir James seems to have been keener to describe the pleasures of the table ('excellent dinner, stewed trout at the head, chine of beef at the foot, soup in the middle, a little pie at each side and four trifling things at the corners...') than the architecture, though he did call Castle Ward the 'finest place in this kingdom' and noted that the floor of the Hall, 'all inlaid with oak and mahogany', was 'diced and kept so smooth with rubbing and beeswax that you are in danger of slipping every moment'.

His host and hostess, for their part, soon slipped asunder. Having achieved such a remarkable agreement to differ architecturally, they could not reach an accommodation in their personal lives. The surviving fragment of an anguished letter from Lady Anne (or Lady Bangor, as she had become on her husband's elevation to a Barony in 1770), gives a flavour of their estrangement:

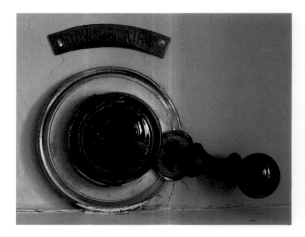

Ring, or rather pull, for service.

> I must repeat what I believe I have said twenty times befor that I cant think that a husbend or any set of people has a wright to Buly a women [or] that it is her duty to bear the treetment I have met without any hope of amendment.

LEFT The ironing and airing room of the Victorian laundry (housed in a late 18th-century outbuilding), hung with linen.

RIGHT Seconds out in the Morning Room for a good, clean fight: the Squirrels' Boxing Match in five scenes. This bizarre example of Victorian taxidermy is almost identical to the set exhibited by the taxidermist William Hart at the Great Exhibition of 1851.

The Gothick facade: Lady Anne's delight with its ogee arches, battlements and pinnacles.

Bully or not, Bernard was advanced to a Viscountcy shortly before his death in 1781, when Castle Ward and the titles passed to his bachelor son Nicholas, previously MP for Bangor. In his days as a politician Nicholas had attracted the attention of the chronicler Sir John Blaquiere, who wrote that he was 'more than half an idiot, [and] requires watching'. This turned out to be all too true and he was eventually confined as a lunatic. The consequence was that Castle Ward became the shuttlecock in a series of family disputes; the original contents were removed and the estate was described in the 1837 *Survey of Ireland* as 'totally out of order'.

By this time, though, the 3rd Viscount Bangor, Nicholas's nephew, had begun to take matters in hand. His son the 4th Viscount considered making large-scale Victorian alterations to the house by the Belfast architect Francis Stirrat, but fortunately these were not carried out, apart from the new porch in 1870, when the main entrance was switched to the east from the south-west. The Hall, with its Rococo plasterwork featuring festoons of musical instruments and gardening tools, became the music room – though the National Trust's visitors of today once more enter through the Georgian Hall, rather than the Victorian porch.

Castle Ward's most bizarre feature also dates from the Victorian era of the 4th Viscount Bangor. This is the hilarious 'Squirrel Room', more properly the Morning Room (another of Lady Anne's Gothick interiors), which contains

The Classical entrance front. The house was built of Bath stone and may well have been designed by an architect from that area.

five cases of stuffed squirrels engaged in a carefully choreographed boxing match. The taxidermist William Hart specialised in this sort of jolly anthropomorphism and exhibited a similar set at the Great Exhibition of 1851.

Thirty years after the Great Exhibition, Captain Henry Ward, a veteran of the Kaffir Campaign, succeeded his bachelor brother as 5th Viscount Bangor. His first wife, Mary King, was a talented artist, whose work can be admired in the old billiard room in the basement of Castle Ward. This is one of a number of attractions ingeniously devised by the National Trust, who took over the place after the death of the 6th Viscount Bangor, Speaker of the Northern Ireland Senate, in 1950.

Castle Ward was accepted by the Government in part payment of death duties, and presented to the Trust with an endowment. In the stableyard, linked to the house by an underground passage, the Trust has established an instructive and enterprising 'Victorian pastimes centre', where children can dress in clothes from the period and play with popular Victorian toys; and there is also a well-stocked laundry, complete with machinery and examples of the linen with which the Wards consolidated their fortunes. Old Castle Ward stands in the farmyard, together with a sawmill and the recently restored cornmill. Altogether it is a most beguiling place.

16

CLANDEBOYE

MUCH OF the magic of Clandeboye has been captured in the recent paintings by its energetic *châtelaine*, the Marchioness of Dufferin and Ava, otherwise the artist Lindy Guinness. With her acute painterly eye, she has vivid memories of her first impressions of the place when she came to Clandeboye as a girl in 1962.

She remembers walking up 'in blurred amazement' through the two extraordinary entrance halls built by her future husband's great-grandfather, the Victorian proconsul the 1st Marquess of Dufferin and Ava, to house his astonishing assortment of relics from his days as an Imperial paladin. And the next morning she recalls looking out from her bedroom, 'Rome' (the 1st Marquess named the rooms after places where he had been *en poste*), 'to see a magnificent interlocking landscape of greens that led down to a lake. It was particularly beautiful: there were low horizontal bands of Irish mist allowing only certain parts of the landscape to be sharply defined; those mists that hung over the lake have a Japanese water-colour quality'.

As Lady Dufferin says, the Clandeboye we see today – though owing much to her own indefatigable tree-planting and her late husband's magpie-like love of collecting – is still essentially the Clandeboye created by the 1st Marquess. 'Every part of the house and estate is a fulfilment of his passionate energy and love of the place', she wrote in a vivid account of Clandeboye for the Ulster Architectural Heritage Society. 'It amuses me to imagine him as Governor-General of Canada or Viceroy of India during prolonged state meetings allowing his mind to wander back to his Irish estate and, surreptitiously, filling his notebook with ideas for improvements, and architectural fantasies to house his ever-increasing collection of books and objects.'

By no means all of these fantasies came to fruition. There were abortive plans for an Elizabethan pile (by William Burn), a French *château* (by Benjamin Ferrey) and a stupendous Baronial affair by the Belfast architect William Henry Lynn, whose scheme, in the words of Lord Dufferin's nephew Sir Harold Nicolson 'suggested, at one and the same time, François Premier and the Prince Consort'. Yet indubitably Lord Dufferin realised enough of his building dreams to transform the unpretentious late Georgian family seat into a great house.

The two entrance halls alone, as Lindy Dufferin points out, are a perfect illustration of the 1st Marquess's 'romantic vision'. Harold Nicolson's awe-struck descriptions of his uncle's Imperial interiors in his book *Helen's Tower* (1937) still cannot be bettered, even if some of the details may have changed:

> The steps which led down to the front door were flanked by a double row of curling stones from Scotland and from Canada, some of which bore silver plaques commemorative of curling triumphs at Inverary or at Montreal. To the left of these unwieldy playthings stood an enormous block of Egyptian granite carved with the semblance of the cow-headed Hathor and bearing the ibis cartouche of Thutmosis I. Balanced upon this pink monolith was the stuffed and startled head of a rhinoceros... The wall behind... had been covered with wire netting on which were affixed dirks, daggers, cutlasses, pistols, lances, curling brooms, and a collection of... fly-whisks...

PREVIOUS PAGES The east front of Clandeboye from across the lake.

RIGHT The Inner Hall: heraldry and heads. The 1st Marquess created the two Halls out of the scullery and kitchen of the old house at Ballyleidy which, with characteristic romanticism, he renamed Clandeboye.

BELOW Welcome to my world: the romantic vision of the Victorian proconsul the 1st Marquess of Dufferin and Ava is fully evident from the front door. The Outer Hall is a heady mixture of curling stones, tiger skins, stuffed bears, ancient artefacts and fearsome weaponry.

Nicolson had a soft spot for a Red Indian fertility idol ('on the whole, a friendly beast'), though he found a huge stuffed grizzly bear somewhat menacing. They are no longer in evidence, but two smaller members of the ursine fraternity still stand sentinel.

The new Halls, outer and inner, were created out of the old scullery and kitchen, whereas the original entrance hall was made into the Library by knock-

The spacious Gallery, which still retains the flavour of the early 19th-century remodelling of the house by R.A. Woodgate, an apprentice of Sir John Soane

ing it into the adjoining study. The result, as Nicolson simply wrote, is 'one of the pleasantest rooms on earth'. In the best Irish way this lovable interior combines grandeur with informality. For all its handsome proportions and Classical touches – the bookcases inscribed in gilt with the names of Greek gods and goddesses – the Clandeboye Library has a mellow, comfortable atmosphere that makes one feel blissfully at home. This intimate quality is nicely caught in a study of the room at Christmas by Lindy Dufferin; it has also been painted by David Hockney.

The Library was a particular favourite of John Betjeman – an Oxford friend of Lindy Dufferin's father-in-law, the 4th Marquess of Dufferin and Ava – who first came to stay here in the 1920s. He delighted in the secret jib-door covered by dummy book spines with such jolly titles as *Humorous Versicles* by the Rt. Hon. W.E. Gladstone, *Gull upon Quacks* and *The Lost Poems of Sappho*.

A predecessor of Betjeman's as Poet Laureate, the great Alfred Tennyson, also has an association with Clandeboye for he wrote a poem specially for the 1st Marquess to adorn the upper room in the remarkable turreted folly in the demesne known as Helen's Tower (and recently restored). This was built in 1862, to the designs of Burn, in honour of the 1st Marquess's mother, Helen, a granddaughter of the playwright Richard Brinsley Sheridan. Tennyson's poem expresses the theme of love between mother and son:

> Helen's Tower, here I stand
> Dominant over sea and land
> Son's love built me and I hold
> Mother's love in lettered gold.

The architectural historian Gavin Stamp, however, has suggested that Helen's Tower (originally inscribed 'Gamekeeper's Tower' on William Burn's plans) may not originally have been intended as an architectural tribute to his mother, but rather as part of the extensive improvements to the Clandeboye estate undertaken by Lord Dufferin to relieve the unemployment caused by the Famine. In any event, as Stamp says, it has become a symbol not just for Clandeboye but

Detail of carving on Irish mahogany table at Clandeboye.

ABOVE 'One of the pleasantest rooms on earth': Sir Harold Nicolson's description of his uncle the 1st Marquess of Dufferin's Library. This lovable interior was created by knocking the former entrance hall of the old house into the study.

LEFT View through the arch in the Gallery to the double or 'Imperial' staircase. Woodgate's original architecture was elaborately decorated by William Henry Lynn for the 1st Marquess in the 1860s.

for all Ulster. A copy of the Tower was erected in France in 1921 to commemorate the men of Ulster who fell in the First World War.

Helen's Tower would have been virtually the last building in Ulster the men saw on their way to the slaughter (5,000 soldiers of the Ulster Division, who had trained on the Clandeboye estate, were killed on the first day alone of the Battle of the Somme in July 1916). For the Clandeboye estate lies along the southern shore of Belfast Lough.

It was here in the early 17th century that the ancestors of the Marquesses of Dufferin and Ava, the Blackwoods, scions of a Scottish family (like so many of the Ulster settlers), leased the estate of Ballyleidy from the local landowners, the Hamiltons, Viscounts Claneboye (*sic*) and Earls of Clanbrassill. They went on to acquire the freehold and become prominent landowners in Co. Down. Robert Blackwood helped the family fortunes along by marrying two heiresses (the first, Joyce Leeson, was a sister of the 1st Earl of Milltown, builder of Russborough, Co. Wicklow – *qv*) and was created a Baronet in 1763. His son Sir John Blackwood, 2nd Bt, did even better for himself by marrying Dorcas Stevenson, heiress to a large part of the original Hamilton estate in these parts – including Claneboye, or Clandeboye.

LEFT and BELOW Two views of the Dining Room at Clandeboye, recently redecorated in apple green. The pair of Ionic columns, in the manner of Sir Richard Morrison were painted by Felix Harbord in the 1950s to resemble grey scagliola. The 18th-century chimneypiece was installed here in 1960; the 19th-century French needlework carpet is also a recent addition. The 1st Marquess of Dufferin's portrait, showing him wearing the sky-blue riband of the Order of St Patrick, hangs above the fireplace.

Sir John also benefited from one of the Hamiltons' 'pocket boroughs', the parliamentary seat of Killyleagh, but as a staunch Whig he was no political puppet. Strongly opposed to the Act of Union with Great Britain, he was, as Sir Alfred Lyall wrote, 'proof against the overtures made by the Government for the purchase of his support by a peerage'. The story goes that an emissary from Dublin Castle examined Sir John's plate at dinner and said: 'Your crest is a very pretty one, but would be improved by a coronet'. Sir John replied: 'The motto, *Per vias rectas* ["Straight forward"], has escaped your notice'.

None the less, after Sir John's death in 1799, his widow accepted the Barony of Dufferin and Claneboye in recognition of their son James's support of the Union. James – who became the 2nd Lord Dufferin and was described by Lyall as 'a choleric yet kind-hearted gentleman, with a reputation for courage and humanity' – decided that the house at Ballyleidy needed a radical overhaul.

Between 1800 and about 1820 the previously plain 18th-century box (with its single-storey wings, which had been added later) was replaced by the elegantly Classical late Georgian house that – the 1st Marquess's flamboyant flourishes notwithstanding – we still see today. The 2nd Lord Dufferin's architect was an apprentice of Sir John Soane's, R.A. Woodgate, who had worked at Baronscourt, Co. Tyrone (*qv*).

As Peter Rankin has pointed out, the east front of Clandeboye, with its shallow bowed Saloon in the centre, corresponds closely to the east front of Soane's Baronscourt (of 1794). Behind the Drawing Room, Saloon and Dining Room on this front, lay an impressive double, or (anticipating the 1st Marquess) 'Imperial' staircase, opening with an arch into an adjoining room to form what was known as the Gallery.

Woodgate died young, in 1805, and it appears that Sir Richard Morrison may have taken a hand in finishing off the house. The ceiling of the Saloon, for instance, is, as Mark Bence-Jones has observed, 'a typically 1820 ceiling of

17

CASTLETOWN

COUNTY KILKENNY

SUCH IS the glorious 'Renaissance of Restoration' proceeding at the dawn of the new Millennium among Irish country houses – as discussed in the Introduction – that this book could easily have been filled with pictures of scaffolding, people in hard hats and craftsmen (and craftswomen) painstakingly carrying out their time-honoured tasks. We make no apology, however, for including at least one 'work in progress' as a symbol of this sea change in Irish architectural and social history – and there could be no better example than Castletown, Co. Kilkenny, where Mr and Mrs George Magan kindly allowed us a preview of what promises to be a triumphant restoration.

Castletown is sometimes known as Castletown 'Cox' (an allusion to its mid-Georgian builder, Michael Cox, Archbishop of Cashel) to distinguish it from the more celebrated Castletown 'Conolly', Co. Kildare, the earliest and largest of the great Irish Palladian houses. While Castletown 'Conolly' may be more famous, many observers (as the Knight of Glin remarked in his *Country Life* articles on the work of the Archbishop's architect Davis Duckart) consider Castletown 'Cox' to be 'Ireland's most beautiful house'.

Castletown 'Conolly', too, has also been undergoing a major overhaul; at the time of our visit there it was exclusively a hard hat area, which precluded photography. However, whereas Castletown 'Conolly', which is now the property of the Office of Public Works, is being restored with the help of public funds, the Castletown 'Cox' restoration is very much in the great tradition of private patronage.

George Magan is a merchant banker descended from a long-established Irish landed family chronicled in *Burke's Irish Family Records*. The ancient Irish name of their original seat in Co. Westmeath, *Umma-More*, was the title chosen by George's father, Brigadier William Magan, for a remarkably perceptive book of reflections on the history of Ireland. The Brigadier has also written an evocative memoir of his Irish boyhood in the foxhunting country of The South Westmeath; he went on to become its Master.

Following his own father's death, Brigadier Magan reluctantly decided in 1967 to sell Killyon Manor, Co. Meath, together with its demesne – all that remained of the formerly substantial family estates (which at their apogee had extended to more than 30,000 acres of agricultural land in Ireland). This undoubtedly spurred George Magan's determination one day to re-establish the family in a fine Irish country house. Finally, in 1991, the opportunity to acquire one of the most architecturally important Palladian palaces in Ireland, the masterpiece of Davis Duckart, proved too good to miss.

Having bought the house, he fortuitously was able to buy back the heart of the demesne running to some 500 acres. The perfectionist Magan decided to take his time over the wholesale restoration in order to get it absolutely right. At the time of writing, eight years after the purchase, there is still more to be done to complete the restoration of the interior of the house – though the external renovation work, including the demesne, is virtually complete.

To help him undertake this marathon labour of love, George Magan assembled a team of all the talents: a project manager, architects, surveyors, historic buildings consultants, artisans, craftsmen, structural engineers and an industrious group of local contractors and builders. He was also fortunate in securing a first-class estate management and gardens team. For the creation of the new formal gardens, Magan turned to the Marchioness of Salisbury, whose grandparents Colonel W.H and Lady Eva Wyndham-Quin, made their home at Castletown earlier in the century before the Colonel succeeded a cousin in the Earldom of Dunraven and the Tudor-Revival Adare Manor, Co. Limerick (now an hotel). And in the demesne a landscaping scheme involving the planting of over 80,000 trees has more than compensated for the removal of the trees previously planted too close to the house, where they had latterly obscured its architecture.

The Magans were determined to 'open up' Castletown's wonderful setting against the backdrop of the Co. Kilkenny mountains and to show off Davis Duckart's supreme composition of house, arcades and cupolas to the full. The park was accordingly remodelled, the lake dredged, a ha-ha wall built, the gardens levelled and the parterres (originally laid out by Lady Salisbury's grandfather) moved. A new walled garden is currently being planned and Maxine Magan, George's mother and a keen garden enthusiast, is actively involved in its creation.

George Magan, an engagingly modest and straightforward proprietor, points out that the theme of all this restoration work at Castletown is 'Repair not

PREVIOUS PAGES and ABOVE Two views of Castletown from across the re-landscaped parkland, showing the central block flanked by arcades and domed pavilions. The house was built by Archbishop Cox to the designs of Davis Duckart in 1767 and is now undergoing a thorough restoration by Mr and Mrs George Magan.

RIGHT View of arcade, domed pavilion and knot-garden. The 'fish-scale' slates on the domes have recently been carefully restored.

Renewal'. Yet no effort has been spared on the exterior and the interior of the house, the arcaded wings and pavilions. The weathered stonework has been thoroughly rejuvenated; the roofs and the windows renovated; the power systems comprehensively replaced (so that the state-of-the-art boiler room in the basement resembles the control room of an ocean-going liner); and the great joy of the interior, the Rococo plasterwork by the Waterford stuccodore Patrick Osborne, brought back to its pristine glory.

What strikes one about the Castletown restoration is the astonishing attention to detail, the accentuation of accuracy, the uncompromising standards of quality. It is particularly instructive to note the high level of expertise that still exists in Ireland when the opportunity to undertake top-flight work is made available. The old myth that 'you can never get the right quality of crafts-manship these days' has proved to be nonsense. In fact, the good craftsmen of today are better than ever.

On our visit, for instance, we saw lime render for the plasterwork repairs being made in the traditional method, complete with goats' hair. And, up on the top floor, craftsmen were to be found cheerfully reconstructing walls in the proper, intricate way of combining lath and plaster that was used centuries ago.

Going back in time, the Castletown estate, near Carrick-on-Suir, was part of the vast landholding of the great 'Old English', or Anglo-Norman, family of Butler (Earls of Ormonde from 1328), who from their castle of Kilkenny used to rule over what was more like a kingdom than an estate. Indeed they actually held palatine rights over the neighbouring county of Tipperary, the border of which is close to the Castletown demesne. The Cavalier 12th Earl of Ormonde was created a Duke, and is known to history as 'The Great Duke of Ormonde' on account of his wisdom and integrity as King Charles II's Lord Lieutenant of Ireland. His grandson the Jacobite 2nd Duke (described in Macky's *Characters* as 'One of the most generous, princely, brave men that ever was, but good-natured to a fault...') at first leased and then sold the Castle-town estate to the lawyer Sir Richard Cox of Dunmanway, Co. Cork, who was appointed Lord Chancellor of Ireland in 1703 and created a Baronet three years later.

Although Sir Richard was the father of the present house's builder, Michael Cox, Archbishop of Cashel, the succession was not as simple as that, for Sir Richard seems to have either sold or sublet Castletown to Edward Cooke of Cookestown, who died in 1751. It then passed to Michael Cox (Sir Richard's fifth and youngest son), who happened to be the widower of Cooke's sister Anne.

The Archbishop seems to have had the traditional sporting instincts of the Irish clergy, as he laid out a racecourse within the demesne. He was also a legendary trencherman. Dorothea Herbert, who lived not far from Castletown, has left us a memorable picture of Cox's character:

> It happened that there was a fine Turkey for Dinner dress'd with remarkable Selery Sauce for his Graces own Eating he being a great Epicure – Mr Hare [Dorothea's brothers' headmaster] calld for some of the turkey – Pooh! Pooh! Man (said the Abp.) Eat Beef, Eat Beef Sir – Mr Hare freely told him he could get Beef and Mutton enough at home amongst his Boys, but when he dined with his Grace he preferred Turkey and high Sauce – The ArchBishop was himself an odd character – He was very close and often blew out the Wax lights before half of his Company dispersed – The Clergy trembled at his Nod and few of them escaped a severe stricture at his Visitations – He

Work in progress: restoring the plasterwork at Castletown. The total cost of the original work, as detailed in an extant bill, came to £696 10s 5d.

Scaffolding in the Staircase Hall as the exhaustive restoration continues.

ABOVE Detail of carved Irish furniture.

RIGHT Formal hall furniture from the Magan family collection arranged inside one of the domed pavilions.

BELOW Detail of the Magan family crest: a boar's head 'couped, tusked and bristled'. The full motto underneath reads '*Virtute et probitate*'.

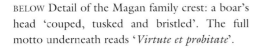

was excessively fond of Cards but so cross at them that few would venture to be his partner...

'Close' he may have been, but he commissioned Davis Duckart to build a house of distinction with echoes, as the Knight of Glin has pointed out, of the *Petit Trianon* and William Winde's Buckingham House. Duckart – otherwise Daviso de Arcort – is a somewhat shadowy figure, an architect-engineer of Franco-Italian descent who came to Ireland in the mid-18th century and died in the early to mid-1780s. He may also have been responsible for the arcaded wings at Florence Court, Co. Fermanagh (*qv*).

The wings at Castletown also have arcades, though with the delightful bonus of culminating in pretty pavilions topped off with octagonal cupolas. (The 'fish-scale' slates have been carefully restored.) The central block of the house is built of dressed sandstone and unpolished Kilkenny marble, with the stonework very finely cut to give an exquisitely crisp effect. The Corinthian motif of the two principal facades is continued inside in the Hall, which has a screen of mono-lithic fluted Corinthian columns of lightly polished Kilkenny marble (which is such a luxurious feature of Castletown), and also a stone chimneypiece with terms. The Hall, Dining Room and Staircase Hall have richly decorated plaster panels on their walls as well as plasterwork ceilings. The total cost of the magnificent plasterwork is given in a detailed bill, still extant, as £696 10s 5d.

LEFT Detail of doorway, with broken pediment and exquisite carving.

RIGHT The Library, in the centre of the garden front.

The Archbishop adorned the garden front with his coat of arms impaling those of his second wife, another Anne, who had died in childbirth in 1746. The second Anne was the daughter of James O'Brien, MP for Youghal, and a granddaughter of the 3rd Earl of Inchiquin. Fortunately, her baby son survived and Castletown, largely unchanged, remained in the Cox family until the middle of the next century, when it passed to Lieutenant-Colonel William Villiers-Stuart, a younger son of the family seated at Dromana, Co. Waterford, who married Katherine, the heiress of Michael Cox of Castletown.

It was their son Henry, another Colonel, who sold the place to the Wyndham-Quins in 1909. Next, in the late 1920s, after the Wyndham-Quins had furnished the gardens with statuary, followed Major-General Edmund Blaque and his wife, Kathleen, daughter of the colourful Admiral Lord Beresford ('Charlie B' from the nearby Curraghmore – *qv*). 'Charlie B's' famous foxhunting tattoo would doubtless have earned the admiration of the Archbishop and indeed of Blaques' son and successor Charles, Master of the Kilmaganny Harriers. Charles Blaque sold Castletown in 1976 and, after some uncertainty about its future, it was acquired three years later by Uli de Breffny, whose husband the late Brian de Breffny, was a well-known writer on Irish architecture, genealogy and culture.

At the end of a chequered century at Castletown it is gratifying to report that the future of this exceptionally elegant house, now being so immaculately restored by George and Wendy Magan, looks reassuringly secure. The work in progress illustrated here encourages one to think that we may be witnessing a new Golden Age for the Irish country house.

18

BANTRY HOUSE

COUNTY CORK

*B*ANTRY, deep in the south-west of Ireland, is a sublime sight worth going a very long way to see. Its spectacular situation puts this endearingly overblown Baroque palace in a class of its own.

For the spreading family seat of the Shelswell-White family – happily still *in situ*, having been the first owners in the British Isles to open a country house regularly to the public back in 1946 – is set against a steep hillside above the southern shore of the vast natural harbour of Bantry Bay. Climb the 100 steps behind the house in the Italian Gardens, the 'stairway to the sky', and you truly feel on top of the world. There, spread before your amazed eyes, is surely one of the most breathtaking views in Europe: the garden statuary and great house in the foreground and, beyond, the Bay, which seems like a grand private lake. The vista culminates in the Caha mountains.

Sprinkled around Bantry Bay are islands with jolly names such as Hog, Rabbit, Horse and the irresistible Lousy Castle. The largest of these islands – not visible from the Bantry side of the Bay, which is just as well as it is now an oil tanker terminal – is Whiddy, on which the White family first settled in the late 17th century. These Whites were a branch of a Limerick mercantile and mayoral dynasty which, as the late writer and novelist Terence de Vere White suggested in *Burke's Irish Family Records*, may well link up with the White family prominent in this city in medieval times.

In the middle of the 18th century Richard White, an increasingly prosperous landowner, managed to acquire the property known as Blackrock, where the present Bantry House stands. The Hutchins (later Hutchinson) family had been leasing it for the previous century from the Annesleys, Earls of Anglesey. In 1750 it was recorded that one Samuel Hutchinson had 'a good house' on the site; this is presumably the nucleus of the house we see today – the square, three-storey, five-bay building that forms the centre of the present east and west fronts of Bantry.

PREVIOUS PAGES Bantry's Library, more than 60 feet long, with its screens of Corinthian columns. It replaced a conservatory in the mid-1860s at the end of the 2nd Earl of Bantry's magnificent series of improvements to the house and gardens. Concerts are held in the great room; and musically inclined visitors are encouraged to try out the Bluthner grand piano.

LEFT View out of an upstairs window across Bantry Bay to the Caha mountains, with garden balustrade and statuary in the foreground.

BELOW Pompeian panels inset into the floor of the Outer Hall. They were collected in 1828 by the connoisseur Viscount Berehaven, later 2nd Earl of Bantry, who transformed Bantry into a Baroque palace.

In any event, White was definitely in the saddle by 1763, when, as John Cornforth pointed out in *Country Life*, he was already making alterations. Cornforth poses the always intriguing question of where the cash came from; perhaps, as he intimates, the profitable trade of smuggling may have played its part, though Richard's wife, Martha, was from respectable Church of Ireland stock.

Their son Simon was called to the English Bar, though he did not practise, and sent his own son, another Richard, to Harrow, where he distinguished himself by participating in a rebellion against the headmaster. This rebellious streak was, though, a thing of the past by December 1796, when an incident occurred that had a decisive effect not only on Richard White and his family but also on the course of European history.

For in that month a French armada sailed from Brest in order to help Wolfe Tone and 'the United Irishmen' liberate Ireland from British rule. Some 50 warships carried nearly 15,000 soldiers towards the south-west coast of Co. Cork, but chaotic ship-to-ship communication and appalling weather conditions dispersed the fleet. None the less, 19 ships with 6,500 men on board were off Bere Island in Bantry Bay on Christmas Eve, ready to land the next day.

View of the Staircase at Bantry. The assortment of treasures led the house, the first to be opened to the public on a regular basis in the British Isles, to be hailed as 'the Wallace Collection of Ireland'.

Baffled by this unexpected Christmas present, Richard White sent a pinnace out into the Bay to ascertain if these strange ships were friendly. The boat and its crew of 10 were never heard of again. Duly alarmed, White sent word to the British headquarters in Cork, organised local defences (the Bantry Cavalry, whose standard still hangs proudly in the Hall of Bantry House) and placed his home at the disposal of the military. (One General wrote to thank him 'for all your kindness – Venison, hares, Woodcocks, Scollops, Oisters and what not'.) It must have been a tense time, but then came anti-climax: savage easterly gales blew the ships out to sea.

However, this turned out to be only a temporary respite. The wind changed. Early in the New Year of 1797 a dozen or so French vessels were anchored

LEFT Bantry's most theatrical interior: the Dining Room, dominated by the pair of State portraits of King George III and Queen Charlotte. Copies of the Allan Ramsay studies, they were presented to the 1st Earl of Bantry and are sensationally framed with dramatic carvings.

RIGHT Detail of the elaborately carved base of the mirror above one of the chimneypieces in the Library. The chimney breast is lined with painted silk in the Louis XIV style.

off Whiddy Island, awaiting a second chance. An enterprising local trader went on board to sell some food to the French. Asked how many troops were on shore by way of defence, he indulged in a bit of Irish hyperbole. There were, he asserted, some 20,000 men in the neighbourhood of Bantry (in fact, there were barely 400).

This intelligence proved too much for the thoroughly seasick would-be invaders. They promptly headed for home, leaving behind the veteran frigate *La Surveillante*, which was scuttled – and is now an official Irish National Monument. A model of the frigate featured in a special exhibition mounted in the handsome Stables (with their pediment and cupola) at Bantry to mark the French armada's bi-centenary in 1996. There was also a memorable tableau of the wretched Wolfe Tone cursing in his cabin. 'We were', he noted in his diary with frustration, 'close enough to toss a biscuit ashore'.

As it turned out, what one might call the Bantry biscuit was taken by Richard White, who was hailed as the hero of the hour for repelling the French fleet and created Baron Bantry. At about this time, and certainly following his marriage in 1799 to Lady Margaret Hare, daughter of the 1st Earl of Listowel, Lord Bantry appears to have made various alterations to the house – probably including the north wing.

Lord Bantry was advanced to a Viscountcy in 1800 and then an Earldom in 1816, but latterly he seemed to prefer basing himself at his shooting-lodge at Glengariff, about eight miles away. Well before his death in 1851 the 1st Earl of Bantry had made over Bantry to his eldest son, who bore the courtesy title of Viscount Berehaven.

Lord Berehaven was a collector and connoisseur on the grand scale, much travelled on the continent of Europe, who in the 1840s transformed the still fairly modest family seat into the sprawling 14-bay-fronted palace we see today. Inside, he filled it with such a remarkable range of treasures that Bantry was to become known as 'the Wallace Collection of Ireland'.

Although today some of Lord Berehaven's eclectic collections have, inevitably, been dispersed, there remains much to see. What strikes one is an atmosphere of serene fantasy about the interiors, an air of heady theatricality. The Rose Drawing Room, for instance, is a dream-like vision of Aubusson tapestries made for Marie Antoinette, and there are more magnificent Gobelins tapestries next door. Nothing could be more flamboyantly stagey than the Dining Room, a riot of royal blue and gilt foliage with a screen of marble columns carrying on the Corinthian motif of the giant redbrick pilasters on the exterior. Dominating the room – or the set, one is tempted to say – are a pair of state portraits of King George III and Queen Charlotte, sensationally framed with dramatic carvings. These pictures, copies of the celebrated Allan Ramsay studies, were presented to the 1st Earl of Bantry.

The 2nd Earl, as Lord Berehaven became, was also responsible for laying out the Italian Gardens with their balustrades and statues. Recently restored by the present owners, Egerton and Brigitte Shelswell-White, with significant help from various grants (notably one from the European Union), these gardens have a potently exotic character which suits the semi-tropical vegetation that flourishes in the generally balmy climate (the French armada's queasy experiences notwithstanding) of the Gulf Stream at their feet. Mr and Mrs Shelswell-White based their restoration of the layout on old photographs taken in about 1870, only a couple of years after the death of the 2nd Earl.

The Earldom of Bantry expired with the childless 4th Earl in 1891, when the estate passed to his sister's son Edward Leigh, from a long-established Cheshire family, who assumed the additional surname of White. In the early 1920s, after the only hospital in Bantry town had burnt down in the Troubles, Edward's widow offered the house as a temporary substitute for the nursing nuns of the Convent of Mercy; a chapel was sanctified in the 2nd Earl's sunlit Library, with its two screens of Corinthian columns and compartmented ceiling on the south front.

Then, in 1926, the indomitable elder daughter, Clodagh, came into her inheritance. In the same year she married Geoffrey Shelswell, who took the additional surname of White. After some years in Africa and the Middle East, where Geoffrey worked for the British Colonial Service, the family returned to their beloved Bantry, where soldiers from the Irish Army were billeted during the Second World War.

Clodagh's bold decision to open the house to the public after the Army departed in 1945 was to help secure Bantry's future. Scores of visitors have rejoiced in its wonderfully friendly, unassuming and welcoming spirit over the years. In a typically informal touch, musically inclined visitors are encouraged to try out the Bluthner grand piano in the Library. Concerts are held regularly in this impressive interior, more than 60 feet long, which replaced a conservatory on the garden front in the 1860s. Clodagh's son and successor Egerton Shelswell-White is himself an enthusiastic trombonist with a local band.

Following his mother's death in 1978 Egerton, who had been teaching out in Alabama at the romantically named Indian Springs School, returned to take over the reins at Bantry. With the help of grant aid from the 'Bantry Package' (money made available by the Irish Government to the Bantry area when the operators of the oil terminal on Whiddy Island sold their interest to the state-owned Irish National Petroleum Corporation) and the Heritage Council, Egerton and his wife, Brigitte, have carried out a sympathetic restoration of the great house and its demesne. Brigitte has been particularly busy in the gardens, which have recently benefited from the EU's admirable Great Gardens of Ireland restoration scheme (mentioned earlier in the chapter on Ballinlough Castle – *qv*).

The upper floors of the west wing, together with the entire east wing, both unused since 1945, were restored in the late 1980s and now offer guest accommodation. The Shelswell-Whites belong to the 'Hidden Ireland' association of private heritage owners who provide traditional country-house hospitality. Those fortunate enough to stay at Bantry – an experience warmly recommended, and not to be missed – have the benefit of a private dining room, sitting room and even a full-scale billiard room. The only difficulty is that one never wants to leave. For Bantry, with its charmingly faded grandeur, is a blissful glimpse of paradise. Its spell bewitches you to return again, and again.

LEFT The cupola above the Stables. The stone stork is the White family crest.

BELOW Top of the world: the spectacular view from the 'stairway to the sky' in the Italian Gardens, with the garden facade of the great house in the foreground.

19

LISSADELL

COUNTY SLIGO

*L*ISSADELL, seat of the Gore-Booth Baronets, on Sligo Bay underneath Ben Bulben, has been celebrated in the 20th century by its neighbouring bard W.B. Yeats ('*The light of evening, Lissadell, great windows open to the south*'); as the family home of the fighter for Irish Independence, Constance de Markievicz (first woman to be elected to the British House of Commons); and as the subject of a public scandal when it was alleged that the estate had been mismanaged during the Wardship of Sir Michael Gore-Booth, 7th Bt. Somehow, amid all this celebrity and controversy, the early 19th-century distinction of Lissadell's architecture (described by Edward McParland in *Country Life* as 'the finest Greek-Revival country house in Ireland') has tended to be overlooked. And of no less interest, too, is the way the present owner, the scholarly and enterprising Sir Josslyn Gore-Booth, 9th Bt, is adapting and improving Lissadell for the 21st century.

'The trick is', explains Sir Josslyn, 'to work out how to use the building in a way that preserves its principal purpose – that of a house – while allowing the public access and not compromising its architecture. I find that a fascinating task.'

Sir Josslyn has worked out an ingenious plan whereby two self-contained residential apartments are being created on the top floor. The principal rooms on the ground floor which are open to the public will be left much as they are – though the lofty Hall and Gallery (described by Yeats as the 'great sitting room as high as a church') now enjoy increased natural light following the replacement of the roof lights, and the more intimate bow room, with its 'great windows' immortalised by Yeats, will revert to its intended purpose as a Library.

The obvious advantage of Sir Josslyn's practical scheme for his family's private apartment on the top floor is that it will benefit from the wondrous views, whether southwards across Sligo Bay to Knocknarea and the Ox Mountains or eastwards to Ben Bulben. Unfortunately the ground-floor rooms have not enjoyed this advantage in recent years owing to the heavy planting of trees around the house, though Sir Josslyn and his admirable property manager Nicholas Prins were busy on a clearance programme during our visit to Lissadell.

This 'opening up' of the landscape surrounding the house will surely lead to a new appreciation of Lissadell's architectural quality. For the Arcadian setting was undoubtedly a key factor in the effect of the house's contrasting austerity. Lissadell responds to such romance, as Dr McParland nicely put it, 'not with Gothick drama, but with Attic reserve'. Certainly Lissadell's architect, Francis Goodwin, was fully aware of its importance. 'The country around', he wrote of Lissadell in his book *Domestic Architecture* (1833/4), 'presents such a striking combination of mountain scenery and water, that it is hardly possible for language to convey an adequate idea of the varied charms of this highly picturesque tract of landscape'.

The previous house at Lissadell, a bow-fronted 18th-century structure, was even closer to the sea, indeed on the shores of Drumcliff Bay along the avenue from the present house. This was demolished in the early 1830s at about the time the new house became ready for occupation.

Back in 1597/8, Paul Gore, who was the seventh son of a London alderman (from whom descend the family of Gore-Langton, Earls Temple of Stowe), came to Ireland as a commander of a troop of horse, serving under Mountjoy. He married a niece of Thomas Wentworth, Earl of Strafford, and settled in Co. Donegal, being granted an Irish Baronetcy in 1622 and some land. Sir Paul and his wife had six sons and seven daughters. His descendants gradually established themselves in the neighbouring counties of Fermanagh, Leitrim, Mayo and Sligo, where his fourth son, Sir Francis Gore, built or took over Ardtermon Castle, only three miles along the coast from Lissadell. Sir Paul's eldest son became ancestor of the now extinct Earls of Ross (not to be confused with the Earls of Rosse at Birr – *qv*); another the ancestor of the Earls of Arran and the Lords Harlech; and between them all they provided, in 1753, no fewer than nine members of the Irish House of Commons, known as the 'Nine Gores'.

The Booth connection came about through the marriage of Sir Francis's grandson, Nathaniel to Letitia the heiress of Humphrey Booth, one of the *Tituladoes* of Sligo town under Cromwell, whose family had long been prominent in Salford and Manchester in the north-west of England. It was at some stage during Nathaniel's ownership that Ardtermon was (accidentally) burnt out. The now vanished bow-fronted house, known as Lissadell, must have been built by his son Booth, who was created a Baronet in 1760.

PREVIOUS PAGE: The Drawing Room, with its Corinthian columns and whimsical chimneypieces containing inset mirrors and a clock. To the right is a model of Lissadell, 'the finest Greek-Revival country house in Ireland', built in the early 1830s by Sir Robert Gore-Booth, 4th Bt, to the designs of Francis Goodwin.

ABOVE Detail of the wrought-ironwork on the double or 'Imperial' Staircase, which is made of blocks of Kilkenny limestone polished to resemble marble.

LEFT The south and east fronts of Lissadell, notable for its superb masonry. The bow in the centre of the south facade contains the 'great windows open to the south' immortalised by W.B. Yeats, a friend and neighbour of the Gore-Booth family.

'The great sitting room as high as a church': Yeats's description of the apse-ended Gallery at Lissadell, with engaged Doric piers along one side and Ionic columns the other. Sir Josslyn Gore-Booth, the present Baronet, who is undertaking a sympathetic restoration of the house, is seated to the right.

The 2nd Bt, also called Booth, inherited the extensive Booth estates in the increasingly industrial area around Manchester (which was, incidentally, to have significant architectural consequences for Lissadell); though it was not he that added the surname of Booth – perhaps he felt it might have been over-egging things to be 'Sir Booth Gore-Booth' – but his brother and successor, Sir Robert Gore-Booth, 3rd Bt, in 1804.

Sir Robert, who had lived a lonely life at Lissadell for over 60 years looking after his elder brother's property while Sir Booth led a more fashionable bachelor's life in Bath and London, then promptly married to produce an heir to the estates, but died when his eldest son and namesake was only nine. The young Sir Robert, 4th Bt, travelled on the continent of Europe and took a keen interest in Classical architecture. Sir Josslyn, the present Baronet, points out that in architectural and other matters Sir Robert, without a father himself, is most likely to have come strongly under the influence of the 1st

ABOVE The Staircase Hall looking up to the columnar gallery above the stairs. Assorted sporting memorabilia on the walls add to Lissadell's extraordinary character and charm.

RIGHT The Dining Room, with its pilaster-murals by Casimir Markievicz depicting members of the family and their staff. Markievicz's celebrated wife, Constance, the fighter for Irish independence, is portrayed with her sister, Eva, as the little girls in the wood above the fireplace.

Viscount Lorton (previously General Robert King, a younger son of the 2nd Earl of Kingston), who in 1810 had built the magnificent Classical house of Rockingham, in the neighbouring county of Roscommon, to the designs of the great John Nash.

Sir Robert married Lord Lorton's daughter Caroline (who died in childbirth), and – according to Sir Josslyn Gore-Booth's intriguing theory – was so impressed with his father-in-law's pile that he decided to produce a similar house, though on a much tighter budget. There are indubitably some instructive parallels between the two houses: Rockingham (tragically gutted by fire in 1957 and subsequently demolished) was Nash's only complete neo-Classical house in Ireland and Lissadell (begun in 1830, a couple of years after Caroline Gore-Booth's death) was the last Irish country house to be built in that style. Neither house had a 'back' nor an attic, and thus both had extensive servants' quarters in the basement and a tunnel for approach. Moreover, both houses had an impressive double, or 'Imperial', Staircase and a central, top-lit Gallery; and both had their principal bedroom on the ground floor.

Stylistically, though, it must be said that the two houses were far from identical. In any event, Sir Robert's architect, Francis Goodwin, was an

accomplished Classicist in his own right, whose noble town halls in Manchester and Salford would have been familiar to Sir Robert from his visits to the Booth estates in north-west England. As Dr McParland notes, the recessed tetrastyle Ionic portico which features in Goodwin's Manchester building was to reappear in the Gallery at Lissadell. Built at a cost of about £11,000, Lissadell was virtually finished by 1833.

At first glance, Lissadell's architecture could be considered to have taken Hellenic purity rather too far – indeed to the extremities of the Atlantic coast. On a wet and windy day, one can see what Yeats, in less romantic mood, meant when he described the largely unadorned exterior as 'grey, square and bare'. Yet when the spellbinding light of the West of Ireland catches the sparkling precision of the crisply carved local limestone, a model of masterly masonry, Lissadell's austere beauty comes into its own. The severity yields its magical secret.

Inside, there are treats in store, not least a series of sumptuous Egyptian-style marble chimneypieces. The two-storey Hall is a dramatic combination of the Doric and Ionic Orders, and the Staircase is of Kilkenny marble. The mighty apse-ended Gallery has engaged Doric piers along one side, and Ionic columns along the other. The Billiard Room shows off Goodwin's love of experimenting with geometric mouldings.

In his book on *The North-West of Ireland* (1862), Henry Coulter describes the way Sir Robert transformed 'wild, miserable and poor looking' land into 'one of the most highly cultivated and beautiful estates in the United Kingdom'.

LEFT and RIGHT Lissadell's lumber is an atmospheric study in itself. Sir Josslyn Gore-Booth, who has celebrated it in print, is taking pains to preserve this aspect of the place's character while adapting the house to the needs of the 21st century.

These agricultural improvements were consolidated by his son and successor Sir Henry Gore-Booth, the 5th Bt, very much a 'hands-on' proprietor, whose popularity as a benevolent landlord was undimmed during the agrarian troubles of the 1880s. Away from agriculture, his passions were for yachting, fishing and Arctic exploration (Yeats noted on a visit to Lissadell in the winter of 1894/5 that Sir Henry 'thinks of nothing but the North Pole').

The intrepid Sir Henry's jolly collection of stuffed birds, together with such items as the skull of a bottle-nosed whale and walrus tusks, is a memorable feature of any tour of Lissadell, though the most haunting impression tends to be made by the Dining Room, with its pilasters sensationally painted with a series of full-length portraits by Casimir Markievicz. The self-styled 'Count' had met Constance Gore-Booth, Sir Henry's eldest daughter (who features, together with her sister Eva, the poet, in the evocative portrait by Sarah Purser, also in the Dining Room, of the little girls in the woods), when they were art students together in *fin-de-siècle* Paris, and they married in 1900.

Markievicz's murals depict, in a strikingly Slavonic style, members of the family as well as the Lissadell forester and gamekeeper and the legendarily eccentric butler Kilgallon, who seems to have strayed from the stories of Somerville and Ross. In his book *Life in An Irish Country House*, Mark Bence-Jones relates the unfortunate occasion in 1913 when Kilgallon took it upon himself to order the bemused Stafford-King-Harman brothers, over from Rockingham on what they had understood to be a three-day stay, out of the premises after barely one night. Possibly Kilgallon had taken exception to one of the young men, on arrival at Lissadell, mistaking Sir Josslyn Gore-Booth, the 6th Bt, and an ardent cricketer, for the butler.

For her part, Sir Josslyn's sister Constance used to relish being sent away by the servants when she would turn up disguised as a beggar girl. As Yeats perceptively wrote, the Gore-Booths 'were a very pleasant, kindly, inflammable family ever ready to take up new ideas and new things'. The idea that inflamed Constance was Irish Nationalism. After being sentenced to death for her active role in the Easter Rising (or Rebellion) in 1916, a sentence subsequently commuted to penal servitude, she went on to become Minister for Labour in the first Republican administration but was incarcerated again during the Civil War by the Free State forces. At her funeral in 1927 300,000 people lined the streets of Dublin.

Notwithstanding the folk heroine's contribution to the new Ireland, and her brother Josslyn's enlightened stewardship of the family estates (it was reputed that he was the first landlord to accept the political necessity to offer his tenants their lands under the terms of the Wyndham Land Act), his death left an unfortunate vacuum. His successor in the title, Sir Michael, the 7th Bt, had never recovered from a mental breakdown at Cambridge, and it had been planned that the property would be managed by his younger brother Hugh, who was killed on Leros in 1943. The estate went into Chancery, and Sir Josslyn's widow and two of her daughters became embroiled in litigation over its management. In 1968 his extensive home farm, which formed the bulk of the estate, was sold to the Land Commission.

Happily all this unpleasantness, so inappropriate to the beauty of Lissadell, is now a thing of the past. In recognition of its importance as a tourist attraction, the Office of Works has been generous with technical advice and the Heritage Council has grant-aided the systematic replacement of the roof leads and the supporting timbers. The present Sir Josslyn's sympathetic restoration of the great house and its demesne promises to breathe new life into this extraordinarily atmospheric place without losing any of its potent poetry.

ABOVE Looking south, from the roof, across Sligo Bay to Knockrarea.

RIGHT Sir Josslyn shuts one of the great studded doors of the *porte-cochère*, which Goodwin ingeniously designed to protect arriving visitors not just from the rain but the Atlantic gales.

20

MOUNT STEWART

COUNTY DOWN

T HE GLORIOUS gardens at Mount Stewart which flourish in the temperate climate of the Ards Peninsula are so highly regarded in horticultural circles, and so much have the appearance of having been here for generations, that it comes as something of a surprise to realise they were only laid out by the mother of the present *châtelaine*, Lady Mairi Bury (who completed the transfer of the property to the National Trust in 1977). Indeed much of what we see today at Mount Stewart, both inside and out, owes a great deal to Lady Mairi's mother, Edith, Marchioness of Londonderry, wife of the 7th Marquess of Londonderry, Secretary of State for Air in the British Government of the early 1930s, and a considerable figure in her own right.

As Edith Londonderry recalled in her invaluable guidebook to the 98-acre gardens, when she first saw Mount Stewart before the First World War (in which she commanded the Women's Legion) she 'thought the house and surroundings were the dampest, darkest and saddest place' she had ever stayed in during the winter. But then, when she came to live here after her husband accepted the post of Minister of Education in the first Parliament of Northern Ireland in 1921, she discovered 'the really exciting and important thing about Mount Stewart': its climate, which proved congenial to plants, trees and shrubs usually grown only in greenhouses. The gloom of the hitherto encroaching trees around the house was banished, and one of the greatest gardens in the British Isles (worth a volume of its own) took shape – complete with its Sunk Garden, Shamrock Garden, Italian and Spanish Gardens, lake and Dodo Terrace.

The carved creatures on the Dodo Terrace recall Lady Londonderry's coterie of friends known as 'The Ark', each of whom was named after an animal of some sort. Thus Ramsay MacDonald was 'Hamish the Hart', Winston Churchill 'the Warlock', the 1st Viscount Hailsham 'the Wild Boar' (his family name was Hogg), the historian H. Montgomery Hyde 'Montgomery the Mole', and so forth. The legendary hostess herself was 'Circe the Sorceress'.

Similarly, Circe's spell brightened and transformed the interior of the house, which had remained largely untouched since the alterations made by William Vitruvius Morrison for the 3rd Marquess of Londonderry in the 1830s. The rooms took on a more stylish and cheerful 1920s feel, combining bold colour schemes (the Drawing Room, for instance, was given salmon-pink walls) and subtle lighting effects from a wonderfully bizarre assortment of lamps, including several brought back from a trip to China in 1912. She redid many of the colours in the early 1950s.

Lady Londonderry's enjoyably eclectic tastes are illustrated in her Sitting Room, where such items as a Dutch oak display cabinet, Spanish and Italian walnut tables and a French writing table of the Louis Philippe period (all acquired by herself) cheerfully co-exist. The early 18th-century English walnut card table in this room has a hinged top lined with a view of the west front and garden at Mount Stewart in Edith Londonderry's own *gros* and *petit point*.

The central room on the garden front, previously an inner galleried hall, was panelled and converted into a Smoking Room. The flavour of this comfortable, cluttered room, so redolent of the 1930s, is nicely captured in Julian Barrow's charming portrait of Lady Mairi Bury, with her cockatoo perched on her shoulder. Lady Mairi, the Londonderry's youngest daughter, inherited her father's passion for flying and qualified as a pilot. Her father, the 7th Marquess, deserves more credit than he has received for managing, while at the Air Ministry in London, to preserve the nucleus of the Royal Air Force despite the policy of disarmament; for setting up the committee which developed the discovery of radar; and for promoting the designs of the aircraft that would help win the Battle of Britain, the Hurricane and the Spitfire.

Such achievements, in the view of the family's historian H. Montgomery Hyde, were worthy to rank 'Charley' Londonderry not far short of his illustrious predecessor the 2nd Marquess, known to history as Castlereagh – who as Secretary of Ireland put down the Rising (or, as he would have seen it, Rebel-

PREVIOUS PAGES The giant Ionic portico – wide enough to serve as a *porte-cochère* – which dominates the north front at Mount Stewart. The 11-bay facade, which became the entrance front, was the result of the remodelling carried out in the 1830s for the 3rd Marquess of Londonderry by the architect William Vitruvius Morrison.

ABOVE A corner of the Smoking Room, featuring a Clifford watercolour of Edith, Lady Londonderry's mother, Lady Florence Leveson-Gower, in hunting habit at her future husband Harry Chaplin's family seat of Blankney, Lincolnshire. Lady Florence was the elder daughter of the 3rd Duke of Sutherland, whose gardens at Dunrobin Castle in Scotland partly inspired Edith, Lady Londonderry's creation at Mount Stewart.

LEFT The comfortable clutter of the Smoking Room which was converted from an inner galleried hall. The portrait over the fireplace is Philip de László's romantic study of Edith, Marchioness of Londonderry ('Circe'), wife of the 7th Marquess of Londonderry, Secretary of State for Air in the British Government of the 1930s.

The spacious Drawing Room, created by William Vitruvius Morrison, *circa* 1835. The two screens of Ionic columns mark the approximate area in the centre which formerly housed the drawing room in the 18th-century house, Mount Pleasant. The interior was redecorated by Edith, Lady Londonderry, and formed a stylish setting for her parties.

lion) of 1798, and engineered the Act of Union three years later, and as British Foreign Secretary directed the strategy that overthrew Napoleon and dominated the subsequent peacemaking at Vienna.

Castlereagh (appropriately commemorated in the Castlereagh Room at Mount Stewart and by the Empire chairs used at the Congress of Vienna now on display in the Dining Room), like Charley Londonderry, has had his critics, though the great Duke of Wellington considered that 'he possessed a clear mind, the highest talents, and the most steady principle – more so than anybody I ever knew'. That principle was perfectly embodied in Castlereagh's statesmanlike words after the fall of Napoleon: 'It is not our business to collect trophies, but to bring back the world to peaceful habits'.

Even the gossipy diarist Charles Greville had to concede that the 'dignified and imposing' Castlereagh was 'affable in his manners and agreeable in society. The great feature of his character was a cool and determined courage'.

ABOVE The Castlereagh Room, originally the dining room in George Dance's plans. The veneered Regency bookcases and shutters (lined with mock books), probably made by the master-carpenter John Ferguson, must have been moved here from the old library (now Lady Londonderry's Sitting Room) when Morrison's new Dining Room was completed in the 1820s. The bust to the right, by Joseph Nollekens, is of the great statesman who gives his name to the room.

RIGHT The monumental central Hall at Mount Stewart, a vast octagon with double pairs of Ionic columns, painted to resemble green marble, and lit by a dome above the gallery. This Classical interior was probably conceived during William Vitruvius's partnership with his father, Sir Richard Morrison; it is reminiscent of their domed rotunda at Ballyfin for the Coote family (now a college). The nude statues were carved by Lawrence Macdonald in Rome 1856. The room was repainted in 1961 by Lady Mairi Bury, the present *châtelaine*.

LEFT The first-floor room of the Temple of the Winds, designed by James 'Athenian' Stuart for the 1st Marquess of Londonderry, 1782–85, with plasterwork by William Fitzgerald and marquetry by John Ferguson. The inlaid floor reflects the pattern of the ceiling – a design feature also to be seen in George Dance's Music Room in the main house.

RIGHT The exterior of the Temple of the Winds, an octagonal banqueting house – 'solely appropriate for a Junketting Retreat', as the 3rd Marquess of Londonderry insisted – designed by 'Athenian' Stuart in homage to the Tower of Andronicus Cyrrhestes in Athens ('the Tower of the Winds').

The spiral staircase in the Temple of the Winds. The Temple is the finest garden building in Ireland.

None the less, he once fought a duel with his political rival George Canning (who was shot in the thigh) and his life ended tragically in 1822 when, driven by overwork, he cut his throat.

As a boy, Castlereagh – then plain Robert Stewart – had been fortunate to escape death by drowning in the surprisingly treacherous waters of Strangford Lough which abut the demesne of Mount Stewart. The boat in which he and a friend were sailing capsized, but fortunately Robert's sharp-eyed tutor happened to spot the incident from the vantage point of the then newly built 'Temple of the Winds', on a promontory to the east of the house with a splendid view of Strangford Lough.

This octagonal banqueting house, designed by the great neo-Classical pioneer James 'Athenian' Stuart in homage to the Tower of Andronicus Cyrrhestes in Athens (better known as 'the Tower of the Winds'), must rank as the finest garden building in Ireland. It was built in the early 1780s for Robert Stewart's father and namesake, MP for Co. Down, whose own father, Alexander Stewart, a prosperous linen merchant, had bought the estate – then called Mount Pleasant – in 1744. After Castlereagh's death, it was suggested that the Temple might be turned into a mausoleum, but, quite rightly, his half-brother Charles, the 3rd Marquess of Londonderry (with whom he had enjoyed an adventurous boyhood at Mount Stewart), was having none of it:

> I am entirely against the Idea... I have no Taste for Turning a Temple built for Mirth & Jollity into a Sepulchre – The place is solely appropriate for a Junketting Retreat in the Groundes.

The boys' father, who entered the peerage as Baron Londonderry in 1789 and was subsequently advanced to the Viscountcy of Castlereagh, the Earldom and finally (in particular recognition of his elder son's public service)

the Marquessate of Londonderry, also considered remodelling his own father's house to the designs of James Wyatt. But in the event, the 1st Marquess merely added a temporary wing to the west of Alexander Stewart's Mount Pleasant (as it was still called) in the 1780s. Some 20 years later this structure was replaced by the present, and satisfyingly permanent, west wing built to the designs of the London architect George Dance.

Inside the west wing, the marquetry doors, dados and floors were made by John Ferguson, who had earlier worked on the Temple of the Winds. Other decorative survivals of the Dance era include three original ceilings of delicate plasterwork, notably the one in the octagonal Music Room, and the elegant Staircase Hall, lit by a dome, which, from a purely architectural point of view, is the finest interior at Mount Stewart.

The character of the rest of the house reflects the tastes of the 1820s/30s, as adapted by those of a century later. The 3rd Marquess of Londonderry – known as 'the Soldier Marquess' and a survivor of two duels – married the autocratic and immensely rich Frances Anne Vane-Tempest, heiress of the coal-owning magnate Sir Henry Vane-Tempest of Wynyard, Co. Durham and immortalised by Benjamin Disraeli (who described her as 'half ruffian and half great lady') as the Marchioness of Deloraine in his novel *Sybil*. Flushed with cash, the Soldier Marquess set about aggrandising Mount Stewart in the late 1820s with the help of William Vitruvius Morrison.

ABOVE View of the south front of the house and the Italian Garden created by Edith, Lady Londonderry, which runs the entire length of the house. The general idea of the stonework was taken from the Villas Gamberaia and Farnese. To the right, two dodos guard the entrance.

BELOW The Dodo Terrace, with the Ark in the centre. Edith, Lady Londonderry's coterie of friends were known as 'the Ark', each of whom was named after an animal of some sort.

Morrison's major remodelling resulted in a vast new entrance front of 11 bays, boasting a giant portico of four Ionic columns and balustraded roof parapets. A single-storey portico of coupled Ionic columns also adorned the no less impressive new garden facade. Inside, the most striking feature of Morrison's work is the monumental central Hall (boldly repainted by Lady Mairi Bury in 1961), a mighty two-storey affair with screens of Ionic columns and a balustraded gallery. There are yet more Ionic columns in the spacious Drawing Room, which must have been a magnificent setting for Edith Londonderry's parties; it overlooks the Italian and Spanish Gardens she created.

The 3rd Marquess of Londonderry is commemorated at Mount Stewart by Scrabo Tower, erected on a hill in the demesne by his son 'Young Rapid', the 4th Marquess, who continued the Stewart tradition of duelling. *The Complete Peerage* rather sniffily notes that

> In June 1838 he was shot through the wrist in a duel at Wormwood Scrubs by Monsieur Gérard de Melcy, husband of the famous opera singer Grisi, to whom, without having received any encouragement, the Viscount [Castlereagh, as he was then styled by courtesy] had addressed a declaration of love.

Later in the 19th century the family resumed its place in public life when the 6th Marquess became Viceroy of Ireland. He and his wife, Theresa (portrayed unsympathetically as the Roehamptons in Victoria Sackville-West's novel *The Edwardians*), were early protagonists of Ulster Unionism. Theresa, an accomplished hostess, was able to win over influential politicians to the cause. 'A clever young lawyer from Dublin who may be useful' was how she described Edward Carson when he came to Mount Stewart for the first time.

In July 1903 the Londonderrys entertained King Edward VII and Queen Alexandra at Mount Stewart to the delight of the neighbourhood. A local newspaper broke into verse:

> All hearts are loyal in our town
> Loyal and true in County Down...
> We thank our noble landlord who
> Brought our good King and Queen to view
> To Londonderry we give here
> A loud and very hearty cheer!

The mythical menagerie at Mount Stewart

The King and Queen planted the two handsome copper beeches which still stand facing the north side of the house. In the visitors' book Queen Alexandra wrote: 'Beautiful place, but very damp'.

The first impressions of the Londonderrys' daughter-in-law Edith had not been dissimilar, but she came to love the place, which she herself enhanced to a degree that it can now be loved by all. She went on working in the gardens she created (and presented to the National Trust) until the end of her life in 1959. Her daughter Lady Mairi Bury (who subsequently gave the house to the Trust as well) recalls that her mother was frequently mistaken for one of the gardeners. But Lady Londonderry took such confusions in good part, for Mount Stewart is a supremely welcoming place. It reflects great credit upon both Lady Mairi – who very much remains in residence and farms her own estate here – and the National Trust that this friendly and informal atmosphere continues to complement the beauty of its surroundings.

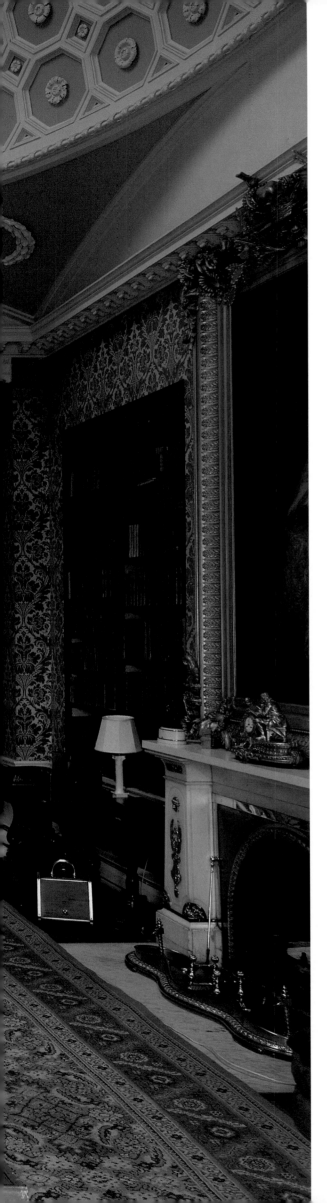

21

CALEDON

POSTERITY, on the whole, has not been kind to the work of the great Regency architect John Nash. Although some of his exercises in the 'castle' style have survived – including Lough Cutra, Co. Galway, which was restored in the 1960s after becoming almost derelict – many of his best Classical designs have disappeared, such as Rockingham, Co. Roscommon (mentioned earlier in connection with Lissadell – *qv*). Or at least their interior decoration has. Therefore Nash's happily extant touches at Caledon, the splendid seat of the Alexanders, Earls of Caledon, make this great, if hitherto underappreciated, house all the more important.

Indeed Christopher Hussey of *Country Life* suggested that Caledon might well be taken to represent Nash among the country houses of the British Isles. Hussey's colleague Margaret Jourdain, the furniture expert, considered it 'the most complete example that has survived of a house furnished in the style favoured by the Regent and his architect during the last years of the Napoleonic War'.

Yet a subsequent generation of architectural historians has been keen that Nash's opulent alterations for the 2nd Earl of Caledon should not totally overshadow the more refined neo-Classical hand of the lesser-known Thomas Cooley, who began the present house in 1779 for James Alexander, a prosperous East Indian 'Nabob' subsequently created 1st Earl of Caledon. Thus, even of Nash's magnificent Library at Caledon, with its coffered dome, Corinthian columns of porphyry scagliola and superlative Regency furniture – an interior hailed by Hussey as 'probably the best preserved of any great room designed by Nash outside Buckingham Palace' – Alistair Rowan drily notes in his scholarly *North West Ulster* volume of *The Buildings of Ireland* series: 'grand, but lacking the delicacy of Cooley's work'.

Professor Rowan also points out that the present late Georgian and Regency house is probably the fourth great house on the estate. During the ownership of the O'Neills, when the place was known as Kinard and occupied a strategic military position (being above the River Blackwater), there was an old castle. This was replaced in the early 17th century by a 'strong house', which was over-run after the Battle of Benburb in 1646, when the O'Neills' Ulster Rising was finally crushed. Next, after the Cromwellian confiscations, came a house built by the Hamiltons from Scotland – hence the change of name to Caledon.

This late 17th-century structure was described in 1738 by the 5th Earl of Orrery – who came into the property that year on his marriage to the Hamilton heiress, Margaret – as 'old, low and, though full of rooms not very large'. Lord Orrery (who also inherited the Earldom of Cork from the branch of the Boyle family seated at Lismore – *qv*) was something of a literary figure, though he has received a mixed press. Dr Johnson considered him 'A feeble-minded man... His conversation was like his writings, neat and elegant, but without strength. He grasped at more than his abilities could reach; tried to pass for a better talker, a better writer, and a better thinker than he was'. But Orrery was a friend of Jonathan Swift and Mrs Delany, the botanist and traveller, thought him 'very gentle in his manners, and mighty polite'.

Such qualities doubtless helped him land a no less mighty dowry. *The Complete Peerage*, not normally given to wild exaggeration, even suggests that Miss Margaret Hamilton of Caledon possessed 'one of the largest fortunes in Europe'. Yet, though, Lord Orrery – who, as Mrs Delany tells us, 'delighted in building and gardening' – apparently toyed with the idea of a new house on a different part of the Caledon estate, he seems to have concentrated his energies on landscaping improvements. Of his Rococo gardens at Caledon, only the bizarre Bone House, with its pillars and arches faced with knuckle bones (supposedly from the midden of an old O'Neill encampment), survives.

Unfortunately, the Hermitage has long since vanished. It sounds enchanting from the 1748 description of the gardens by Mrs Delany:

PREVIOUS PAGES John Nash's magnificent domed Library at Caledon, added in 1812 for the 2nd Earl of Caledon, who had acquired the book collection of Bishop Percy, editor of *Reliques of Ancient English Poetry*. The Corinthian columns are of porphyry scagliola.

RIGHT Detail of a male figure adorning one side of the neo-Classical chimneypiece in the Saloon. Executed in Roman cement and painted to look like stone, the chimneypiece's high relief modelling suggested to Christopher Hussey the hand of Richard Westmacott, who provided the chimneypieces for Castle Coole (*qv*) not far away.

ABOVE and LEFT Two views of the Saloon, designed in the neo-Classical style by Thomas Cooley as the original entrance hall for 'Nabob' Alexander's new house in 1779. The columns are yellow scagliola; the plasterwork above the door leading to the Oval Drawing Room shows a pair of sphinxes in the Adam manner. The gilt furniture is of the Regency period.

LEFT View through the centre of the house from the Inner Hall created in the final remodelling of 1833, when the entrance was switched from the north to the east and Thomas Cooley's original entrance hall became the Saloon.

BELOW Service bell. Before the First World War there was an indoor staff of 13 at Caledon.

... about an acre of ground – an island, planted with all the variety of trees, shrubs and flowers that will grow in this country, abundance of little winding walks, differently embellished with little seats and banks. In the midst is placed an hermit's cell, made of the roots of trees. The floor is paved with pebbles; there is a couch made of matting, and little wooden stools, a table with a manuscript on it, a pair of spectacles, a leathern bottle; and hung up in different parts, an hourglass, a weather glass and several mathematical instruments, a shelf of books, another of wooden platters and bowls, another of earthen ones, in short everything that you might imagine necessary for a recluse. Four little gardens surround this house – an orchard, a flower garden, a physick garden and a kitchen garden – I never saw so pretty a whim so thoroughly well executed.

The Orrerys' son Edmund, the 7th Earl of Cork and Orrery, proved to be anything but a hermit. According to Sir Herbert Croft's racy volume *The Abbey of Kilkhampton* (1780), he was 'devoted to the most wretched voluptuousness' and this is confirmed by his appearance in the notorious '*tête-à-tête* portraits' of peers and their mistresses published in *Town and Country Magazine*. Preferring the English fleshpots to the sylvan scenery of Ulster, the errant Earl sold Caledon to 'Nabob' Alexander in 1778.

ABOVE The Oval Drawing Room, transformed by Nash into an opulent Regency interior through the ingenious use of gilt paper silhouettes and mouldings.

The Nabob was a younger son of Alderman Nathaniel Alexander, a Londonderry merchant who had returned to Ireland having amassed a large fortune in the East Indies. Altogether he spent the staggering sum of some £600,000 on acquiring property in Ireland, including the borough of Newtownards, Co. Down. A staunch Tory, he became MP for Londonderry and was a strenuous supporter of the Act of Union. The Nabob entered the peerage in 1790 as Baron Caledon and was subsequently advanced to a Viscountcy (1797) and then, in 1800 (on the day 18 Irish peerages were conferred on persons who already possessed a peerage of that Kingdom), to the Earldom of Caledon.

Having established himself as a landed proprietor at Caledon, the Nabob wasted no time in commissioning Thomas Cooley, who had recently completed the Royal Exchange building in Dublin (and who was later to be associated with the great James Gandon in the building of the Four Courts in that city), to build him an elegant Classical villa on a new site, a flattened knoll in the parkland. Cooley designed a two-storey house with a pedimented breakfront centre on the entrance front to the north and a central curved bow on the garden front to the south.

The Diocletian windows on the ground floor (still to be seen at either side of the bow on the garden front) are known in Ireland as 'Wyatt windows'; and Mark Bence-Jones has pointed out the similarity of Cooley's interior plan at Caledon to the one he adapted from an original design by James Wyatt at Mount Kennedy, Co. Wicklow, for the 1st Lord Rossmore. Inside, Cooley's entrance hall (now the Saloon) was given a screen of yellow scagliola Doric columns and Adamesque plasterwork – though the Doric frieze and central ceiling roundel strike Professor Rowan as seeming 'later than 1780'. (None the less, they can hardly be Nash's work, whereas the chimneypiece here probably is.)

Other surviving features of Cooley's interior decoration at Caledon include the wrought-iron banister of the Staircase; the delicate panelled shutters and doors (topped by a frieze of gilded dolphins) in the Oval Drawing Room; and, above all, the exquisite Boudoir, with its 'Harlequin'-style plasterwork and roundels by Angelica Kauffmann. Professor Rowan regards this as 'one of the finest neo-Classical ceilings in Ireland'. The pretty apple-green Chinese or 'India' wallpaper may well have been brought back from the East by the Nabob himself.

The Nabob died in 1802 and was succeeded by his only son, Du Pre – traditionally known as 'the Governor' at Caledon on account of his being appointed the first Governor of the Cape of Good Hope when the colony was ceded to the United Kingdom in 1806. The Governor remained on the Cape for five years (the Caledon River is named after him) and, as Christo-

LEFT The Boudoir, with its 'Harlequin'-style plasterwork, roundels by Angelica Kauffmann and chimneypiece of piping and lyre-playing nymphs. This interior has 'one of the finest neo-classical ceilings in Ireland', according to Alistair Rowan The 18th-century Chinese wallpaper may have been brought back from the East by Nabob Alexander.

RIGHT A corner of a passageway at Caledon, faded by the sun.

pher Hussey remarked in *Country Life*, the attractive form of veranda known as a *stoep* that he would have enjoyed in the old Dutch houses of the colony could well have fuelled the Governor's desire for the Ionic colonnade that John Nash provided back home at Caledon.

Nash's screen of coupled Ionic columns runs the full length of Cooley's entrance front culminating in flanking (and projecting) domed pavilions. The domes and plaster composition for this work were shipped over from London in 1808; the columns and glass for the cupola light in the Library, which was to fill the western pavilion, followed the next year. By 1810 the cost of Nash's alterations had already risen to nearly £10,000; the Governor's agent John Pringle commented: 'We are certainly at his mercy as to ornaments'.

Besides creating the Library – surely one of the most satisfying interiors in Ireland – Nash transformed the Oval Drawing Room into a riot of Regency splendour through the ingenious use of gilt paper silhouettes and mouldings. The Governor, a considerable connoisseur who was elected to the Society of Dilettanti, bought Bishop Percy's collection of books and toured the continent of Europe on artistic shopping expeditions with his father-in-law, the 3rd Earl of Hardwicke (from whom his wife, Catherine, inherited Tyttenhanger in Hertfordshire).

In 1825 the Governor finally acceded to an old suggestion of Nash's that Caledon needed an attic storey and eight years later Thomas Duff of Newry was brought in to switch the entrance from the north to the east. This resulted in an Ionic *porte-cochère* on the east front and a new internal sequence of Entrance Hall and octagonal domed Inner Hall. Cooley's original entrance hall on the north front became the Saloon.

The Governor died in 1839, much mourned by his tenants in the model town of Caledon, which he had rebuilt and enlarged so sympathetically. A loyal address by the tenantry in 1835 alludes to his 'acts of liberality, munificence and kindness' and there is plenty of evidence to confirm that this was not just the standard guff from feudal forelock-tuggers. 'Lord Caledon', wrote Inglis in his book *Ireland* (1834), 'is all that could be desired – a really good resident country gentleman'. An obituary in *The Journal of the Georgian Society* recorded that 'His relations with his tenants were of the happiest; he built excellent cottages... and spared no expense to improve the neighbourhood'. In short, the Governor fully deserved the monumental column erected to his memory near the gates to the demesne (demolished by a bomb in 1973).

An evocative picture of life at late Victorian and Edwardian Caledon – complete with its own laundry and dairy, gamekeepers dressed in dark green jackets, porters in cockaded hats, an indoor staff of 13 – is given in Nigel Nicolson's biography of *Alex: The Life of Field Marshal Earl Alexander of Tunis* (1973). 'Alex' – or 'Tubby', as he was quite inappropriately known to his family – was the third son of the 4th Earl of Caledon, who from a trip to the Wild West brought back some wapiti and black bears to enliven the park. The Field Marshal – one of the astounding total of half-a-dozen Ulstermen of his generation to reach that exalted rank – recalled Caledon as a wonderful place in which to grow up. His 'glorious, happy days' were filled with outdoor adventures and included the memorable sight, when he crept out of the house early one morning, of 'a full moon struggling against the light of dawn' which inspired him to take up painting.

On the death of the Field Marshal's endearingly eccentric bachelor brother Eric, the 5th Earl of Caledon, who based himself in one room at the house, the title and estate passed to a nephew, Denis Alexander. It was the end of the 1960s, which, to say the least, did not herald an encouraging era in the

Downstairs in the cavernous basement at Caledon. An underground service tunnel connects the house to the stables, as at Castle Coole (*qv*).

RIGHT Detail of the pediment on the north front featuring the coat of arms of the Alexanders, Earls of Caledon, complete with the supporters – a mermaid and an elephant.

history of Ulster. Nothing daunted, the new Earl gallantly set about reawakening Caledon, which had rather gone to sleep during his Uncle Eric's 70-year stewardship. The house had to withstand terrorist attacks – and security continued to be a problem in view of the estate's situation near the border with the Republic – but noble efforts were made at restoration.

Since Denis's death in 1980, his son Nicholas, the 7th Earl of Caledon, who is Lord-Lieutenant for Co. Armagh, has courageously carried on the good work. In the public service traditions of the Alexander family he is actively involved in the Caledon Regeneration Partnership, a cross-community body set up to breathe new life into the Caledon conservation area. The handsome town laid out by the 2nd Earl is certainly worthy of the reinvigoration it is receiving from this admirable enterprise.

The present Lady Caledon has contributed to the enhancement of the house with a flair that is sensitive to the exceptional achievements of both Thomas Cooley and John Nash.

BELOW View of the east and north fronts of Caledon, showing Nash's colonnade to the right and the *porte-cochère* (by Thomas Duff of Newry, 1833) to the left.

22

BARONSCOURT

COUNTY TYRONE

T HE FAMILIAR pattern when writing about country houses is to begin at the beginning and then plod dutifully through the history until one reaches the present day, which tends to merit only the briefest of mentions. Such is the panache with which the present Duke and Duchess of Abercorn, aided and abetted by the late David Hicks, have reinvigorated Baronscourt that one can only respond by scrapping such a pedestrian approach. For through their confident style, sensibility and imagination this triumvirate of taste has effectively redefined country-house life.

The key word here is 'life', for James and Sacha Abercorn determined, when they took over Baronscourt with their young family in the 1970s, that they would enjoy *living*, as opposed to merely curating, in the great house. Their most adventurous stroke was to create a comfortable and practical Family Room in the east wing. William Vitruvius Morrison's vast neo-Classical dining room of the 1830s, with its white walls, yellow scagliola pilasters and half-columns, and rich plasterwork ceiling (all of which features, naturally, remain intact) was ingeniously converted by David Hicks into three separate spaces. These comprise a kitchen unit, a store/flower/drink area and, in the middle, an informal dining and breakfast room. Each space has its own architectural entity. Hicks described the towering green-painted wooden cupboards as 'modern island skyscrapers'.

Those who find this shock of the new too uncompromisingly modern can take reassurance from the fact that Hicks's handiwork here is reversible; the integrity of the original room is not affected by such innovation. One of David Hicks's maxims was that 'good design always goes with good design' and this principle has been triumphantly applied at Baronscourt, where a complex architectural history and the highly eclectic collections of contents could easily have led to a conflict of styles. Yet as the late Gervase Jackson-Stops, that most perceptive of architectural historians, acknowledged in *Country Life*, the boldness of Hicks's redecoration matches the strength and unity of the neo-

Classical interiors by the Morrisons (not only William Vitruvius but also his father, Richard). The result is 'a setting that can well hold its own'.

Indeed, looking back at the career of David Hicks, who died in 1998 at the time we were preparing this book, one is inclined to think that he may have done his finest work at Baronscourt. It is especially significant that his hero was Sir John Soane, perhaps the most original architect since Sir John Vanbrugh and a master of linear ornamentation; Soane's spirit hovers over the ducal seat of the Abercorns.

Although, alas, nothing actually survives of Soane's interior designs for the 1st Marquess of Abercorn at Baronscourt, which was gutted by fire in 1796 almost immediately after they were executed, it was he who remodelled George Steuart's original house for the 1st Marquess's austere bachelor uncle the 8th Earl of Abercorn (who 'never drank anything but water... nor had more relish for the society of women'). Within 24 hours of arriving at Baronscourt in May 1791, he produced a plan to rework the bachelor villa of 1779/82 by Steuart into a suitable family seat for 'Don Magnifico', as the 1st Marquess was known. 'The alterations Mr Sloan [sic] proposes astonishes me not a little', wrote the agent on the estate. 'He just reverses the house; what was the backside is to be the entrance and the front part the rere'. Inside, Soane created an 88-foot-long gallery with screens of columns, and the old central staircase was replaced by a domed, top-lit billiard room. All this, and his other decorative flourishes, were to disappear in the fire a mere five years later.

Yet Soane's influence lingered on during the radical remodelling by the Morrisons between 1836 and 1840 for the 2nd Marquess (and subsequently 1st Duke) of Abercorn. Sir Richard Morrison, in particular, had a yen for sophisticated spatial effects in the style of Soane, as can be seen in the two libraries at Baronscourt. The ceiling in the gorgeous White Library, with its tell-tale shallow saucer-dome, is clearly derived from Soane's Bank of England designs. The idea of the Rotunda had its origins in Soane's top-lit billiard room and the Gallery, again, harked back to his earlier scheme. Upstairs, too, the bedrooms in the east wing have a strong, simple 'Soanic' character.

So David Hicks responded sympathetically to all these Soanic vibrations. In the jargon of the period when he overhauled Baronscourt he knew where the Morrisons were 'coming from'. He was equally responsive to the robustness of their own architecture; as whatever debt may be owed to Soane at Baronscourt, the credit for the rich, deep and muscular plasterwork, which is the great glory of the house, must go to the Morrisons, or, more specifically, to William Vitruvius Morrison, who had a detailed grasp of the Classical orders.

The enfilade of state rooms at Baronscourt is certainly an object lesson in the Doric-Ionic-Corinthian development. In the expert judgement of Gervase Jackson-Stops, the plasterwork at Baronscourt is of the highest quality – 'far richer and more accomplished than anything to be found in England of this period'. (Unfortunately the craftsmen are not known, though the 'J. Smith' who crops up in the accounts may well have worked with Henry Popje for William Vitruvius at Killruddery – qv.)

Hicks's dramatic colour schemes complement the neo-Classical architecture and the assorted works of art remarkably well. Thus the deep red lacquer of the Staircase Hall contrasts effectively with the white columns (which recall 'Athenian' Stuart's Temple of the Winds at Mount Stewart – qv). Hicks derived his dark reds, purples and yellows for the Library from William Vitruvius Morrison's design for a stained-glass skylight above the staircase next door. As Jackson-Stops remarked, this achieves 'an effect of great warmth and comfort – a perfect place to spend a winter evening'.

PREVIOUS PAGES Baronscourt in its beautiful wooded valley underneath the slopes of the Bessy Bell mountain. This view is looking across the middle lake to the north, entrance, front, with its giant Ionic portico of the late 1830s by William Vitruvius Morrison.

ABOVE and RIGHT Two views through the nobly Classical Hall created by the Morrisons on the same site as the vestibule in the burnt Soane house.

ABOVE The Morrisons' magnificent Gallery (itself an adaptation of the original by Soane) as restored and redecorated by David Hicks in the 1970s for the present Duke and Duchess of Abercorn. The screens of Corinthian columns help to break up the 88-foot-long interior into a series of different spaces.

LEFT A corner of the Gallery dominated by a charming study by the Victorian artist Sir Edwin Landseer, a friend of the Abercorns who often stayed at Baronscourt.

In the Rotunda, a thrilling circular 'Tribune' with a Pantheon dome, Hicks preserved the neo-Classical grandeur with a large round table in the centre and a carpet specially woven to his design in the Philippines, with a wide anthemior border. The refurnishing of this spectacular interior has enabled the Abercorns to use it as a dining room for more formal occasions when the Family Room would not be so appropriate.

The present Duke, like his predecessors, is a prominent public figure in Ulster and has done much to encourage progress in the province. Before inheriting the Dukedom he represented Fermanagh and South Tyrone in the House of Commons at Westminster, and in the 1980s he was a director of the Northern Ireland Industrial Development Board before taking on the chairmanship of the Laganside Development Corporation, which has revitalised Belfast. James Abercorn's tall, courteous presence as Lord-Lieutenant of Co. Tyrone has exercised a calming and positive influence during troubled times in Northern Ireland. The many charitable and educational works of his wife, Sacha, include the inspirational 'Pushkin Prize' (the Duchess is a descendant of the great Russian writer), a creative writing competition for Irish schoolchildren from both sides of the border in which she takes a practical interest.

LEFT Looking into the White Library, one of Baronscourt's most 'Soanic' interiors though it was probably designed by Sir Richard Morrison as there is little doubt that none of Sir John Soane's work inside the house survived the fire of 1796.

BELOW Detail of the plasterwork in the mirror-surround in the White Library. The plasterwork in this room is very much in the style of Morrison.

James's father, the 4th Duke of Abercorn, an engagingly Emsworthian figure, was a passionate forester and the woods he planted in the demesne now frame wonderful vistas in every direction that help to make Baronscourt, in its sheltered valley complete with lakes, a place of enchanted beauty. After the Second World War he and his wife, the former Lady Mary Crichton from Crom (*qv*), decided to simplify the house, which had also suffered another fire – this time gutting the east wing. Sir Albert Richardson was brought in to abbreviate both wings and to tidy up the entrance front – though, of course, William Vitruvius Morrison's massive Ionic *porte-cochère* still, more than ever indeed, dominates the scene. Later, in 1970, Raymond Erith provided a well-mannered garage block.

Inside the house, Sir Albert Richardson turned the Morrisons' long Gallery into three rooms (as, in fact, it had been in George Steuart's original house before Soane arrived), but had the foresight to make his alterations easily reversible. David Hicks saw the opportunity: he removed the partitions and brought the great Gallery gloriously back to life for a new generation.

ABOVE Detail of the plasterwork in the frieze of the Rotunda. Gervase Jackson-Stops described the Morrisons' plasterwork at Baronscourt as of the highest quality – 'far richer and more accomplished than anything to be found in England of this period'.

RIGHT The Rotunda, a thrilling circular 'Tribune', with a Pantheon dome and Ionic columns in green scagliola. David Hicks refashioned it in the 1970s as a formal dining room for the present Duke and Duchess of Abercorn; the carpet was specially woven to his design in the Philippines.

A dream-like vision of infinity punctuated by Corinthian columns, the Baronscourt Gallery makes one gasp with delight. Hicks has revealed it once more as a magnificent Morrison interior worthy to rank with any in Ireland (it is actually longer than the gallery at the Palladian palace of Castletown, Co. Kildare). The special quality of the great room is its light airiness – thanks to no fewer than 11 tall windows – and Hicks has consciously enhanced this in his redecoration, deploying several shades of beige and off-white in the walls, ceilings and curtains. The variety of contents lives up to the name of Gallery and, to quote Gervase Jackson-Stops again, 'The harmonious marriage of different nationalities and styles seems effortlessly achieved in these surroundings'.

The heraldic achievements displayed on the scagliola tops of the handsome pier tables remind one of the illustrious history of the House of Hamilton. For unlike most of the other Lowland Scots who came over to Ulster in the early 17th century, the 1st Earl of Abercorn – grandson of the 2nd Earl of Arran, who acted as Regent during the minority of Mary Queen of Scots – was already, as one genealogist put it, 'a very grand personage' in his own right. Lord Aber-

LEFT The Staircase, which formed part of the Morrisons' remodelling of Baronscourt in the late 1830s. In the 1970s redecoration David Hicks gave the walls a deep red lacquer which contrasts dramatically with the white columns and coffered ceiling.

RIGHT The Library boldly redecorated by David Hicks using the reds, purples and yellows of the original stained-glass design of the skylight above the staircase by William Vitruvius Morrison. The geometrical carpet was woven to a Hicks design.

BELOW A 1573 portrait of Lord Claud Hamilton, father of the 1st Earl of Abercorn, above a chimneypiece by Peter Bossi of Dublin in the Duke of Abercorn's Study at Baronscourt. Lord Claud commanded the vanguard for Mary Queen of Scots at the Battle of Langside in 1568 and was subsequently outlawed, but King James VI restored to him his rank and fortune.

corn, who had received seven Scottish peerages, was granted large parcels of land in the Barcny of Strabane, Co. Tyrone, and built an L-shaped castle, the ruins of which are still discernible in the woods about half-a-mile from the present Baronscourt.

The 2nd Earl – who became Heir Male, or Head, of the House of Hamilton when his cousin the 2nd Duke of Hamilton died bearing no son – was a Roman Catholic like his mother, Marian Boyd. The 4th Earl, a staunch Jacobite, accompanied King James II to France after the Battle of the Boyne and the family estates were forfeited for a brief spell.

The anchor embedded on the lawn in front of the Agent's House at Baronscourt comes (according to tradition) from the frigate in which King James and the 4th Earl escaped to the continent. The Agent's House – described in Alistair Rowan's *North West Ulster* volume of *The Buildings of Ireland* as a 'charming little essay in rustic Palladianism... one of the most interesting small classical houses in Ulster, architecturally one of the more ambitious and one of the earliest' – was originally intended as a family seat.

It seems to have been begun in 1741 by the scholarly 7th Earl of Abercorn, a Fellow of the Royal Society and joint-author of a *Treatise on Harmony* (whose strongly Protestant father had revived the family fortunes by marrying an heiress) and finished by his son, the bachelor 8th Earl, who succeeded to the estate only three years later. The architect was James Martin, a local

builder who also worked on Clogher Cathedral, and he appears to have based his design on Sir Edward Lovett Pearce's villa of Bellamont Forest, Cootehill, Co. Cavan. Like Bellamont Forest, it must presumably have had an extra storey – subsequently removed.

The removal of this attic storey probably occurred in the 1780s, when the house was 'demoted' after George Steuart had built the new Baronscourt down the hill. By this time the old bachelor 'Builder Earl' – who had also commissioned Sir William Chambers to design a fine house at Duddingston on recovered Scottish estates – was pushing 70, and considered

> at my time of life it is perhaps necessary to find excuses for
> engagements of this sort. Mine must be that it sets very many people
> to work, who would otherwise be idle.

Such sentiments make one warm to the old water-drinker who, according to one contemporary, did the Grand Tour of Europe in 'so *perpendicular* a style as never to have touched the back of the carriage'.

His nephew and successor at Baronscourt, 'Don Magnifico', the 1st Marquess of Abercorn, also seems to have been something of an acquired taste. Legendarily pompous, he is said to have always gone out shooting adorned with his blue riband as a Knight of the Garter; to have insisted that the housemaids wore

A view of the house from the south-west, showing the bay window on the west installed in 1838 by William Vitruvius Morrison, which replaced a shallow bow by his father, Sir Richard.

– 228 –

RIGHT View from the south-east, up the steep path leading to the Stables. This gives an idea of the original seven-bay house as designed by George Steuart, 1779–82 – though an attic storey and portico were removed by John Soane when he turned the house round in the 1790s. The figures in the foreground are a group of weekend guests playing croquet.

BELOW Looking out to the demesne, which was greatly improved by the plantations of the 4th Duke of Abercorn, who died in 1979.

white kid gloves making his bed; and, according to the gossipy G.E. Russell, to have begged his second wife, when contemplating elopement, 'to take the family coach, as it ought never to be said that Lady Abercorn left her husband's roof in a hack chaise'.

Yet Don Magnifico had his good points, not least that he was an early patron of John Soane, who enlarged his principal residence of Bentley Priory at Stanmore, near London, as well as reworking Steuart's house at Baronscourt. The patron of the Morrisons, who subsequently remodelled Baronscourt, the 2nd Marquess, was another cultivated connoisseur and a voracious collector. In public life he distinguished himself by serving two terms as Lord-Lieutenant of Ireland.

Towards the end of his first term of office, in 1868, he was created Duke of Abercorn; Disraeli claimed that by thus elevating 'Old Splendid' (as he was nicknamed by his doting grandchildren) he had actually increased his physical stature. Following his second term at Dublin Castle, the Duke brought in the landscape gardener Ninian Niven to lay out the terraces on the south front at Baronscourt. His wife, Louisa, daughter of the 6th Duke of Bedford (and, incidentally, the Morrisons' Gallery has echoes of Henry Holland's library at the Bedford seat of Woburn – see *Great Houses of England and Wales*), took an enthusiastic interest in the formal garden.

The redoubtable Duchess lived to 1905, by which time she had accumulated more than 160 descendants: a celebrated photograph was taken in 1894 of 101 of them. The picture is like a key to the network of the great houses of the British Isles, for all Duchess Louisa's daughters had married a Duke, Marquess or Earl. The House of Hamilton may have spread its dynastic wings far and wide but it is gratifying to report that today their beloved base of Baronscourt is in better shape than ever before. The present Duke and Duchess of Abercorn have tackled the task of conservation with a tremendous brio.

23

CASTLE COOLE

COUNTY FERMANAGH

*T*HE ABERCORNS of Baronscourt, featured in the previous chapter, had a lively political rivalry with the 1st and 2nd Earls of Belmore of Castle Coole around the time of the Act of Union, which the Belmores opposed. The part politics plays in the creation of great houses often tends to be overlooked; we are inclined to think of them purely as Temples of the Arts rather than, as it were, Palaces of Power. Recent research in the papers of the Lowry-Corry family, Earls of Belmore, has shown that the 1st Earl's political ambitions were a significant factor in the building of what was the most palatial late 18th-century house in Ireland, celebrated as the masterpiece of James Wyatt.

In his characteristically incisive introduction to the catalogue of the Belmore Papers in the Northern Ireland Record Office, Dr Anthony Malcomson writes that:

> Castle Coole was built as part and parcel of Belmore's plans for his
> own and his family's political and social aggrandisement... it was well
> situated to mark the nucleus of a north-western political power bloc in
> the Irish Parliament... That Parliament, its autonomy enhanced by the
> so-called Constitution of 1782 looked as if it would last forever...
> Castle Coole therefore reflects Belmore's confidence in his own
> political future and in the future of the political institutions of his day.
> It was to be the home of a great Irish political family: not merely a
> place to live in, but a showpiece to proclaim Belmore's position in
> Irish society and influence in the Irish House of Commons.

Unfortunately for Lord Belmore that confidence proved to be misplaced. Although he had inherited various family estates totalling some 70,000 acres (with a rent roll of at least £12,000) and had risen, after 13 years as MP for Co. Tyrone, through the ranks of the peerage – barony, viscountcy and, in 1797,

earldom – ultimately the dreaded Act of Union ended his chances of political influence. All that remained of his ambitions was Castle Coole – and that was really more a source of satisfaction to posterity than to himself, for he had effectively handed over his various properties to his son, Somerset, on his coming-of-age in 1795.

This fact, which neatly nails the old *canard* that the 1st Earl bankrupted himself in building the house, is one of the many instructive discoveries to have been made recently by Peter Marson, formerly the National Trust's administrator at Castle Coole, who is currently writing a family history of the Lowry-Corrys. The first fruits of his admirable researches were published in a booklet accompanying the Family Exhibition held there in 1997.

The family papers also reveal that the 1st Earl played a more 'hands-on' role in the design and building of Castle Coole than has been generally appreciated before. He decided to create the new family seat on his maternal estate in Co. Fermanagh rather than his paternal property in Co. Tyrone on account of Castle Coole's naturally beautiful setting with lakes, woods and mountain views. (According to family tradition, he chose the site on the hill well above the lake owing to his rheumatism.)

PREVIOUS PAGES Looking through the Saloon to the Drawing Room at Castle Coole. Twelve scagliola pilasters flecked with grey and black are set around the Saloon's oval walls worked by Domenico Bartoli in July 1794; the Corinthian capitals were sent over from London by Joseph Rose the following spring. The room was furnished by John Preston, the Dublin upholsterer from 1815 to 1824. The piano to the left is a Broadwood of 1802.

ABOVE and FAR RIGHT The entrance front of Castle Coole: the serene perfection of James Wyatt's masterpiece built in the 1790s for the 1st Earl of Belmore.

RIGHT Detail of leonine decoration on the front door.

The earlier houses at Castle Coole had stood beside the lake. John Corry, a Belfast merchant of Scottish origin, who bought the estate in 1656 and rose to be High Sheriff of Co. Fermanagh 10 years later, rebuilt an old plantation house by Lough Coole. This had been burnt before he bought it, and it was to be burnt again during the Williamite Wars. Next came a Queen Anne house, built for John's son Colonel James Corry, MP for Co. Fermanagh, to the designs of John Curld or Curle (who also worked at Beaulieu – *qv*), but this, too, was to be consumed by a conflagration at the end of the 18th century – just about the time the new Castle Coole was being completed up the hill. The position of the Colonel's house is still discernible in the demesne from the avenue of oaks which led up to it, and the layout of the old formal garden can also be seen.

The male line of the Corrys expired in 1741 on the death of the Colonel's bachelor grandson Leslie Corry, MP for Killybegs. Castle Coole subsequently passed, in succession, to his three sisters. Martha (Mrs Leslie) and Mary (Mrs Armar) both died childless, so it was Sarah Lowry-Corry, mother of Armar, later the 1st Earl of Belmore, who finally scooped the pool in 1774. Ten years earlier she had already inherited another portion of the family estates, when her husband Galbraith Lowry was, in accordance with landed tradition, obliged to add the suffix Corry.

LEFT Looking through the Hall to the Staircase. The red scagliola Doric columns are by Domenico Bartoli; the frieze is also Doric. The doors are Cuban mahogany. The hall chairs were specially designed by Wyatt.

RIGHT The double-return Staircase with a colonnaded screen at the top. The stairs are of Portland stone which was transported from Dorset, finally reaching Castle Coole by bullock cart.

BELOW The two-storey Bedroom Lobby, with especially fine plasterwork by Joseph Rose. This unexpected flourish by Wyatt has been described by John Cornforth of *Country Life* as 'the most exciting architectural feature of the house'.

'Gilly' Lowry was a person of some stature in his own right: MP for Co. Tyrone, where he was seated at Ahenis, close to Caledon (*qv*); sometime High Sheriff of both Tyrone and Co. Monaghan; and a member of the Linen Board. As Peter Marson has pointed out, he gave his son Armar a good grounding in the responsibilities of the large estates he was to inherit in 1779.

Certainly, the following year, the Lord-Lieutenant of Ireland, the 2nd Earl of Buckinghamshire, was impressed enough by the prospect of Armar Lowry-Corry as a son-in-law. He described him as follows:

> Member for the County of Tyrone... the best match in this Kingdom...
> His property is immense. He is universally esteemed, acknowledged to
> be generous without profusion, honourable upon the most correct
> line. He is rather well in his figure. His age is thirty-two [*sic*: actually
> he was about to be 40], and in addition to these capital points his nose
> resembles mine.

Armar was available as a 'match' again because his first wife, Lady Margaret Butler, daughter of the 1st Earl of Carrick, had died in 1776.

Unfortunately the marriage to Lord Buckinghamshire's daughter, Lady Henrietta Hobart, did not turn out well. More than 20 years Armar's junior, she

ABOVE The colonnaded gallery above the Bedroom Lobby. The paired columns in the Adam manner are of no particular Classical Order.

RIGHT The Library, with bookcases by Peacock & Berry and what John Preston & Son, the suppliers in 1811, described as 'large Egyptian couches... in fine Jamaican mahogany'. To the far right is a corner of Richard Westmacott's remarkable chimneypiece carved as marble drapery. The laurel wreath on the curtain rail commemorates Napoleon's defeat in Egypt.

seems to have been rather flighty (her father, for instance, noted once how she was 'subdued by the naked hocks' of 'a blooming Highlander') and Armar's brother-in-law, the 1st Earl of Enniskillen, of Florence Court (*qv*), observed early in the ill-fated marriage how 'there was a visible disgust on the part of Lady Belmore... towards Lord Belmore'.

Perhaps Lord Belmore found relief from marital unhappiness in his ambitious building operations at Castle Coole. In 1789, the year in which as 'a penitent Baron', in the phrase of the then Lord-Lieutenant of Ireland (the 1st Marquess of Buckingham), he was advanced to a Viscountcy, he commissioned a design from the Dublin architect Richard Johnston. The plan he produced was strikingly similar to what was eventually built (and credited to Wyatt): a nine-bay two-storey house flanked by arcaded wings ending in pavilions, with the central block dominated by a giant Ionic portico.

Lord Belmore seemed happy enough to proceed with Johnston's scheme, but then, after the foundations had been dug, he suddenly switched to a more fashionable architect, James Wyatt. Wyatt's first drawings for the revised plans for Castle Coole are dated July 1790, a month after work began on the

long arched tunnel which was to run for more than 50 yards from the east end of the house to the stable and office buildings.

This kitchen passage, as it became, was initially used to bring the stone in carts into the foundations. Lord Belmore was actively involved in the whole procedure: he was his own contractor and organised the importation of the Portland stone from Dorset on his own brig, the *Martha* (presumably named after his aunt), to Ballyshannon. The stone was then taken overland to Lough Erne and shipped to Enniskillen; the last couple of miles to Castle Coole were covered by bullock carts. All this must have been a very expensive undertaking – it is said that the final cost amounted to double Lord Belmore's original estimate.

Although he entrusted the supervision of the daily labour to a Scottish builder called Alexander Stewart, Lord Belmore did his best to keep a close watch on the finances. The family papers record fierce rows with both Stewart and the London plasterer Joseph Rose (much in demand by Wyatt and Robert Adam), who took particular exception to Lord Belmore's interference and criticism. Wyatt, too, had a considerably less free hand in the building and decoration of Castle Coole than has sometimes been portrayed.

Nevertheless, work seems to have proceeded at a fairly brisk pace. The west wing was roofed by 1791; the main house by 1792 (when Lord Bel-

ABOVE The east wall of the Morning Breakfast Room at Castle Coole, dominated by Cipriani's painting of *Castor and Pollux* ('the Heavenly Twins'). The present Earl of Belmore bought this important picture, which had formerly been at Houghton Hall in Norfolk (it was commissioned by the Cholmondeleys in 1783), and lends it to the National Trust for show at Castle Coole.

RIGHT View across the lake to the garden front of Castle Coole, with its curved central bow.

more began divorce proceedings on account of his wife's adultery not with 'a blooming Highlander' but with the Lowlander Earl of Ancram, later 6th Marquess of Lothian, whom she subsequently married); and the portico was up by 1794 (when Lord Belmore married his third wife, Mary Anne Caldwell).

The result was a triumph. For many architectural enthusiasts, the present writer among them, Castle Coole expresses a serene perfection, combining Hellenism and Palladianism, mass and moderation, that is unrivalled. There is a pale, silvery majesty about the place which has been evocatively captured in the paintings by Terry Flanagan commissioned by the present Earl of Belmore. Whatever the restrictions placed on him by Johnston's original design or the 1st Earl's political aspirations, James Wyatt rose above it all to produce something sublime. As Alistair Rowan remarks in the *North West Ulster* volume of *The Buildings of Ireland* series: 'There is a rightness about Castle Coole that is immensely satisfying. None of Wyatt's lines is superfluous: all are carefully calculated, with a few chosen to run right through the design'.

Inside, the craftsmanship is of the finest quality: plasterwork by Joseph Rose, marble chimneypieces by Richard Westmacott, Cuban mahogany doors. The dignified Doric Hall leads to the sumptuous oval Saloon, with its scagliola pilasters by Domenico Bartoli. The Saloon is in the middle of the garden front overlooking the lake and forms a splendid enfilade together with the Drawing Room and the Dining Room.

Up the noble stone double staircase is found Wyatt's most unexpected flourish at Castle Coole, the two-storey Bedroom Lobby, described by John Cornforth in *Country Life* as 'the most exciting architectural feature of the house'. Lit by an oval oculus, this dramatic interior has a colonnaded gallery and more especially fine Rose plasterwork.

By 1795, when the 1st Earl of Belmore handed over Castle Coole to his son Somerset, the decoration and furnishing of the house still had some way

ABOVE and BELOW LEFT Two views of basement rooms at Castle Coole, redolent of 'downstairs' life in a great house.

BELOW The Kitchen Passage, or Servants' Tunnel – 14 feet wide, 12 feet high – which runs for more than 50 yards from the east end of the house to the stable and office buildings. During the building of Castle Coole it was used to bring in the stone in carts.

to go; though Wyatt had designed some special furniture himself, Somerset, who succeeded to the Earldom of Belmore in 1802, shared the opulent tastes (and, it must be said, something of the same tendency to extravagance) of his contemporary the Prince Regent. In 1807 he began splashing out with the Dublin upholsterers, John and Nathaniel Preston; as Gervase Jackson-Stops, architectural adviser to the National Trust, revealed in *Country Life* in 1986 (shortly after Preston & Son's accounts were discovered in a trunk at Castle Coole), the 2nd Earl was to spend £26,367 with the firm over the next 18 years.

Among the rooms the Prestons furnished was the State Bedroom, or Bedchamber, supposedly with a view to a possible visit by 'Prinny' himself, by now King George IV, who came to Ireland in 1821. But the sybaritic monarch headed no further north than Slane Castle, Co. Meath, whose *châtelaine*, the massive Marchioness Conyngham, exerted a strange fascination over him.

Besides doing up Castle Coole in lavish Regency style, the 2nd Earl was a passionate yachtsman who toured the Mediterranean in his 232-ton brig *Osprey*. Like his father, Somerset found himself frustrated in his political ambitions. He hoped for a United Kingdom peerage to give him a seat of his own in the House of Lords at Westminster, but in the event had to settle for a spell as a Representative Irish Peer in the Lords, and then the Governorship of Jamaica. His grandson the 4th Earl, who wrote the engaging *History of Two Ulster Manors*, went out, like Hilaire Belloc's Lord Lundy, to govern New South Wales.

The present Earl's mother, the former Gloria Harker, also happened to hail from Australia, and it was in his parents' time, in 1951, that the house and part of the demesne of Castle Coole were bought with a grant from the Ulster Land Fund and passed to the National Trust. In the 1980s the Trust carried out a magnificent restoration at a total cost approaching £5 million. This involved dismantling the exterior cladding of the entire house and overhauling the stonework. The new stone came from beside the quarry in Dorset from which the original Portland stone had been transported nearly 200 years before. The interior of the house was done up using the strong colours of the Regency decorative scheme favoured by the 2nd Earl and the Prestons – though one of the colours deployed in the redecoration proved rather too strong for some tastes.

The present Earl of Belmore and his wife, the former Lady Mary Meade, second of the six daughters of the 6th Earl of Clanwilliam, together with their young family, continue to live on the demesne and to retain the west wing for their use. Lord Belmore generously loans the contents of Castle Coole to the Trust for visitors to enjoy. A considerable connoisseur, John Belmore has added some interesting pictures to the collection which he has also lent for show in the house – including a fine Cipriani (previously at Houghton Hall in Norfolk – see *Great Houses of England and Wales*) in the Morning Breakfast Room and a series of Irish landscapes by such artists as Hone the Younger, Campbell and George Barret (also represented in the Rohan Collection at Charleville, Co. Wicklow – *qv*).

Latterly concerts have become a popular event at Castle Coole, which Queen Elizabeth The Queen Mother reopened to the public in 1988 after the restoration was completed. Among the other attractions are the Grand Yard, the Servants' Tunnel, the recently restored Ice House, the Dairy, the Stables (by no less an architect than Sir Richard Morrison), the Laundry and a display room featuring the Belmore Coach – proud conveyance of a family that may not quite have become the powerful political dynasty the 1st Earl hoped for but which gave us one of the greatest houses of the British Isles.

View of the stable yard at Castle Coole designed by Sir Richard Morrison in the 1820s.

24

LYONS

COUNTY KILDARE

WHAT Dr Tony Ryan, of Ryanair fame, has achieved at Lyons is not just a restoration but a glorious recreation. For in 1996, when the enterprising founder of the GPA Group acquired the property, the important late Georgian house (begun almost exactly 200 years before by the architect Oliver Grace for the 1st Lord Cloncurry, a prosperous woollen merchant's son, and later remodelled by Richard Morrison for the connoisseur and patriot the 2nd Lord Cloncurry) was in a sorry state of near dereliction. Latterly Lyons had been in institutional use, as an outpost of the Faculty of Agriculture of University College, Dublin, and the once elegant interiors housed offices and laboratories.

Within an almost incredibly short period, however, a quite remarkable transformation has been achieved. It has been rightly said that at Lyons 'Dr Tony Ryan has accomplished the largest, most ambitious and exhaustive programme of restoration ever undertaken in a private capacity in the history of the Irish State'. A total of some 670 'man years' of work was packed into 33 months by his expert and enthusiastic team of architects, artisans, builders, craftsmen and craftswomen. But what shines through this phenomenal project is the sheer romance and excitement of bringing new life to such a great house, and Dr Ryan's passion for the place. 'Despite its semi-ruinous state', Dr Ryan recalls of the daunting task that faced him in 1996, 'Lyons seemed to possess an indomitable spirit and a vast amount of potential'.

The meticulous attention to detail has produced a masterpiece. The work of Grace, Morrison, the Italian landscape artist Gaspare Gabrielli and the sculptor Luigi Antonio Acquisti has been faithfully recreated. Besides a comprehensive overhaul that has encompassed re-roofing and the faithful replication of window sashes, floors, chimneypieces and plasterwork, Lyons has also undergone a sensitive remodelling of its garden facade, in sympathy with the period detailing of the entrance front. The newly rusticated garden facade now incorporates a row of handsome arched windows set into mellow granite, which was specially quarried at Ballyknocken, Co. Wicklow. One of the wings now houses a splendid swimming-pool; the other, a delightfully cheerful Orangery, for informal dining, which features the outstanding prospect of the newly restored formal gardens, with their avenue of yews and column supporting a statue of Venus (excavated at Ostia), leading down to the 27-acre lake (and its dramatic 63-foot jet-fountain) and the picturesque Hill of Lyons beyond.

The historic hill traditionally takes its name from Liamhain, one of four daughters of the ancient King of Desi Bregia, Dubhthach Dubthaire, all slain by their outraged father for breaking the pagan *geis* (or injunction) on their marrying. Liamhain is said to have been buried on *Cnoch Liamhna*, or Lyons Hill.

Subsequently, Lyons became the property of the Aylmers. According to *Burke's Irish Family Records*, in the early 15th century Richard Aylmer of Lyons was Keeper of the Peace for counties Dublin and Kildare, and a century or so later his descendant and namesake was High Sheriff and Chief Serjeant of Co. Kildare. The old castle of Lyons seems to have been destroyed in the Rebellion of 1641 and there is no visual record, apart from old maps, of the house that replaced it; the present house stands to the north-west of where it stood before it was demolished once the new house was built.

The Aylmers of Lyons eventually hit the buffers through the gambling and other debts run up in the late 18th century by the erratic, thrice-married Michael Aylmer. Among his creditors was Nicholas Lawless, son of a rich Dublin draper of humble origin, who duly acquired the Lyons estate in a series of somewhat complex transactions finally completed (at a cost of £37,450) in 1796.

Having consolidated his father's business interests, which included banking as well as the woollen trade, Nicholas Lawless and his wife, Margaret, heiress of the Dublin brewer Valentine Browne, had settled for a spell in Normandy – as a Roman Catholic, he was unable to buy an estate in Ireland during the Penal Times. But then, in the 1770s, had come a change of heart brought about, it seems, by the snobbish attitude of the French towards the son of someone who had begun life selling turf in the Wicklow Hills. Nicholas decided to return to Ireland and conform to the Established Church. In 1776 he entered Parliament as MP for Lifford and was created a Baronet; 13 years later he rose to the peerage as Baron Cloncurry.

PREVIOUS PAGES View from the Hill of Lyons, with Ireland's largest man-made lake in the foreground and the formal gardens recently restored by Dr Tony Ryan, the new owner of the Lyons demesne.

BELOW The triumphal arch at the entrance to the Lyons demesne, complete with pediment, pilasters, volutes and rusticated wicket gates and surmounted by the appropriate lions, formerly stood at the entrance to Browne's Hill, Co. Carlow. It was moved here, thanks to the enterprise of the Irish Georgian Society, during the ownership of University College, Dublin, when Lyons was an outpost of the Faculty of Agriculture.

View through the trees of Lyons's entrance facade, with its unusual double bow front and colonnades. The central portico incorporates three columns of antique red Egyptian granite from the Golden House of Nero and a fourth from the Baths of Titus – some of the treasures acquired in Italy by the connoisseur 2nd Lord Cloncurry.

More of the ubiquitous lions at Lyons – though the name of the place actually derives from Liamhain, one of four daughters of the ancient Irish King of Desi Bregia to be killed by their father for indulging in matrimony.

Snobbery was not exactly unknown in Dublin either at this period. Shortly after his ennoblement, the new Lord Cloncurry found the following verse (attributed to a Miss de Burgh) in his box at a theatre where *Don Quixote* (featuring the scene in which Sancho Panza is 'tossed') was to be performed:

> Cloncurry, Cloncurry, don't be in a hurry,
> To see them toss up the poor squire;
> Tho' high he must go, yet we very well know,
> *Your* blankets have tossed you much higher

Cloncurry's 'hurry' was to advance up the ranks of the peerage. In his acidulous *Review of the Irish House of Commons* (1789), the Reverend John Scott (who does not appear to have been overburdened by Christian charity) noted of the Member for Lifford:

> His person has more of the stiffness of a French dancing master than of the easy disengaged air of a well bred gentleman; and his voice is peculiarly unpleasing, it having a sharp querulous tone grating to the ear, equally destitute of strength or sweetness, melody or compass... The great object on which his heart is fixed, next to the accumulation of money, is the attainment of a peerage and to procure that splendid distinction, he has for some years dedicated himself most assiduously to the service of every administration.

Ten years later, though, when Cloncurry still had only a mere Barony and Baronetcy to show for his efforts, he grumbled to the Viceroy of Ireland, the 3rd Duke of Portland, that 'If I have obtained any honours, they have cost me their full value'. At least when he died later that year, 1799, the 1st Lord Cloncurry had the satisfaction of knowing he had set in train a palatial new pile at Lyons – begun two years earlier to the designs of Oliver Grace, hitherto best known for his work on Cashel Cathedral.

The most striking feature of Grace's granite building was its double-bowed front – a rare, indeed possibly unique, flourish on a major country house of this period. The three-storey central block was joined to its two-storey wings with curved colonnaded sweeps. Mr Grace had achieved an appropriately graceful composition.

The 1st Lord Cloncurry must have been rather less enchanted, however, with the political activities of his son Valentine, who was an active member of the Society of United Irishmen, founded in 1791 (when Valentine was an undergraduate at Trinity College, Dublin) to oppose the projected Act of Union with Great Britain 'and all other Government measures'. Valentine sported green cloth manufactured in Ireland and wrote pamphlets denouncing British rule. During the 1798 Rising ('The Year of Liberty') Valentine was arrested and committed to the Tower of London. After about six weeks inside, he was released, only to be arrested again in 1799. This time he was to remain in the Tower for nearly two years on suspicion of treason.

Back in Ireland, a free man again in the year that the Act of Union finally went through, the 2nd Lord Cloncurry (as he had become while he was in the Tower) 'settled upon a plan for enlarging my house at Lyons'. Richard Morrison, a promising young architect from Cork who had also worked on Cashel Cathedral and was much influenced by the genius of James Gandon of Dublin Custom House fame, was engaged to do the enlarging. He replaced Grace's curved sweeps with straight colonnades (as he was later to do for the 3rd

LEFT and ABOVE Two views of the Hall, with its frieze of ox-skulls and tripods derived from the Temple of Fortuna Virilis in Rome and stucco bas-reliefs of Classical scenes over the doors. The overmantel by Gaspare Gabrielli above the marbleised Portland stone chimneypiece was recently restored.

Duke of Leinster at Carton nearby) and faced the ground floor of both the main block and the wings with rusticated ashlar.

Meanwhile, Valentine Cloncurry toured the continent of Europe acquiring antiquities and works of art with which to embellish his burgeoning palace. Among his most notable purchases were the three columns of antique red Egyptian granite from the Golden House of Nero, which had latterly ornamented the Palazzo Farnese in Rome and which Morrison accordingly incorporated into the new portico back at Lyons. The fourth column in the portico originated from the Baths of Titus.

A less fortunate acquisition on Valentine Cloncurry's travels, as it turned out, was his bride, Georgiana Morgan. For after their return to Ireland from Rome in 1805, Lady Cloncurry was seduced by her husband's old schoolfriend Sir John Piers, Bt, a notorious gambler, duellist and spendthrift. The seduction, which supposedly took place as the result of what James Woods in his *Annals of Westmeath* called 'a diabolical wager', led to a scandalous court case for 'criminal conversation' in 1807, whereby Lord Cloncurry sued the 'monster' Piers for £100,000 damages. The case inspired John Betjeman (who first read about it in the library at Pakenham Hall, now Tullynally – *qv*) to write his epic poem *Sir John Piers*, which includes the couplet:

> The nobility laugh and are all free from worry
> Excepting the bride of the Baron Cloncurry

If Lord Cloncurry had won all the damages he had claimed from the bold, bad Baronet, he might at least have been partially 'free from worry' himself, but in the event he obtained £20,000 – a mere 10 per cent of what he reckoned to have spent on creating what he proudly called 'a fine place'. Besides, as he put it, 'building, draining, planting and cultivating my grounds' (not least laying out the largest man-made lake in Ireland), Lord Cloncurry's most inspired commission was to employ, among 'an army of men', the Italian landscape artist Gaspare Gabrielli.

At Lyons, Gabrielli (who married Lady Cloncurry's maid and found himself dragged into the 'Crim. Con.' case as a witness) adorned the principal rooms with enchanting murals that became the most beautiful painted interiors in Ireland. His subjects included studies of three famous Irish waterfalls (Poulaphouca, the Salmon Leap at Leixlip and Powerscourt) in the Music Room; a view of Dublin Bay in the bow-ended Dining Room; and a group of landscapes inspired by Claude in the Drawing Room.

From the surviving correspondence, it is clear that the 2nd Lord Cloncurry kept his architect Richard Morrison on a tight rein. 'Stop all Morrison's proceedings', Cloncurry complained at one stage, 'and if he dont attend to the business have no more to do with him'. Morrison evidently had his hands full in adapting the architecture and the interior decoration to accommodate his patron's demands. The Hall was given a frieze of ox-skulls and tripods based on the Temple of Fortuna Virilis in Rome, doorcases with fluted entablatures and overdoor panels with Classical reliefs and free-standing antique marble Corinthian columns, as well as sculptures from Lord Cloncurry's vast collection.

As the years progressed, Valentine the young radical developed into a respectable Liberal (and received a Barony of the United Kingdom in 1831). Carpenter's *Peerage for the People* (1849) accorded him 'a high place on the roll of noble patriots... in his politics [he] has ever been a *liberal* as in his more private character'. Daniel O'Connell, 'The Liberator', wrote in 1824 that 'Ireland has not a better friend or one more devoted to her service than Lord Cloncurry. The poor man's justice of the peace; in private life the model of virtue; in public life worthy of the admiration and respect of the people'.

Valentine Cloncurry found contentment with his second wife, Emily (widow of Joseph Leeson, heir to the 3rd Earl of Milltown and to Russborough

LEFT The Music Room or Family Room as it is now called. Gabrielli's magnificent ceiling and roundels have been carefully restored by Mary McGrath and her team from the Courtauld Institute in London.

– *qv*), with whom, as he put it in his *Recollections* (1849), he shared 'uninterrupted happiness and affection for 30 years'. Unfortunately their son the 3rd Lord Cloncurry was a less contented character: he threw himself out of a window at Lyons in 1869, with fatal consequences. The 3rd Lord Cloncurry's daughter Emily Lawless was a well-known poet of Nationalist sympathies and a prominent figure in the Irish Revival of the early 20th century.

Emily's niece Kathleen Lawless inherited Lyons from the 5th (and last) Lord Cloncurry in 1929 and in turn bequeathed the property to a cousin, Mark Winn from Yorkshire, in 1958. A few years later Winn sold the place to University College, Dublin, the principal legacy of whose ownership is the splendid triumphal arch at the entrance to the demesne installed here, thanks to the enterprise of the Irish Georgian Society, from Browne's Hill, Co. Carlow.

Then, in 1990, the estate was sold to Dr Michael Smurfit and today Lyons is the home of Dr Tony Ryan and his burgeoning stud. Everywhere one feasts one's eyes, the pristine perfection of Dr Ryan's painstaking restoration is a source of joy. In the Hall, the Portland stone chimneypiece has been re-marbleised as it was in the early 19th century and Gabrielli's elaborate over-mantel (previously hidden beneath lining paper) restored by Mary McGrath and her team of conservationists from the Courtauld Institute. They have also done a brilliant job in rejuvenating Gabrielli's masterpieces in the Drawing Room and Music Room, or Family Room as it is now called. The formal Dining Room has been given a new ceiling and gilt bookcases in the Georgian manner, but the room of Dr Ryan's delight is the Orangery, with its exquisite sculpted panels by Acquisti depicting the fate of Icarus, a 17th-century Spanish tapestry and floor of Portuguese mocca. The refectory-style table is carved from a single piece of iroko. The view is sensational.

With typical generosity Dr Ryan, a governor of the National Gallery of Ireland, is not keeping all these superlative sights for his eyes only. As he says, 'It is my pleasure to open part of the house to the general public and to return part of Ireland's cultural heritage to the nation'. Visitors can indeed share the sense of pleasure that Dr Ryan feels in having made his home at Lyons.

ABOVE One of the sculpted panels by Acquisti in the Orangery, depicting the story of Icarus.

RIGHT The garden front of the house has been sympathetically rusticated by Dr Tony Ryan in mellow Wicklow granite. The column in the formal gardens is topped by a statue of Venus excavated at Ostia.

25

CHARLEVILLE

A PALLADIAN villa, with robust Regency interiors, and a garden of delights set in the dream-like landscape of the Wicklow Hills. What could be more ideal than Charleville? And surely it has never looked better than it does today, as the cherished home of Ken and Brenda Rohan, who have carried out a stylish and sensitive restoration of the house and gardens.

The house, begun in the late 1790s and then supposedly done up in anticipation of a visit by King George IV when he went to Powerscourt next door, has been sympathetically redecorated and adorned with exceptionally fine furniture and Irish works of art. The demesne, imaginatively remodelled with the help of some notable Irish gardening experts, now features a remarkable series of circular borders, within the vast expanse of the walled gardens that follow the curves of the boundary wall. With their different 'rooms' formed by beech and yew hedges, an amazing beech 'tunnel' and Doric-columned conservatory, all lovingly cared for, the Charleville gardens must rank as one of the most admirable horticultural achievements in Ireland.

Ken Rohan, a prominent Irish industrialist, bought Charleville in 1981. Previously it had belonged for nearly 40 years to Donald Davies, the fashion pioneer, who brought the house to life again after a period when it had been shut up, and established one of his 'shirt-dress' manufacturing bases in the handsome stables, with their cut-stone dressings. Mr Davies's only daughter, Lucy, married the Earl of Snowdon, photographer son of Anne Countess of Rosse of Birr (*qv*) – where, incidentally, the celebrated 'Arlington Suite' of furniture by Thomas Chippendale, originally made for the London house in Arlington Street of the great 18th-century merchant contractor Sir Lawrence Dundas, 1st Bt, and acquired by Mr Rohan for the Drawing Room at Charleville, was formerly housed.

The stables at Charleville appear to be earlier than the present house and may well be a survival from the previous three-storeyed house here, which was destroyed by fire in 1792. The Moncks, who owned Charleville well into the 20th century, first came into the property through the marriage in 1705 of Charles Monck, a barrister, to Agneta, eventual heiress of Major Walter Hitchcock of Charleville.

Charles also inherited his maternal property of Grange Gorman, now a suburb of Dublin. The Moncks, originally from Devon in the south-west of England, had arrived in Ireland in the early 17th century, when Charles's grandfather and namesake became Joint Surveyor-General of Customs in Dublin. Charles's father, Henry Monck, who was attainted by King James II but restored to his estates in Co. Westmeath by King William III, married Sarah, the heiress of Sir Thomas Stanley of Grange Gorman.

The Moncks continued to go up in the world during the 18th century. Charles and Agneta's elder son, another Henry, succeeded to Charleville and married Lady Isabella Bentinck, daughter of the 1st Duke of Portland. Their only daughter, Elizabeth, married the 1st Marquess of Waterford and became the *châtelaine* of Curraghmore (*qv*), while Charleville passed to her cousin Charles Monck in 1787.

This Charles went into politics and represented Newborough, or Gorey, Co. Wexford, for seven years before being caught up in the flood of peerages being offered by the Government for support of the Act of Union with Great Britain. First, in 1797, he accepted a Barony and then, in the fateful year of 1801, a Viscountcy. These trousered inducements are unlikely to have endeared Monck to his neighbour the 4th Viscount Powerscourt, one of only five peers to vote against the Union. Desmond Guinness relates in his book on *Great Irish Houses and Castles* how when a Government emissary turned up at Powerscourt to offer the Viscount an Earldom, by way of a similar bribe, Lord Powerscourt proceeded to kick him down the stairs.

To suit his elevated status, and to fill the gap left by the fire of 1792, the new Lord Monck set about building an appropriate seat at Charleville. His architect, as established by the researches of the Knight of Glin, was Whitmore Davis, whose designs appear to have been inspired by Lucan House, Co. Dublin. This Palladian villa had been built in the 1770s by Agmondisham Vesey, with some tips from Sir William Chambers.

Like Lucan, Charleville has the central feature of a pediment raised on a three-bay attic and carried on four engaged Ionic columns standing on the lower storey which, below them, is rusticated. However, whereas at Lucan the front door is arched, at Charleville it is pedimented; and whereas at Lucan the facade is of only seven bays, Charleville boasts nine. And although, inside, the arrangement of the Entrance Hall at Charleville, with fluted Ionic columns, is also reminiscent of the hall at Lucan, here it leads through to the impressive Staircase Hall, with its cantilevered Portland stone staircase and balustrade of brass banisters – a splendidly swooping affair worthy of comparison with the one at Castletown, Co. Kildare, in the view of Desmond Guinness himself (who saved this grand Palladian palace in the 1960s, when it was threatened with demolition).

Comparisons with yet another great house, Carton, Co. Kildare, are evoked by the floor-length 'Wyatt windows' at the sides of Charleville, which are similar to ones added at Carton in 1817 by Richard Morrison. This raises the interesting question of how much Charleville was altered in the early 19th century barely a generation after it was begun. In her book *The Moncks and Charleville House* (1979), Elisabeth Batt says that the first stage of build-

ABOVE and BELOW Two views of the Drawing Room. The 'Arlington Suite' of furniture by Thomas Chippendale, acquired by Ken Rohan from Birr Castle (*qv*), was originally made for the London house in Arlington Street of the great 18th-century contractor Sir Lawrence Dundas, 1st Bt

The Sitting Room with its barrel-vaulted ceiling and plasterwork encompassing musical instruments, gardening implements and sheaves of corn.

ing was completed by 1799. So the alterations would have been made in the time of the 2nd Viscount Monck, who succeeded his father in 1802 and was created Earl of Rathdowne 20 years later.

The year before, King George IV had made his celebrated visit to Ireland, which took in the neighbouring Powerscourt. The story goes that the waterfall, the highest in the British Isles, was dammed up in order to provide an even more dramatic spectacle for the royal eyes on a specially constructed bridge. But the King dallied over his dinner and never arrived at the bridge – which was just as well for it was swept away when the water was finally released.

It is an article of faith at Charleville that the Moncks refurbished their house in the latest fashion in case the King came to call next door. Other families, such as the Belmores of Castle Coole (*qv*), are said to have done the same, and been equally disappointed by the vagaries of this most unreliable of monarchs. It is significant that Desmond Guinness draws our attention to the fact that plasterwork installed at Powerscourt for the royal visitation, such as that on the staircase (now, alas, no more after the terrible fire which gutted the interior in 1974), is similar to decoration to be found at Charleville.

In any event, there is a strong Regency flavour to the completed interiors at Charleville. The ceilings of rich Grecian Revival plasterwork again suggest the hand of Sir Richard Morrison. The Sitting Room, redecorated in a delicious yellow by the Rohans, has a bold barrel-vaulted ceiling with plasterwork encompassing musical instruments, gardening implements and sheaves of corn. The Dining Room ceiling's centrepiece of shamrock and foliage seems earlier than *circa*

1820, but the acanthus frieze, presumably added to beef up the cornice, is evidently later. The Entrance Hall's fine floor of inlaid parquet probably dates from later still in the 19th century.

Despite the best efforts of his Countess (herself a daughter of the 1st Earl of Clancarty), who bore him two sons, who both died as boys, and no fewer than 11 daughters, the Earl of Rathdowne could not father an heir to the new Earldom and the title died with him in 1848. The Viscountcy of Monck, however, carried on for six months or so in the person of his brother before being inherited by his nephew Charles, who was also his son-in-law, having married one of the 11 daughters, Lady Elizabeth.

The 4th Viscount Monck, as he became, was a Liberal politician and sat in the English House of Commons (as Irish peers were, and indeed are, allowed to do) as MP for Portsmouth before going out to Canada in 1861 as its first Captain-General and Governor. Five years later he was granted a United Kingdom Barony and then, in 1867, given the grandiloquent title of 'Governor-General of British America', a designation soon changed to the more tactful Governor-General of the Dominion of Canada. He entertained W.E. Gladstone at Charleville – the Liberal statesman planted a tree near the house to mark the occasion – but subsequently fell out with the 'Grand Old Man' over Home Rule in 1886. Lord Monck maintained the strongly Unionist views of his family.

The last of the Moncks to live at Charleville was Edith, widow of the 5th Viscount Monck, a veteran of the Egyptian War. Edith, whose elder son had been killed in action in France during the first few months of the First World War, died in 1929, after which the future of the great house seemed unpromising, to say the least.

Happily, though, its potential was spotted by Donald Davies and now, under the dedicated ownership of Ken and Brenda Rohan, it is being immaculately realised. Among the notable collection of Irish works of art with which they have beautified the interior are a set of lyrical Irish landscapes by George Barret and, dominating the Staircase Hall, a tremendous narrative picture of King George IV's departure from Ireland in 1821. In not having seen the perfection of Charleville the old sybarite missed a treat.

26

BALLYWALTER PARK

COUNTY DOWN

A LTHOUGH THE years after the Act of Union saw much architectural activity in Ireland, the appalling Famine of the 1840s put the brakes on the building of great country houses. There were, though, some exceptions and most notable among those which survive in private hands is Ballywalter, the *palazzo* of the Mulhollands, a splendid example of the calm confidence of the early Victorian age with which to end our tour in capital style.

'Capital', in several of its senses, seems the *mot juste* for Ballywalter. For it was built (or, to be precise, comprehensively remodelled and enlarged) with the well-earned profits of Belfast's booming linen industry and exudes a city-like sophistication. As Alistair Rowan, who has written so perceptively about Ballywalter in *Country Life* and in the Ulster Architectural Heritage Society's series on country houses, put it, the building has 'a metropolitan air and all the architectural trappings of a London club, dropped as if by chance in the open country on the north Irish coast'. Certainly, as one luxuriates in the stupendous central galleried Hall, with its Doric and Corinthian columns, there is a heady feeling that one has been transported to the heyday of those two great Pall Mall clubhouses the neighbouring Travellers' and Reform, both designed by Sir Charles Barry, whose exercises in the *palazzo* style must surely have inspired the Belfast architect Sir Charles Lanyon.

At the time the 4th Lord Dunleath inherited Ballywalter in 1956 such bold expressions of Victorian taste tended to be regarded as anachronistic monstrosities, embarrassing white elephants. His father, the 3rd Lord Dunleath, had considered abandoning the vast pile, or at least radically reducing it in size. (Sir Albert Richardson was actually commissioned to draw up a plan for removing the top floor and dismantling Lanyon's Conservatory.) The 4th Lord Dunleath, then still in his twenties, was wondering whether to follow suit when a *deus ex machina* arrived on the scene: John Betjeman came for tea.

'When he saw the house', Henry Dunleath recalled not long before his untimely death in 1993, 'he displayed signs of ecstasy'. Betjeman pointed out to the young peer that the Conservatory (a noble domed affair fronted with more Corinthian columns) was an essential element in Lanyon's concept for the rear elevation of the house, and should be preserved at all costs. He added that if the entire house as originally designed could be preserved for another 25 years (this was in 1961), it would become a mecca for architectural historians and enthusiasts.

The far-seeing poet was, of course, absolutely right. Fortunately, Henry Dunleath (who had not been quite sure whether Betjeman was pulling his leg) accepted this, as he ruefully put it, 'expensive advice' and he and his wife, Dorinda, set about essential repair work. They battled against dry rot and, following a devastating fire in 1974, put back the glazing-bars in the windows which had been replaced with plate glass around 1900, and also redecorated the state rooms.

The fire occurred the day after Henry Dunleath's cousin, Brian Mulholland, first took his future wife, Mary Whistler, to see Ballywalter. Now the present Lord and Lady Dunleath, Brian and Mary are looking at various ways of enabling Ballywalter to survive and take on an active role in the 21st century. The public-spirited Dunleaths are very much aware of the responsibilities that go with owning an officially designated Heritage House; they hold many open days for the public to enjoy the beautiful gardens and see the state rooms, as well as holding charity events, such as musical evenings.

Such community spirit is certainly in the responsible tradition of the Mulholland family. When Andrew Mulholland, a great philanthropist as well as a tycoon, was elected Mayor of Belfast in 1845, the fateful year in which the failure of the potato crop first caused the Famine, he dedicated himself to encouraging 'anything that may tend to the improvement or amelioration of the conditions of the operatives'. He called for

> the establishment of public walks or gardens, in some of the suburbs; public baths connected with washhouses; and also fountains where a constant supply of pure water could be produced free of expense; a library and reading room (with a rate of charges that would be merely nominal); and also coffee shops.

When the Ulster Hall was being built in Belfast he presented the great organ there (the Mulholland Grand Organ, recently restored) to the people of Belfast 'for the improvement of their minds and taste'.

The Mulholland family business presided over by the philanthropic Mayor had been founded by his father, Thomas Mulholland, a shrewd businessman notwithstanding his supposed illiteracy (he signed his name with an *X*), who established his sons in a cotton business in Belfast. But then, in 1828, a fire destroyed the brothers' mill. What could have been a disaster turned out to be a blessing in disguise for the Mulholland brothers had hit on an opportune time to switch from cotton (the Irish cotton trade was by then being bested by the Lancastrians) to linen. Their York Street premises pioneered flax-spinning and became one of the biggest mills of its kind in the world.

Andrew Mulholland, who initially worked in partnership with his brother St Clair until buying him out, consolidated the firm's phenomenal success. 'Belfast', wrote a fellow mill-owner, Hugh MacCall, 'can never forget how much she owes to the house of Mulholland'. And the Mulhollands' profits, as MacCall mused, were beyond their 'dreamiest imaginings'.

PREVIOUS PAGES A corner of Ballywalter's sensational central galleried Hall: niches, statuary, Corinthian columns, all contributing to the *palazzo* effect created by Sir Charles Lanyon for the Belfast linen tycoon Andrew Mulholland.

BELOW A view through the columns of the *porte-cochère* on the entrance front to the pedimented Corinthian aedicule on one of the wings.

View of the garden front of Ballywalter, with the conservatory to the left. Sir John Betjeman pleaded successfully for its preservation in the 1960s.

The entrance front.

Naturally enough, the dream of this pillar of the so-called 'Linenocracy' was to celebrate his good fortune with an appropriate country seat. In the spring of 1846, following his admirable year as Mayor of Belfast, Andrew Mulholland bought the Springvale estate, beside the attractive seaside village of Ballywalter, for £23,500.

Springvale had formerly been the seat of the Matthews family, who, in turn, had acquired it from the Montgomerys of Grey Abbey in 1729. An earlier house on the site of the present Ballywalter Park, formerly called Ballymagown, is mentioned in Walter Harris's *Ancient and Present State of County Down* (1744). This was rebuilt by George Matthews, a noted collector of curios (Harris refers to 'several Figures of Mummies in divers kinds of Earth, in wood that is never said to decay, called *Lignum Ficulnum Aegypitacum Pharaonis*'), and renamed Springvale. His grandson and namesake appears to have carried out a major remodelling of the house in the early 19th century – and it was this building that Lanyon was to transform for Andrew Mulholland.

Although nothing of the old Springvale is readily discernible today, apart from the atmospheric stable range which survives to the north, investigation of the basement area confirms that the central block of Lanyon's refashioned house retained the original structure. Basically, Lanyon, a friend and fellow councillor of his patron, turned the bulk of the old two-storey house into the huge Hall, 60 feet long and the full height of the new building, which accommodated an additional floor. The entrance was switched from the south to the east, where Lanyon added the *porte-cochère*, with coupled Doric columns

LEFT The comfortable Victorian Library. The pedimented bookcases were installed by the 1st Lord Dunleath, who succeeded to Ballywalter in 1866 and was created a peer in 1892.

BELOW *The Infant Samuel* by Patrick McDowell in the Saloon section of Ballywater's great Hall.

and end piers, surmounted by a latticed balustrade. And single-storey wings (with elaborate windows on the entrance front framed by pedimented Corinthian aedicules) were added to balance the central block.

Later, in 1863, Lanyon added a further wing, prolonging the garden front, to house a billiard room and, at right angles to it, the celebrated Conservatory. John Betjeman's prediction that architectural historians would eventually come to appreciate Ballywalter's beauty came true sooner than even he anticipated. For barely half-a-dozen years after he prophesied this to Henry Dunleath, the scholarly Alistair Rowan was writing with sympathy in *Country Life* of Andrew Mulholland's architectural aspirations at Ballywalter: 'The ponderous grandeur of its facades, the richness and weight of its marble and mahogany, the solid comfort of the place – these are the qualities that he had learnt to approve and appreciate in the world of business'.

It is exactly that feeling of 'solid comfort' which strikes one so strongly in these spacious surroundings. The expansive proportions of Lanyon's sumptuous interior encourage the visitor to walk tall; his gloriously grand designs flatter the visitor to feel at home in such a princely *palazzo*, in much the same way as Barry's buildings bolstered the egos of clubmen and politicians. And even those who might find the opulence of the magnificent Hall, part saloon, part picture-gallery, adorned with statues and urns, a trifle overwhelming, will surely rejoice in the cool elegance of the Ballroom, with its bow-fronted apse, screen of Corinthian columns and coved and coffered ceiling.

A particularly cosy and comfortable room in which to find solace is the Library, where Andrew Mulholland's son John, who succeeded to Ballywalter on his father's death in 1866 (three years after Lanyon completed the Conservatory), installed the ornate pedimented bookcases. The rich glow of the mahogany and the leather bindings, the coved ceiling and the deliciously deep sofas combine to make this a haven of Victorian content.

The Ballroom, with a screen of Corinthian columns, bow-fronted apse and coved and coffered ceiling. There is a notable collection of keyboard instruments at Ballywalter.

John Mulholland continued to expand the York Street Flax Spinning Company (which benefited from the American Civil War virtually cutting off the supply of raw cotton) and was elected MP for Downpatrick in the House of Commons at Westminster. His obituary in *Truth* described him as 'a Tory of the old Ulster school... an admirable speaker on commercial subjects... and... a most popular landlord'. In 1892 he was created a peer as Baron Dunleath.

The *Truth* obituary of three years later also described the 1st Lord Dunleath as 'an enthusiastic yachtsman', which was something of an understatement. His 77-foot schooner *Egeria* was celebrated as 'the fastest schooner afloat' and won over 60 major prizes, including five Queen's Cups.

In the Edwardian heyday of Ballywalter the Mulhollands relished the outdoor life. The 2nd Lord Dunleath, John's son, laid out the demesne to the east of the house as a private nine-hole golf course (now vanished); to the west, a stream was led through the grounds, forming pools, and his wife, Norah Ward from Castle Ward (*qv*), known as 'Gogo' to her grandchildren, installed a tropical aviary. (The park had previously been landscaped in Andrew Mulholland's day: in 1846 alone he planted 41,000 trees and shrubs.) Cricket, then enjoying its Golden Age, was another favourite pursuit of the Mulhollands, and to accommodate visiting teams the 2nd Lord Dunleath built a service wing of *circa* 1902 by the Belfast architect W.J. Fennell to contain the full cricketing complement of 11 bedrooms. This structure, known as the Bachelors' Wing, was partially demolished in the late 1950s and early 1960s.

When it was wet, the Mulhollands could always resort to a game of billiards inside, or even to badminton – underneath the carpet in the Library the markings of a court are still to be found. 'Gogo' Dunleath was also a keen photographer, with her own darkroom in the house. The cheerful atmosphere at Ballywalter under her reign, which extended into the 1930s, is beguilingly evoked in the surviving albums – especially an unusual visitors' book chronicling, complete with joky asides, the poundage at which they weighed in and out. Survivors from the still palmy days between the two World Wars recall scintillating house parties at Ballywalter; a highpoint was the visit of the Duke and Duchess of York (later King George VI and Queen Elizabeth, now The Queen Mother) in the 1920s.

The Second World War, with much more finality than the First (in which Gogo's eldest son, Edward, was killed in action at Ypres), put an end to the old style of country-house living. The 3rd Lord Dunleath pared staff to a minimum and shut off parts of the house. His son, the 4th Lord Dunleath, carried this process one stage further, so that by the 1980s there were no live-in staff.

Under the present ownership of Brian Dunleath (whose grandfather, Harry, the third son of the 2nd Lord Dunleath, served as Speaker of the Northern Ireland Parliament and was created a Baronet in 1945) and his wife, Mary, Ballywalter promises to enjoy a rejuvenation. 'We believe', say the Dunleaths, 'that for Ballywalter to survive and fulfil any meaningful role in the next century it is necessary to be a *whole house*, not just a few "show rooms". As a result, we are battling with long overdue modernisation and decoration, which includes the complete re-rendering of the outside, and at the same time we are searching for ways to make this charming anachronism find a purpose in the modern day.' In short, the Dunleaths epitomise the sensible and practical-minded new generation of owners dedicated to discovering a fresh approach to carrying on the lively contribution made by the great houses of Ireland.

RIGHT Palatial splendour: the staircase in the central galleried Hall.

LEFT Assorted lumber in the upper floors of Ballywalter.

Acknowledgements

THIS BOOK was born in the happiest of circumstances, at the photographer's wedding in the autumn of 1997, when a chance conversation with those two Hibernian heroes, Desmond Guinness, the founder-president of the Irish Georgian Society, and the Knight of Glin, his successor and a champion of Irish decorative arts, inspired us into action.

Although, as the dedication of the book intimates, we had both loved touring Ireland since boyhood, visiting our respective – if, happily, not always respectable – relations, and had naturally hoped to round off this series of books on the Great Houses of the British Isles with an Irish volume, we had come to fear that the ground might have been too well trodden. But, with glorious generosity of spirit, Desmond Guinness, himself the author of two volumes on great Irish houses and castles (the first in collaboration with William Ryan, published in 1971, the second with Jacqueline O'Brien, in 1992) and the Knight, encouraged us to give it a go. What they impressed on us was that within the previous few years there had virtually been a sea change of attitude towards 'the Big House' in Ireland; that stirring restoration schemes were currently being undertaken by not only long-established owners but more significantly by *new* owners; and that there were some remarkable fresh stories to tell. So it has proved.

Therefore a very big Thank You to the 'Two Desmonds' is our first priority. We are also extremely grateful to the Knight for his subsequent scholarly guidance, and to both him and his wife, Olda (Olda FitzGerald, whose book on Irish gardens was published recently), for having us to stay so frequently at Glin. Much wise counsel and cheerful hospitality was also generously given to us by William and Daphne Montgomery in the north.

An enormous debt of gratitude is owed to the great pioneer in this field, Mark Bence-Jones, the Irish mentor of the present writer, as well as an old and dear friend (and distant kinsman), with whom it was a privilege to work on several books in the 1970s, including *Burke's Irish Family Records* and *Burke's Guide to Country Houses, Volume I: Ireland* – the original Bence-Jones compendium which he subsequently revised as *A Guide to Irish Country Houses.*

The standard of scholarship and writing on Irish architecture is uncommonly high – the Irish Heritage lobby has rightly been described as the most eloquent in Europe, if not always, as the Knight of Glin would robustly counter, the most effective – and we have been fortunate indeed in following in some very distinguished footsteps. We salute, in alphabetical order, Sir Charles Brett, Christine Casey, John Cornforth, Maurice Craig, Mark Girouard, the late Gervase Jackson-Stops, Edward McParland, Kevin Nowlan, Peter Rankin and Alistair Rowan.

Without the owners' co-operation, as some of them have been at pains to remind us, we could not, of course, have produced the book. Although we must confess that there has been the *odd* occasion when we found ourselves inwardly invoking an old Turf adage – that any fool can train racehorses, it's dealing with the owners that demands the real skill – we rejoice in expressing our sincere and heartfelt thanks for the wonderfully generous welcome, consideration, kindness, concern, hospitality and constructive criticism we received from the owners of the great houses, as well as from administrators, experts, friends and relations (respectable and otherwise) all over Ireland.

We would particularly like to thank the following, all of whom helped us along the way: the Duke and Duchess of Abercorn, Lola Armstrong, Frances Bailey, Viscount Bangor, Hugh Barrett, Evelyn Beattie, Lady Beit, John Bellingham, the Earl and Countess of Belmore, the Trustees of the Birr Scientific and Heritage Foundation, Betty Brittain, Mary Brown, Lady Mairi Bury, the Earl and Countess of Caledon, Frank Carr, Claire Carter, Triona Caslin, Jim Chestnutt, Cholmeley Cholmeley-Harrison, Henry Clark, Woody Clarke, Alec Cobbe, John Coote, Joanna Cramsie, Monica Daly, David Davies, Gabriel de Freitas, the Duke and Duchess of Devonshire, Michael Dillon, Luke Dodd, Bob Duff, the Marchioness of Dufferin and Ava, the Lord and Lady Dunleath, Viscount Dunluce, Austin Dunphy, Nancy Countess of Enniskillen, the Earl and Countess of Erne, Fingal County Council and the Trustees of the Cobbe Family Collections, Ann FitzSimons, Mike Gaston, Spud and the late Rosamund Gibbon, Sir Josslyn Gore-Booth, Bt, George and Susan Gossip, the late Mariga Guinness, Penny Guinness, the Marquess and Marchioness of Hartington, Nicholas Haslam, Gary Hewitt, the late David Hicks, Bevis Hillier, Harry Hutchman, Breda Ievers, Norman Ievers, Patrick James, Declan Jones, John Joyce, Ann Kelly, Charles Kidd, Tim Knox, William Leaf, Julian and Victoria Lloyd, Todd Longstaffe-Gowan, Robert and Angela Lowry, Candida Lycett Green, Michael Lynch, Charles Lysaght, Rosie McBriar, Harry and Joan McDowell, Robert and Cherith McKinstry, Mary McNeela, Matt McNulty, Ian McQuiston and all the staff of the National Trust (Northern Ireland Region), John and Lucy Madden, George and Wendy Magan, Elizabeth Malcolm, Connor Mallaghan, Peter Marlow, Peter Marson, the Earl and Countess of Meath, the late Earl of Meath, and Elizabeth Countess of Meath, Hugh and Valerie Montgomery, John and Marsali Montgomery-Massingberd, Teresa Moore, Maria Morgan, Martin and Carmel Naughton, Sir John and Lady Nugent, Thomas and Valerie Pakenham, William Packer, Michael Penruddock, Anthony and Lady Violet Powell, John Powell, Nicholas Prins, SallyAnne Robertson, John Martin Robinson, Ken and Brenda Rohan, the Earl and Countess of Rosse, Lord Rossmore, Deirdre Rowsome, Dr Tony Ryan, Egerton and Brigitte Shelswell-White, the Marquess and Marchioness of Sligo, Gavin Stamp, Sir Tatton Sykes, Bt, Robert Tainsh, Hugo Vickers, Sidney Waddington, the Marquess and Marchioness of Waterford, Geoffrey Wheatcroft, Richard Wood, and Jack and Betty Wrisdale.

Finally, we must pay tribute to Mary Scott, Philip Cooper and, especially, Laura Church at the publishers for turning our dreams of Erin into reality; to the designer Karen Stafford, with whom it has continued to be a pleasure to collaborate for the third time; and to the careful copy editor Matthew Taylor. The indefatigable Cynthia Lewis did yet another fine job of typing the manuscript, coping admirably with the pressures of time and illegibility. The writer's offspring Harriet and Luke Massingberd, press-ganged into service as drivers/research assistants, added immeasurably to the pleasure of the project. And our wives, Ripples and Isabella, bravely bore our prolonged absences across the Irish Sea.

HMM
CSS
St Patrick's Day 1998 – St Patrick's Day 1999

Amory, Mark (ed.), *The Letters of Evelyn Waugh*, London, 1980

Annual Register

Anson, Lady Clodagh, *Victorian Days*, London, 1957

Atkinson, A., *The Irish Tourist*, Dublin, 1815

Bateman, John, *The Great Landowners of Britain and Ireland*, London, 1883 (4th edn)

Batt, Elisabeth, *The Moncks and Charleville House*, Dublin, 1979

Bence-Jones, Mark, *The Remarkable Irish*, New York, 1966

— *Burke's Guide to Country Houses. Volume 1: Ireland*, London, 1978

— *Twilight of the Ascendancy*, London, 1987

— *A Guide to Irish Country Houses*. London, 1988 (revised edn)

— *Life in an Irish Country House*, London, 1996

— 'Building Dreams of a Viceroy' [Clandeboye, Co. Down], *Country Life*, October 1 and 8, 1970

Bence-Jones, Mark, and Montgomery-Massingberd, Hugh, *The British Aristocracy*, London, 1979

Bennett, Geoffrey, *Charlie B*, London, 1968

Beresford, Admiral Lord Charles, *Memoirs*, London, 1914 (2 vols)

Berleth, Richard, *The Twilight Lords*, New York and London, 1979

Bernelle, Agnes (ed.), *Decantations. A Tribute to Maurice Craig*, Dublin, 1992

Betjeman, John, *Collected Poems*, London, 1958

Brett, C.E.B., *Buildings of Belfast, 1700–1914*, London, 1967

Buckland, Patrick, *Irish Unionism*, Dublin and New York, 1972

— *Ulster Unionism*, Dublin, 1992

Burke, Sir Bernard, *Burke's Peerage, Baronetage & Knightage*, London, 1826–1970 (105 edns)

— *Burke's Landed Gentry*, London, 1833–1972 (18 edns)

— *A Visitation of the Seats and Arms of the Noblemen and Gentlemen of Great Britain and Ireland*, London, 1852–5 (4 vols)

— *Vicissitudes of Families*, London, 1883 (2 vols)

— *Burke's Landed Gentry of Ireland*, London, 1899–1958 (4 edns)

— *Burke's Dormant and Extinct Peerages*, London, 1969 (reprint)

Campbell, Colen, *Vitruvius Britannicus*, London, 1715–25 (3 vols)

Casey, Christine, and Rowan, Alistair, *North Leinster*. in *The Buildings of Ireland* series, London, 1993

Civil Survey of Ireland, 1654–1656, Dublin, 1942

Cloncurry, 2nd Lord, *Recollections*, Dublin, 1849

G.E.C [okayne], *The Complete Peerage*, London, 1910-59 (13 vols); Gloucester, 1982 (microprint, 6 vols)

— *The Complete Baronetage*, Gloucester, 1983 (reprint. with Introduction by Hugh Montgomery-Massingberd)

Colvin, H.M., *A Biographical Dictionary of British Architects, 1600–1840*, London, 1978

Cornforth, John, 'Bantry House, Co. Cork', *Country Life*, July 27 and August 3, 1989

— 'Castle Coole,Co. Fermanagh', *Country Life*, December 17, 1992

— 'Glin Castle, Co. Limerick', *Country Life*, June 11, 1998

— 'Russborough, Co. Wicklow', *Country Life*, December 5, 12 and 19, 1963

Country Life: see Bence-Jones, Cornforth, FitzGerald, Girouard, Glin, Jackson-Stops, Jourdain, McParland, Rowan

Cox, Sir Richard, *History of Ireland*, Dublin, 1689–90

Craig, Maurice, *Classic Irish Houses of the Middle Size*, London and New York, 1976

— *The Architecture of Ireland*, London and Dublin, 1982

Craig, Maurice, and Glin, the Knight of, *Ireland Observed*, Cork, 1970

Croft, Sir Herbert, *The Abbey of Kilkhampton*, London, 1780

Crookshank, Anne, and Glin, the Knight of, *Painters of Ireland*, London, 1978

— *The Watercolours of Ireland*, London, 1994

Crookshank, Anne, *et al*, *Irish Houses and Landscapes*, Dublin, 1963

Cruickshank, Dan, *A Guide to the Georgian Buildings of Britain and Ireland*, London, 1985

Davie, Michael (ed.), *The Diaries of Evelyn Waugh*, London, 1976

de Breffny, Brian, *Castles of Ireland*, London, 1977

— *Heritage of Ireland*, London, 1980

— *Ireland: A Cultural Encyclopaedia*, London, 1983

de Breffny, Brian, and ffolliott, Rosemary, *The Houses of Ireland*, London, 1975

de Moubray, Amicia, 'Glin Castle, Co. Limerick', *The World of Interiors*, February, 1983

de Vere White, Terence, *The Anglo-Irish*, London, 1972

Dictionary of National Biography

Eiffe, June, 'Lyons, Co. Kildare', *Irish Georgian Society Bulletin*, 1984

Enniskillen, Countess of, *Florence Court, My Irish Home*, Monaghan, 1972

FitzGerald, Brian, 'Russborough, Co. Wicklow', *Country Life*, January 23 and 30, 1937

Fletcher, Sir Banister, *A History of Architecture*, London, 1954 (16th edn)

Foster, R.F., *Modern Ireland, 1600–1972*, London, 1988

Gaughan, J. Anthony, *The Knights of Glin*, Dublin, 1978

George, M., and Bowe, Patrick, *The Gardens of Ireland*, London, 1986

Girouard, Mark, 'Beaulieu, Co. Louth', *Country Life*, January 15 and 22, 1959

— 'Birr Castle, Co. Offaly', *Country Life*, February 25 and March 4 and 11, 1965

— 'Castle Ward, Co. Down', *Country Life*, November 23 and 30, 1961

— 'Curraghmore, Co. Waterford, *Country Life*, February 7, 14 and 21, 1963

— 'Glin Castle',Co. Limerick', *Country Life*, February 27 and March 5, 1964

— 'Lismore Castle, Co. Waterford', *Country Life*, August 6 and 13, 1964

— 'Mount Ievers Court, Co. Clare', *Country Life*, November 8, 1962

— 'Modernising an Irish Country House' and 'Comforts for a Victorian Household' [Tullynally Castle, Co. Westmeath], *Country Life*, December 23 and 30, 1971

Glin, Knight of, *Irish Furniture*, London, 1978

— 'A Baroque Palladian in Ireland' [The Architecture of Davis Duckart], *Country Life*, September 28 and October 5, 1967

Glin, Knight of, *et al*, *Vanishing Country Houses of Ireland*, Dublin, 1988

Greeves, Lydia, and Trinick, Michael, *The National Trust Guide*, London, 1989 (4th edn)

Greville, Charles, *Journals of the Reign of Queen Victoria, 1837–52*, London, 1885 (3 vols)

Guinness, Desmond, *The Irish House*, Dublin, 1975

Guinness, Desmond, and Ryan, William, *Irish Houses and Castles*, London, 1971

Guinness, Desmond, and Sadler, J.J., *The Palladian Style in England, Ireland and America*, 1976

Hansard, *History of Waterford*

Hare, Augustus, *Life and Letters of Maria Edgeworth*, London, 1894

Harris, John, *Sir William Chambers*, London, 1970

Hastings, Selina, *Evelyn Waugh*, London, 1994

Haverty, Anne, *Constance Markievicz*, London, 1988

Herbert, Dorothea, *Retrospections*, London, 1929–30

Hillier, Bevis, *Young Betjeman*, London, 1988

Hussey, Christopher, 'Caledon, Co. Tyrone', *Country Life*, February 27 and March 6, 1937

— 'Castle Coole, Co. Fermanagh', *Country Life*, December 19 and 26, 1936

— 'Mount Stewart, Co. Down', *Country Life*, October 5 and 12, 1935

Hyde, H. Montgomery, *The Londonderrys*, London, 1978

Irish Architectural Archive: The Architecture of Richard Morrison and William Vitruvius Morrison, Dublin, 1989

Irish Georgian Society Bulletin, 1958 onwards

Jackson-Stops, Gervase, 'Barons Court, Co. Tyrone', *Country Life*, July 12, 19 and 26, 1979

— 'Crom Castle, Co. Fermanagh', *Country Life*, May 26 and June 2, 1988

— 'A Temple Made Tasteful' [Castle Coole, Co. Fermanagh], *Country Life*, April 10, 1986

Jourdain, Margaret, Regency Furniture at Caledon, *Country Life*, September 26, 1936

Killanin, Lord, and Duignan, Michael V., *The Shell Guide to Ireland*, London, 1967 (2nd edn)

Lecky, William, *A History of Ireland in the Eighteenth Century*, London, 1892–6

Lees-Milne, James, *The Bachelor Duke*, London, 1991

— *Diaries*, London, 1975–98 (7 vols)

Llanover, Lady (ed.), *Autobiography and Correspondence of Mrs Delany*, London, 1861 (3 vols)

Loeber, Rolf, *A Biographical Dictionary of Architects in Ireland 1600–1720*, London, 1981

Lycett Green, Candida (ed.), *John Betjeman: Letters*, London, 1994–5 (2 vols)

— *John Betjeman: Coming Home*, London, 1997

MacLiammóir, Micheál, *All for Hecuba*, London, 1946

MacLysaght, Edward, *Irish Life in the Seventeenth Century*, Cork, 1950 (2nd edn)

McParland, Edward, *James Gandon*, London, 1985

— 'Sir Richard Morrison's Country Houses', *Country Life*, May 24 and 31, 1973

— 'Lissadell, Co. Sligo', *Country Life*, October 6, 1977

— 'A Bibliography of Irish Architectural History', *Irish Historical Studies*, November, 1988

Magan, William, *Umma More*, Tisbury, 1980

Malins, Edward, and Bowe, Patrick, *Irish Gardens and Demesnes from 1820*, London, 1980

Malins, Edward, and Glin, the Knight of, *Lost Demesnes: Irish Landscape Gardening 1660-1845*, London, 1976

Marreco, Anne, *The Rebel Countess*, London, 1967

Marson, Peter, *Castle Coole* ('Family Exhibition' booklet), Enniskillen, 1997

Masters, Brian, *The Dukes*, London, 1980 (2nd edn)

Montgomery-Massingberd, Hugh, *Great British Families*, London, 1988

— 'Heritage' articles in *The Field*, 1976–87, and *The Daily Telegraph*, 1987–96

— 'The Knight of Glin and the Irish Georgian Society', *Town & Country*, October, 1993

Montgomery-Massingberd, Hugh (ed.), *Burke's Irish Family Records*, London and New York, 1976

— *Burke's Introduction to Irish Ancestry*, London, 1976

— *Burke's Guide to Country Houses, Volume I: Ireland*, by Mark Bence-Jones, London, 1978

— *The Daily Telegraph Book of Obituaries*, London, 1995–99 (5 vols)

National Trust Guidebooks: Castle Coole; Castle Ward; Florence Court; Mount Stewart

Neale, J.P., *View of the Seats of Noblemen and Gentlemen in England, Wales, Scotland and Ireland*, London 1818–23 (6 vols); London, 1824–9 (5 vols)

Nevill, Ralph, *Sporting Days and Sporting Ways*

Nicolson, Harold, *Helen's Tower*, London, 1937

Nicolson, Nigel, *Alex: The Life of Field Marshal Earl Alexander of Tunis*, London, 1973

O'Brien, Jacqueline, and Guinness, Desmond, *Great Irish Houses and Castles*, London, 1992

O'Faolain, Sean, *Countess Markievicz or The Average Revolutionary*, Dublin, 1934

O'Leary, Declan (ed.), *The Future of the Country House*, Dublin, 1993

Pakenham, Thomas, *The Year of Liberty*, London, 1969

— *Meetings with Remarkable Trees*, London, 1996

Pilkington, Matthew, *The Gentleman's and Connoisseur's Dictionary of Painters*, Dublin, 1770

Powell, Anthony, *Messengers of Day*, London, 1978

Powell, Violet, *The Departure Platform*, London, 1998

Rankin, Peter (ed.), 'Ulster Houses Series' (Ulster Architectural Heritage Society): *Ballywalter Park*, Belfast, 1985; *Clandeboye*, Belfast, 1985

Rowan, Alistair, *North West Ulster*, in *The Buildings of Ireland* series, London, 1979

— 'Ballywalter Park, Co. Down', *Country Life*, March 2 and 9, 1967

Russell, G.E., *Collections and Recollections*, London, 1898

St Helier, Lady, *Memories of Fifty Years*, London, 1909

Sayer, Michael, and Massingberd, Hugh, *The Disintegration of a Heritage: Country Houses and their Collections 1979–1992*, Wilby, 1993

Scott, Reverend John, *Review of the Irish House of Commons*, Dublin, 1789

Sheehy, J., and McCarthy, J.J., *The Gothic Revival in Ireland* (Ulster Architectural Heritage Society)

Smith, Charles, *Ancient and Present State of the County and City of Waterford*, 1746

Somerville Large, Peter, *The Irish Country House*, London, 1995

Swan, Abraham, *Collection of Designs*, 1757

Sykes, Christopher Simon, *Black Sheep*, London, 1932

— 'Glin Castle, Co. Limerick', *House & Garden*, January 1995

Tillyard, Stella, *Aristocrats*, London, 1994

Topographical and Chronological Survey of the County of Down, 1740

Ulster Architectural Heritage Society, Lists and Surveys, 1969 onwards

Walpole, Horace, *Letters*, Oxford, 1903–8 and 1918–25, London, 1937–onwards

— *Memories of the Reign of King George III*, London, 1894 (4 vols)

Wheatcroft, Geoffrey, *The Randlords*, London, 1984

Wood, James, *Annals of County Westmeath*

Young, Arthur, *A Tour in Ireland*, London, 1780

Index